Edited for Television

EDITED FOR TELEVISION

CNN, ABC, and the 1992 Presidential Campaign

Matthew Robert Kerbel

Westview Press

Boulder • *San Francisco* • *Oxford*

Published in 1994 in the United States of America by Westview Press, Inc., 5500 Central Avenue, Boulder, Colorado 80301-2877, and in the United Kingdom by Westview Press, 36 Lonsdale Road, Summertown, Oxford OX2 7EW

Library of Congress Cataloging-in-Publication Data
Kerbel, Matthew Robert, 1958–
    Edited for television : CNN, ABC, and the 1992 presidential
campaign / Matthew Robert Kerbel.
        p.   cm.
    Includes bibliographical references and index.
    ISBN 0-8133-1699-5 (hc.)—ISBN 0-8133-1700-2 (pb)
        1. Presidents—United States—Election—1992.   2. Television
broadcasting of news—United States.   3. Television in politics—
United States.   I. Title.
E884.K46   1994
324.973'0928—dc20   93-45690
                                                                    CIP

Printed and bound in the United States of America

The paper used in this publication meets the requirements
of the American National Standard for Permanence of Paper
for Printed Library Materials Z39.48-1984.

10   9   8   7   6   5   4   3   2   1

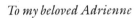

To my beloved Adrienne

Contents

PART I   The 1992 Campaign: Pictures on Television

PART III   Conclusions

Tables and Figures

Preface and Acknowledgments

I am a student of the mass media and a former television newswriter. I have been on camera on occasion in a professional capacity as one of so many "talking heads," and like everyone in my generation I have watched television all my life. But not until January 21, 1993, while in the midst of writing this book about television election coverage, had I ever been in the center ring of the media circus. That "opportunity" came when my wife's postcard was selected by chance from among 90,000 citizen requests, each submitted to the National Park Service in the hope of beating long odds to be among 2,000 people invited to a White House "open house" on President Clinton's first day in office. Until that day, I had stood behind the cameras as news practitioner and astride them as observer; I was about to find out how it felt to stand in front of them.

What I experienced was an event that seemed more likely to have been arranged by NBC than by the National Park Service. Network and local television cameras panned the line of ticket holders awaiting entry to the White House grounds. Waves of reporters and crews bearing minicams sought pictures and sound bites they believed would interest the home audience: How did you get invited? (answer: "We were lucky"); What will you tell the new president? (answer: "Congratulations"). Once inside, a different array of cameras followed our steps along the South Lawn. As we approached the West Wing, the procession of visitors ground to a halt at a table where everyone was assigned a number—not for security purposes, but because the cable network C-SPAN wanted a record of presidential visitors.

As we were each in turn introduced to President Clinton and Vice President Gore, our words were captured by microphone and our images recorded on videotape. Reporters and their paraphernalia occupied a space as prominent as that of America's new leaders, crowding four rows deep behind the backs of the guests. Even as the visit ended, the press encounter lingered. At the foot of the White House driveway, reporters held signs bearing the names of their home cities and states, trying to connect with hometown residents for interviews with a local flavor (to obtain local answers to questions like, "How did you get invited?" and "What did you tell the new president?").

I see the impact of the media on this open house as a personal metaphor for one of the central themes of this book: The impact of television is such that it has grown beyond simply covering the story, beyond even shaping the story, to the point where it often *is* the story. Just as the trip to the White House to meet the president became a trip to the White House to meet the press, news coverage—or at least television election coverage—quite often offers no more than a story about the reporters themselves: what they endure, how they feel, the way they do their jobs. It is a story of great interest to those who write it but of questionable utility, even potentially harmful, to those who consume it. Harmful because at a time when political parties have declined beyond recognition, television finds itself brokering the relationship between candidate and voter to an unprecedented extent. But television is not designed to function like a political party; it has neither the ability nor the desire to aggregate interests and facilitate a candidate-voter dialogue. Responsive to its need to hold and entertain an audience, television pays untold attention to what it finds most engaging and interesting. When this amounts to little more than television's own role in the process, the result is a cynical incantation of what it takes for candidates to win high office in the mass media age.

These observations come from the study that forms the basis for this book: a year-long examination of the content of regularly scheduled evening news broadcasts about the presidential election as they appeared on broadcast (ABC) and cable (CNN) television, supplemented by 44 interviews with members of each network's election news unit. The methodology employed in conducting the content analysis and the interviews is discussed in the appendix. At one level, I investigate what the election looked like on the two networks: its thematic content, its analytical nature, the portrayal of individuals, institutions, and their relationships. At another level, I compare traditional broadcast coverage with its cable counterpart, which only recently has emerged as a respected and powerful media force. At yet another level, I draw conclusions about the nature of the mediated message itself: Using the election as a case study, I examine how television covers events and assess the mixture of organizational, procedural, and personal factors that help to explain why television coverage looks the way it does.

*   *   *

Like media coverage itself, this book was of course shaped by many influences. I would particularly like to acknowledge the kind assistance of those who helped me at various stages in the life of this project. The book assumes the form it does in part because of the helpful comments of Pamela Shoemaker, Michael Traugott, Kim Kahn, and my colleagues at Villanova, Len Shyles and David Barrett, all of whom took the time to comment on my initial proposal. Dan Amundson assisted me in the development of the coding scheme, and numerous people gave me insight and support as I considered who to interview and what to ask. I am particularly grateful to Norman Ornstein and Larry Sabato for sharing their insights about the television news community, to Bill Porter for helping to guide my initial contacts at the two networks, and to Brooks Jackson and Gene Randall at CNN for their early support of this project.

Several people offered valuable insights at various stages of manuscript development. I would particularly like to thank Ann Crigler, Timothy Cook, Marion Just, Tom Patterson, Robert Spitzer, Holli Sometko, and Michael G. Hagen for their help and guidance; I hope I have done justice to their many fine suggestions. At the two networks, interviews were facilitated and expedited by executive-level support and encouragement, particularly from Hal Bruno at ABC and Tom Johnson and Tom Hannon at CNN. My wonderful research assistants, Sara Robins and David Howell, contributed hours of their time to learn the complex content analysis coding scheme used here and without complaint carried a good deal of the burden for delivering the data effectively and in rapid order. If they never again have the stomach to watch network news, it is a consequence of the invaluable contribution they made to this book.

At Villanova, Susan Burns and Diane Mozzone patiently put up with an ongoing set of requests for copies of new chapters and weathered the inevitable ups and downs of manuscript writing with grace and good humor. At Westview, Jennifer Knerr and Eric Wright labored diligently despite an unbelievably crowded agenda to guide this book swiftly to publication. Working with them was both a pleasure and a privilege, for they never lost sight of an author's needs. Likewise, I was blessed with the patience, love, and support of my wife, Adrienne, who not only eased the burden of the endless hours and relentless tasks required to produce this book but also provided editorial guidance that helped to make the final version better than I could have made it alone. She is a partner in this project, and it is dedicated to her.

Finally, I would like to thank the correspondents and producers at CNN and ABC who probably could not afford the time they spent unselfishly answering my questions. This book would not have been possible without them.

Matthew Robert Kerbel
Villanova, Pennsylvania

1

Introduction

We are heading for a presidential campaign that within the next twelve years will take place either within a TV studio or at least within television's special confines. I am not sure I know what to do about it.

—Roger Mudd[1]

It was that kind of year.

A real vice president sends a real gift to the fictional child of a fictional television character. A billionaire becomes a media celebrity and a serious independent presidential contender, only to self-destruct—twice—under television's searing hot lights. Larry King emerges as an electoral force, perhaps the first-ever host of a presidential campaign.

The 1992 national election did not simply unfold on television; it was of and about television. Presidential candidates masquerading as pitchmen hawked toll-free phone numbers and feel-good imagery on forums ranging from the traditional ("Meet the Press" and "Today") to the unorthodox and downright bizarre ("The Arsenio Hall Show" and MTV),[2] as all the while television reporters dutifully legitimated these events by making them the focus of coverage. There were "electronic town meetings" and "infomercials," with candidates serving as ginsu knife substitutes. Ross Perot went so far as to reduce his reborn quest for the presidency to a series of commercial messages, which the major television networks felt worthy of news coverage in their own right. Roger Mudd erred only by allowing twelve years for his prediction to come true.

Television's domination of the electoral spotlight was far more insidious than these events suggest. Some of it may be understood in terms of what Mudd calls "television's special confines," in which the medium sets the conditions for what millions come to know as the presidential campaign. Television, secure in its cardinal role as the primary institution connecting Americans with their political candidates, is free to cover what it feels is important.

And quite often, nothing is more important to television than television itself. Consequently, the campaign story on the evening news was often about little more than how the press covered the election.

During the 1992 campaign, reporters routinely inserted themselves and their experiences into election text, becoming co-stars in a drama of their own creation while sending a strong, cynical message to the audience about the evils of the political system. The problematic nature of candidate-reporter relationships, the backstage efforts by candidates at television image-making, the underlying motivations for candidate behavior toward the press—these constitute the reporter's experience as she fights boredom and campaign operatives in search of something new. Although such topics are of dubious utility to the news viewer, in 1992 they became the news.

Beyond this pervasive interest in the self, television coverage of the 1992 election may be most noteworthy for what it was *not*. It was not about institutions that were uninvolved in electoral competition, like interest groups. In fact, it wasn't really about institutions at all, favoring as it did individuals over groups or organizations in all facets of coverage. Even such political structures as the major parties and their representatives were rarely mentioned. And only certain individuals were favored: Most nonpolitical or apolitical individuals received little notice. Absent as well were ideological arguments and members of groups that might espouse them. Finally, for all the fanfare surrounding the advent of narrowcasting, election coverage was not much different on cable television than on the traditional broadcast networks.

This is surprising. In the aftermath of cable coverage of the Persian Gulf War, television news reporting appeared to have entered a new era. Live battlefield images were carried by satellite and cable into our homes, creating not just a living room war but an around-the-clock, real-time living room war. Only cable news, with its twenty-four-hour-a-day capability, could provide such unprecedented saturation coverage. When media watchers proclaimed a new dawn, they were only reiterating what was obvious to anyone with a cable box.

However, the war itself was an atypical news item. Constantly changing developments fueled an international obsession with knowing the latest information, as high-stakes conflict riveted attention on the Persian Gulf. The situation played to cable television's strengths: For the viewer with a hunger to know the latest, CNN was always there, going so far as to transmit live from ground zero in Baghdad.

Coverage of the Persian Gulf War capitalized on conflict, drama, uncertainty, and audience need-to-know. Routine news stories may offer some of these elements, but without the crisis moniker, they lack, by definition, the sort of intensity that brought high ratings to CNN's continuous war coverage. The presidential election is a good example of this contrast. Laden with conflict and uncertainty, election news attracted the concerned and the curious, especially as November neared. Lacking the nailbiting concerns raised by the Gulf War, however, it did not draw, nor did CNN pay, constant, cutting-edge attention.

In this most typical of news situations, CNN's offering was far more familiar than it was revolutionary. Reporters followed campaigns, delivering assessments of the political situation. Pundits interpreted opinion polls, and staged candidate appearances were announced and discussed. With only a few exceptions, it would be difficult to distinguish this sort of coverage from that available on CNN's competitors. These reports were available on a twenty-four-hour basis, of course, but that is a matter of quantity, not content. With its much-heralded ability seemingly to go anywhere at any time, CNN would appear to be positioned to cover an election in any number of ways. On the eve of an age in which we are promised (or threatened with) hundreds of cable channels, CNN could provide us with an alternate approach to the news—a different appreciation of what an election is about. But the network distinctly did not do this in 1992.

As if following a formula, newsworkers at CNN and ABC regularly and predictably showed us the same pictures of the presidential campaign again and again, and these images seemed to reflect a consensus in the news community. The camera's eye focused on the usual suspects: major candidates, generic members of the public, the press itself, rendering the televised election story highly personalized, politicized, and homogenized. It was about people rather than institutions, winners rather than losers, and power rather than ideas.

All the same, the coverage was not tilted by the partisanship of those who produced it. Despite arguments by conservatives that television favors liberal ideals and candidates,[3] the televised election story was largely mum on matters of political preference. Yes, George Bush got bad press on both cable and broadcast television in 1992. So did Bill Clinton. This was not because of the partisan predispositions of the television news community but a result of how those in the news community determined what was germane to campaign coverage. An incumbent presiding over a protracted recession is going to hear stories he doesn't like simply because his name will be associated with unfavorable economic statistics and the unpleasant pictures that accompany them. This is how television newsgathering works; partisan affiliation matters not at all.

Where bias existed, it revealed a preference for the procedural self-interest of those reporting and producing the news: the process by which newsworkers struggled to get the story on the air, the reporter's unseemly battle with candidates and campaign workers. This is the stuff of the reporter's experience. It is bias of a structural nature, derived from how newsworkers perceive their work and their world. It led television to present the election in terms best understood by those who were reporting it, which is to say as a nonideological power play in which they have a critical role. Daniel Hallin writes, "Serious journalism tends to treat politics as a contest rather than a discussion of social values: it asks 'Who is winning?,' not 'Who is right?' or 'What should we do?'"[4] To this, we might add that television reporters ask, in the best tradition of Ross Perot's running mate, Admiral James Stockdale, "Who am I and why am I here?"

We will ask a different version of this question of television news: What is it, and why is it so? Taking these summary observations of television's version of the 1992 campaign as a starting point, I will examine the many similarities and few differences between cable and broadcast television's approaches to the campaign; the themes both networks emphasized; their portrayal of individuals, institutions, and relationships among principal actors; and their dogged determination to tell you about themselves.

Then, I will explore how this picture of the campaign came about. I will consider the interaction of several factors long considered to have an impact on news coverage: the structure and operation of news organizations; the routines used to gather the news; and the personal perspectives of the newsgatherers toward their work, their goals, and the news itself. Working backwards from the picture of the campaign drawn by television, I shall connect product with producer in order to better understand the former by observing the latter.

Five Themes or "Miniseries"

In theory, television stories about the election may constitute a broad range of things. In practice, they tend to converge around several topics of interest to the subculture to which reporters (and, for that matter, candidates and campaign officials) belong.[5] As this subculture envelopes both cable and broadcast news, these topics emerge in similar fashion on CNN and ABC.

Traditionally, election coverage is dichotomized by those who examine it into "horserace" stories, which detail arduous competition among candidates, and more substantive "issue" stories, which address candidate policy positions and performance.[6] I have expanded the dichotomy to encompass five discrete thematic devices, each with distinct origins in the media-campaign subculture: horserace, issue, process, image, and nonissue.

Horserace coverage references the various campaigns and derives from reporter assessments of electoral competition. Issue coverage alludes to stories about policy concerns that newsworkers generally consider to be of substantive importance to the public, even if they are uncertain how long their viewers are willing to listen to them.[7]

To these, I add what I call "process" coverage, which is about the media in general and the methods by which they cover a campaign. Self-referential by definition, this category encompasses all things related to the media's role in the presidential race. Often, process news is simply coverage of the coverage, the story of what television does to bring its audience the story of the campaign.

"Image" coverage is about the persona of the office-seeker. It looks at the character and capability of the candidates and their posturing and preening on the stump. Originating as it does with the words and actions of the candidates, image coverage is less substantive than issue coverage. Likewise, while related to the horserace, it may be distinguished by its emphasis on matters of personality rather than competition.

"Nonissue" coverage involves discussion of specific occurrences that have no bearing on policy issues but that are more distinctive than simple image references. At minimum, they are fleeting references to such things as a candidate's judgment, personal history, or health; at maximum, they endure and become campaign crises. Nonissue items are always about a candidate, but unlike stories involving policy issues, rarely draw a connection between the candidate and the public. Instead, the nonissues are portrayed as matters of concern to the candidate, with no mention of how the viewer may be involved.

Obviously, portrayal of *all* of these topics derives from the decisions of newsworkers, regardless of whether the public, the candidate, or the media serve as the point of reference. Each theme becomes part of the television story of the campaign only with the blessing of the gatekeepers. Thus, television's rendition of an election may be understood as the concurrent depiction of five thematic "miniseries" that collectively constitute the televised picture of the campaign. These miniseries document the campaign as television news personnel saw it and related it. Slice through television coverage at any given time, and you will find a series of subtexts, often overlapping one another in the same story, relating to some or all of these five topics. Over time, these thematic devices evolve, disappear, reemerge. Collectively, they constitute the picture of the election we see on cable and broadcast television.[8]

In past years, television has paid more attention to the horserace than to the issues, leading observers who equate issues with essence to question the substantive value of election coverage. In 1992, the horserace remained the most prominent topic of campaign coverage, but it was far from the only story. Horserace coverage shared the spotlight with process references, a never-ending but ever-changing stream of nonissues, and a healthy dose of image coverage.

And in a departure from past elections, television also paid greater attention to a select set of issues. Although foreign policy and most domestic policy issues were all but ignored, economic matters marshaled a large share of attention, especially at times when horserace conflict was low. Two distinct elements contributed to this coverage. First, given a primary field composed of unknowns (or "supporting players"), television news could not find a convincing way to portray electoral competition. Second, economic figures, public opinion polls, and reporter judgments indicated that an enduring recession had planted itself in the American pocketbook and psyche. For those reporters and producers who anticipate audience interest, pictures of domestic suffering rivaled metaphors of athletic competition; the circumstances were right for issue coverage, at least of the bread-and-butter variety.

Cable Versus Broadcast:
New Ways of Watching Television

Until very recently, discussions of television election coverage have focused on the three major broadcast networks. The reason for this is clear: CBS, ABC, and NBC together boasted the largest electronic news audience. CNN, once derided as the "Chicken Noodle Network," came of age in the 1980s as the audience for cable television grew. Today, CNN boasts a regular viewership in the half-million range and is still growing. In the wake of the Persian Gulf War, CNN began to receive acclaim for its ability to report undigested news—live pictures of the bombing as it was happening. In 1992, CNN had a well-developed election news unit and aired an ambitious series of election-oriented programs. Claims to being a "fourth" news network no longer sounded far-fetched.

The coming of age of cable news provides an interesting basis for comparison and a forum for better understanding how election news appears on television and why it looks as it does. The numerous similarities in how cable and broadcast television conceptualized and portrayed the 1992 presidential campaign occurred despite sharp distinctions in how broadcast and narrowcast media operate. In fact, looking simply at the organizations behind cable and broadcast news might lead one to expect differences in what they produce. But this is not the case.

Although both outlets depend on advertising revenue, individuals use cable television and broadcast television differently and so the commercial imperatives of the two are somewhat dissimilar. Network news operations are components of large entertainment vehicles broadcasting to a mass audience. Executives count on evening news programs to capture and hold sizable audiences for subsequent entertainment programming. Until recent years, news divisions were regarded by the networks as investments. The evening news drew people into the hours of prime time programming. Before the advent of the remote control, cable alternatives, and the VCR, viewers could be expected to seek out their favorite evening news broadcast and park themselves on that channel all night. So, although expensive to operate, news divisions were allowed to lose money, provided they paid dividends by delivering a nightly audience. Today, with more competition from new services and with operating budgets under far greater scrutiny, networks are less forgiving of the high cost of news. Nevertheless, the enduring presence of highly paid anchors and expensive news broadcasts to usher in the evening signals the continued commitment of all the networks to news as a vehicle for attracting an audience, at least for now.

Cable, by contrast, is an information medium that feeds large quantities of material over numerous specialized channels to a more select audience.[9] Typically, cable subscribers have access to at least fifty separate options. Because the capability to increase that number is limited only by the availability of ideas for new services, the cable smorgasbord grows ever larger. Hence, the concept of "narrowcasting," or sending information on a particular topic (like news, weather, music, or movies) over distinct channels. In this type of shopping environment, patrons are expected to hop from channel to channel, settling perhaps for a few minutes on a particular program before moving somewhere else. Indeed, if the remote control had not already existed, cable companies surely would have invented it. The objective is not to hook the viewer for the evening but to keep him coming back.

Viewers may select CNN programming at any time from among their cable options as they bounce from channel to channel to satisfy precise interests or desires. So specific are cable services that CNN offers two channels, fine-tuned to satisfy different types of news needs. Their primary channel, examined in this book, tenders a never-ending pastiche of regularly scheduled news programs, generally one hour long, interspersed with talk programs and full-length specialty shows on such topics as finance, entertainment, and politics. The second is a headline service (aptly named "Headline News") that cycles every thirty minutes through select news stories, business, sports, weather reports, and feature items. Although marketed as two distinct services, the CNN channels are commonly operated and share news reports. Many cable systems offer both channels as part of their basic service agreement.

It is reasonable to assume that the requirements of a broadcast setting, where the daily allotment of news time may be measured in minutes, might lead to a more circumscribed picture of the election than what one may find on cable news. Indeed, some key differences emerge. On nightly news broadcasts, ABC was consistently more analytical than CNN in its treatment of the election, mediating material for the viewer in the confines of brief, two-minute stories. Likewise, the rhythm of the contest was more regular on CNN, where each day provided numerous opportunities to address election details and material was more likely to be laid out for the audience in descriptive fashion. On ABC, where campaign news competed with other items for scarce broadcast time, the intensity of election coverage more closely followed the ebb and flow of the horserace. Differences in cable-broadcast news cycles and production needs gave the story a distinct form on each network, generating on cable a more even, descriptive, less horse-drawn election picture.

By and large, though, the differences rested more in the realm of form than of content. The five election topics were given strikingly similar emphases on broadcast and cable television, and the overall picture of events was notably comparable. With only a few important exceptions, regular viewers of the Cable News Network received the same central ideas about the campaign that they would have obtained as patrons of ABC's "World News Tonight," indicating a consensus about what constitutes election news common to two media with distinct audiences. Regardless of personal preferences, people who depended on television to inform them about the campaign received the same basic messages regardless of where they turned.

From Content to Process

These similarities were the result of forces at work behind the scenes at both networks. News coverage doesn't just happen; it is produced. The simple belief that television news reflects the world in a mirror has been widely disregarded by those who have examined the cultural context in which news is created as well as by many journalists who once relied on the mirror analogy to claim objectivity in their reporting. News is more accurately understood as the product of choices made by newsworkers operating under a complex of organizational constraints, shared ideological beliefs, common values, and clearly defined work routines. In theory, news may be anything; in practice, it is defined by the expectations and beliefs of those who create it.[10]

A host of such influences have been offered to explain why news coverage often assumes its regular, predictable form.[11] Large-scale environmental forces, such as economic pressures and market influences, are widely assumed to influence television programming.[12] So are technological advances such as satellite transmission of videotape and portable minicams, which enable reporters to capture, process, and transmit footage from remote locations at great speeds.[13] Then there are the routines of newsgathering, which developed out of the need to minimize uncertainty in the face of the demand for fixed quantities of news reports at regular times.[14] On a more personal level, a host of values, beliefs, and norms are held by those who gather and produce the news,[15] ranging from ideological predispositions[16] and political opinions[17] to beliefs about the audience[18] to the norm of journalistic objectivity.[19]

In this book, I will not only look at each of these factors in turn but also consider how they combine to create the news that home viewers see. Correspondents, off-air reporters, producers, and executives respond not just to an intricate set of influences but to the interplay of forces at work in the newsroom and out in the field. Only through examining the interaction of these environmental, procedural, and individual forces can we better understand how election news is produced.[20]

Specifically, comparing and contrasting cable and broadcast news production during the 1992 campaign reveals how these factors interacted in two different settings. I will address the distinct organizational pressures in force at CNN and ABC; in addition, considering that both networks produced similar versions of election news, I will devote a great deal of attention to factors of a nonorganizational nature common to the process of covering an election for television. Drawing on specific links between the various newsroom influences and the product viewers see, I will focus on the assumptions made by the people creating network news—assumptions that transcend differences in the institutions for which they work. I will show how the process of newsgathering, the use of sources, and in particular, the shared orientations about what is important and relevant combine to structure the words and pictures that represent "the way it is" to the viewing audience.

What emerges from this analysis is that the overriding influence on election coverage in 1992 was a set of perspectives or orientations shared by political reporters and producers at both networks. Part value-based, part attitudinal, these perspectives functioned to guide newsworkers toward a specific definition of election news to the exclusion of all other possibilities. From the outset, they led newsworkers directly to the political campaigns in search of information. They confined coverage to political, personal, often self-oriented material only sporadically relevant to the home viewer but distinctly revealing of how political reporters understand politics.

This scenario played out against the noise and confusion of the presidential campaign, which simply compounded television's frantic pace. Newsworker orientations about what should be covered guided their steps in a marathon dance with political personnel in which running, shoving, sleep deprivation, and the struggle for control of information were constant facts of life. Newsworkers described it as life inside a bubble, where there was no escape from the incessant pressures of life on the road with the same people making the same speeches and the same demands. Internal sensors took over, guiding correspondents toward a common understanding of what to report and how to report it. These were their orientations speaking, their internalized sense of what was and was not news. Colleagues shared them, as did the producers and executives back at home base, so silently their judgments were reinforced. Without time to pause or think or get away, reporters relied on what felt like their instincts to pull them through. And, in the end, there was election news—the same election news on cable as on broadcast television.

It is important to understand these influences because they inform a news product consumed by millions, transmitted by a medium that plays an increasingly central role in domestic politics. The weakening of political parties in the latter half of the twentieth century has coincided with the growing prominence of television in the electoral process. The proliferation of popular primaries, with candidates winning nomination by appealing directly to the public for votes, was an open invitation for greater mass media influence.[21] Nominees win election by building name recognition and creating positive "atmospherics." Television, rather than the party, is the primary source of political information,[22] the new intermediary between candidate and public. Televised candidate appeals to voters are the back-room deals of the 1990s; media consultants wield the power once held by the party elite.

But television is not set up to perform this function. Its purpose is to entertain by informing, not necessarily to educate, and certainly not to broker coalitions or build political support. At times, television appears to undermine candidates and the process of electoral competition in its quest to connect with the audience. The candidates that survive are the ones that figure out how best to feed television's hunger for horserace and process, sound bite and picture; they may or may not be those best suited to office. Television's role in the system underscores the importance of understanding the interplay of influences that generate the product viewers see on the evening news. Thus, television should be regarded as a political institution, much as one might approach Congress, the judicial system, the presidency, the executive branch, and political parties.

A Note About Method

This book relies on three primary sources of data. The first consists of the actual words spoken by correspondents on CNN and ABC over the course of regularly scheduled, prime-time election coverage on the two networks. The second is a more systematic approach to those words and accompanying pictures in the form of a content analysis of every statement made about the 1992 election on two of those shows—ABC's "World News Tonight," and CNN's "PrimeNews"—starting on the first of the year and continuing until election day. Statements are analogous to sentences, and their treatment reflects the way a sentence might be parsed. Data were collected on the subject, direct object, and topic of each statement, along with a number of other items related to the form and substance of election coverage.

I chose these programs to represent election coverage on the two networks for substantive and practical reasons. Although we must not overlook the fact that both networks offered election coverage in venues ranging from interview programs to documentaries, it was neither necessary nor possible to examine every word uttered about the campaign in order to understand the perspectives underlying the reporting. "World News" and "PrimeNews" were chosen because they are both geared toward a general news audience in a similar, familiar anchor-reporter format. Furthermore, each program is the early evening flagship broadcast for its network, featuring its marquee anchors in prime time.[23] Whatever the networks decided the election was about would invariably appear in these two newscasts; they are appropriate windows through which to view television election coverage.

For the third source of data, I conducted free-ranging interviews with forty-four members of the CNN and ABC election news units. Correspondents, producers of various rank, and news executives were contacted in two waves, one preceding and one following the fall campaign. They were asked to speak about items that they felt influenced how they covered the campaign and to assess the content of their work.

At times in this book, the campaign is addressed in terms of six specific stages. These are based on the electoral calendar that placed distinct markers on the campaign race track: the New Hampshire stage, which stretched from the start of the calendar year to the New Hampshire primary (January 1–February 18, 1992);[24] the Super Tuesday stage, which began the day after New Hampshire and terminated with the flurry of mostly southern primaries held on March 10; the New York primary stage (March 11–April 7); the California primary stage (April 8–June 2); the summer convention stage, which completed the nomination process (June 3–September 6); and the General Election stage, bridging Labor Day and Election Day (September 7–November 3).

Those interested in a more detailed discussion of the data and methods employed here may find it in the appendix.

How This Book Is Structured

This book is divided into three parts. Part I discusses the words and pictures that constituted *coverage* of the 1992 presidential campaign on cable and broadcast television: who and what it was about and how it evolved over time. It compares cable coverage with broadcast coverage and examines the five thematic elements or "miniseries" of the televised campaign: process, issue, nonissue, horserace, and image. It assesses the mixture of institutions and individuals that starred in the election drama and the relationships among them in order to ascertain how television portrayed the dynamics among those it covered most: the candidates, the public, and the press. And it details the degree to which CNN and ABC news analyzed as opposed to described the campaign.

Part II assesses the mix of *factors* that informed election coverage. It examines the relative impact on news coverage of corporate and organizational constraints, the routines of newsgathering, and individual newsworker orientations. Part III addresses the *implications* of the news product for the viewing audience and the *impact* of the forces that create television news on the political system.

For the reader interested in a brief overview of the content of campaign coverage before moving on to a discussion of the influences that generated that coverage, chapters 3, 4, and 5 are recommended. The reader concerned with comparisons between cable and broadcast television is advised to see chapters 2 and 7. For everyone else, Part I provides a detailed assessment of how the 1992 presidential contest appeared as words and pictures on television.

PART I

The 1992 Campaign: Pictures on Television

2

Cable Versus Broadcast Coverage: Form and Content

Several months before television began to display interest in Campaign '92, an experienced Washington producer expressed what many believed when he observed, "Since [CNN] is not bound to the rigid demands of the 30-minute evening news program, ... the dynamics of television coverage will be altered dramatically."[1] When CNN coverage is taken as a whole, there is truth to this statement, especially given the ability of the twenty-four-hour news network to carry live coverage of press conferences, major addresses, campaign appearances, and "breaking" news. For the news connoisseur, the 1992 election was indeed a brave new world. But the impact on the rest of us was not as profound. The newly emerging realm of around-the-clock coverage did not dent television's airtight consensus about what constitutes election news. Casual viewers of the evening news received strikingly similar messages regarding what the election was about regardless of whether they heard it from Bernard Shaw or Peter Jennings.

At the level of the individual news program, the CNN format mainly affected how the election was portrayed rather than what was portrayed. Some of the notable differences in the shape of election coverage on CNN encompassed such things as who was telling the story, how prominently the story was displayed, and—most important—how analytical and interpretive the story was. These were matters of consequence, but their contextual nature made them more likely to influence how the election was perceived relative to other news than how it was interpreted in its own right.[2]

More striking, and perhaps more noteworthy, is how similarly both networks conceptualized the campaign story. Despite CNN's revolutionary capabilities, the election was consensually portrayed on television as a political, personal, nonideological event relating candidates to a vague conception of "the public," where television's own mediating role often became the focus

15

of coverage. In this chapter I will first consider subtle differences in how the networks reported election news and then turn to the bold similarities in the content of what they reported.

Differences of Form

The most prominent differences between CNN and ABC during 1992 were distinctions of form. Though not related to content, these variations were not simply cosmetic; they presented the viewer with different impressions of the importance of the election through variations in the amount, style, and prominence of coverage. Some of the differences, such as the quantity of material reported and the style of presentation, were obvious results of distinct format requirements present at each network. Others were neither obvious nor inevitable, such as variations in the amount of attention paid to the story over the course of the campaign and the prominence of election coverage within the newscast.

Amount of Coverage

Throughout the campaign, ABC reported more statements about the election on "World News Tonight" than CNN did on "PrimeNews." Overall, six in ten election statements were broadcast on ABC, a figure that varied little between campaign stages. When these statements are grouped into stories, we find much the same thing: More election stories were carried on broadcast than on cable.[3] But this should not be interpreted to mean that CNN paid less attention to the campaign than ABC; both organizations aired far more election coverage than what appeared on the evening news, and it may be argued that CNN's twenty-four-hour all-news format provided more opportunities for election coverage than found on the broadcast networks.

The disparity is in part attributable to the fact that CNN had a regular forum for election coverage in the form of "Inside Politics," an afternoon program that dedicated thirty minutes (one hour during the final weeks of the campaign) to campaign information. Given the ability—some at ABC call it the luxury—to devote large amounts of time solely to election news, CNN could generate volumes of campaign coverage, knowing that most if not all of what it produced would eventually see the light of day, although perhaps not in prime time.

In this regard, CNN's choice of how to present the election on programs such as "PrimeNews" becomes even more interesting, for it reflects decisions about how to portray the campaign story to the less specialized viewer. The CNN schedule is a nonstop array of hour-long general news programs interspersed with full-length feature shows (like "Inside Politics," as well as similar programs about medicine, entertainment, and the like). Consequently, to satisfy its immense news needs, CNN typically cycled news stories through several programs on both its comprehensive network and its headline channel. Thus, many items appearing on "PrimeNews" were first reported on "Inside Politics," and items appearing on "PrimeNews" would often appear on subsequent CNN general news programs. Of course, most "Inside Politics" pieces would *not* make it to the prime-time newscast. Thus, stories selected for use on "PrimeNews" are good indicators of what the network felt warranted attention in a general news format.

Attention to the Campaign

Over the months, the two networks differed in the amount of interest they paid to the campaign. CNN chose to represent the election to its evening audience as a regular story worthy of fairly steady attention. This approach differed from ABC coverage, which peaked sharply during periods of intense horserace competition. Figure 2.1 illustrates the number of election statements appearing on each network program on a weekly basis over the course of the campaign. For much of 1992, CNN and ABC paid about the same amount of attention to the election. But interest surged sharply on ABC during the weeks bridging the New Hampshire and New York primaries and again during the general election campaign.

These were the periods during which the horserace winners and losers were sorted out. In 1992, both networks reported the field to be muddied early on by the lack of a clear frontrunner. This uncertainty was clarified in the period between the New Hampshire primary and the Clinton and Bush victories in New York. The horserace was again reported to intensify during the general election, especially in the waning days when Ross Perot reentered the competition and the Bush campaign made its final and most effective effort.

CNN also devoted more attention to the campaign when horserace interest peaked, but the increase was not as great as it was on ABC; thus, the overall pattern of coverage on CNN had a more consistent feel. In general, CNN's "PrimeNews" was oriented more toward giving the evening viewer a steady helping of campaign information along with coverage of other news of the day. Additional material could be found in abundance elsewhere at different times during the twenty-four-hour cycle, for the political junky or simply for the curious. During the final days of the campaign, evening political coverage increased only slightly, but "Inside Politics" was expanded to an hour, providing a veritable banquet of campaign news. At ABC, election coverage competed with other news primarily for time on the evening broadcast. Reports not carried on "World News Tonight" could not simply appear later in the evening on another news program. Because of this constraint, news broadcasts more strongly reflected qualitative decisions about the importance of campaign items relative to all other available news items. By and large, these choices were informed by the amount of heat generated by the horserace. The *content* of election news on ABC was about far more than competition, how-

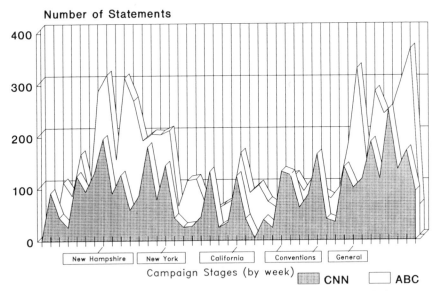

Number of Statements

Campaign Stages (by week)

New Hampshire   New York   California   Conventions   General

CNN   ABC

Figure 2.1   Number of Campaign Statements on CNN and ABC, by Week

ever; many of the statements comprising the ABC general election bulge were about campaign issues. ABC simply chose to broadcast these items in September and October, assuming that interest in anything related to the election would increase as the finish line came into view.

The feel for the campaign as portrayed by ABC underscored the assumption that interest in the election would follow the horserace. Hence, the spring and autumn election coverage surges. It may be argued that the same assumption held at CNN, which actually devoted a greater share of attention to the horserace than its broadcast counterpart did. But the availability of other outlets for campaign coverage at CNN allowed for the maintenance of a more steady presentation of evening election news.

Style and Prominence of Presentation

The two networks packaged the election story differently, each relying on a style of presentation suitable to its format. ABC emphasized the anchor-introduced reporter piece, whereby Peter Jennings would lead into a videotaped report of roughly 90 to 120 seconds' duration. CNN utilized this format as well but relied more often on shorter reports relayed directly by the news anchors and, at times, on far longer reporter background pieces. Anchors introduced videotaped reports twice as frequently on ABC as on CNN,[4] but the ABC anchors were less likely than CNN anchors to engage in time-consuming on-air dialogue with correspondents or analysts.[5]

Because CNN (literally) had all day, it could vary videotaped reports with both shorter anchor-delivered stories and long (several minute) backgrounders. For instance, on October 12, CNN "PrimeNews" devoted eight minutes and forty-two seconds to a "Special Assignment" profile of Vice President Quayle, followed two days later by an eight-minute twelve-second background piece on Senator Gore. Both pieces had run previously on "Inside Politics." In between, on October 13, ABC "World News Tonight" broadcast background stories about the vice presidential candidates, devoting seventy seconds each to Quayle and Gore. The contrast in length is typical of the two networks; at no time did an item as long as either CNN report appear on ABC, where eight minutes represents one-third of the available news allotment.

There were differences as well in the placement of campaign stories in the newscasts. Whereas both networks realized variations in the prominence of election news stories over the course of the campaign, each network followed a distinct pattern. Through Super Tuesday, the networks aired most of their election coverage during the first segments of "PrimeNews" and "World News Tonight," treating viewers to their election news before going to the first set of advertisements for hair coloring or nicotine treatment. But, as Figure 2.2 indicates, the two networks diverged in their placement of the story during the New York primary stage. ABC continued to highlight campaign coverage during its first segment; on CNN, the campaign story sank further into the broadcast as the spring progressed.[6] During the summer convention months, the two networks once again gave comparable headline attention to the election, albeit less than during the early primaries. The springtime pattern reversed itself during the general election, as CNN highlighted the campaign almost exclusively in its opening segment while ABC distributed election coverage more generally throughout its newscast.

This difference in story placement does not suggest a difference in news judgment between CNN and ABC about the value of individual stories. Quite to the contrary, both networks featured the campaign during the most heated periods of primary competition,[7] and each offered less lead material during what was perceived as the "slower" California primary and convention stages. Instead, it indicates how format differences—the thirty-minute news show versus twenty-four-hour news programming—can alter how prominently a story is portrayed.

The general election stage offered an excellent example of this effect. Given the enhanced sense of competition that reporters and producers feel as the end of a race approaches, the campaign would naturally be featured prominently on both networks during the final stage. This was obviously the case on CNN, where 81 percent of election-related material appeared during the first segment. On ABC, the figure was only 57 percent. But the percentage of statements reported as lead newscast items was very similar.[8] Placement dif-

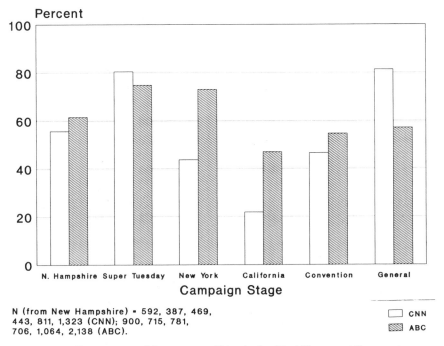

Percent

N (from New Hampshire) = 592, 387, 469,
443, 811, 1,323 (CNN); 900, 715, 781,
706, 1,064, 2,138 (ABC).

☐ CNN
▨ ABC

Figure 2.2   Percentage of Statements Airing in the First Newscast Segment, on CNN and ABC

ferences reflected the greater presence of "back of the book" items on ABC. Stories about "public concerns" and many close-up reports on "candidate positions" occupied the third segment of "World News Tonight," while the occasional retrospective or, at times, humorous story would close the newscast.

CNN did it differently. During the fall campaign, election news was generally grouped together in the same segment and did not appear again later in the program. There were few light features. This was because there was no need to give the appearance of closure necessary to a thirty-minute broadcast. The news doesn't end—it simply continues after the next commercial break. In this regard, "PrimeNews" is less self-contained than "World News Tonight," and the campaign is but one stop on the endless news tour. Whereas the ABC broadcast leads the viewer thematically through videotaped events of the day, carefully building bridges among news items and ending with a final benediction, CNN is just as likely to close with a meteorologist reporting today's low temperature in Rapid City. It's just the last item for this hour. They take a break, then they continue.

Collectively, these differences impart subtle cues to the viewer about the role of the election in the world of news. On CNN, the election "story" rolled along to a fairly steady rhythm where prominence in the newscast could vary greatly but the overall amount of attention paid to the campaign would fluctuate far less. There would be some in-depth reporting, some videotaped stories, and a lot of anchor "talking heads" imparting election news. On ABC, where the format requires tighter packaging, the volume of videotaped pieces—always the staple of the newscast—would rise and fall with the horserace, the crescendo of coverage intensified by the fixed half-hour format, and campaign news would grab a much greater share of the attention at peak times. Both networks turned up the volume in advance of what they agreed were key election benchmarks, but on ABC the sound was louder because the echo chamber was smaller. To the viewer, this approach meant a more all-consuming representation of the campaign. When we consider the content of the message being sent, we will see that it also meant a more predigested account of the campaign, as ABC was more analytical by far in its treatment of every election topic. This is an important matter in its own right and will be addressed in chapter 7.

Similarities of Content

A consensus about the nuts and bolts of the story transcended differences in the vehicles used to deliver the news at CNN and ABC. Despite the potential for CNN to utilize the new world of countless television channels to provide a different perspective on the election, there was remarkable agreement between CNN and ABC regarding who and what the election was about and even how much attention to give newsmakers relative to newspeople. Similarities extended to the attribution, topic, and subject of coverage—in short, to every important measure of election news content.

Statement Attribution

Every statement made about an election on a newscast is attributable to someone: a reporter or political figure, an interest group representative, or a prototype "person in the street." The contours of election coverage begin to emerge when the amount of attention paid to each of these sources is considered. On both networks in 1992, better than three-quarters of all statements were attributable to news personnel—correspondents, anchors, or analysts solicited by the network to make observations about the election. They were, of course, the individuals "telling" the story. But it is noteworthy that both networks aired almost the identical proportion of reporter to nonreporter statements.[9] This similarity indicates a news consensus about the degree to which other first-person references should be included in coverage.[10]

There was also concordance about who those other persons should be, or at least about what venue they should come from. Most of the remaining statements were attributable to partisan figures, giving election coverage something of a myopic perspective. Only a relative handful of statements were attributable to nonpartisan individuals. CNN and ABC paralleled one another in the degree to which they covered partisan actors—and disregarded nonpartisans, who accounted for a mere 5 percent of election content on ABC, 3 percent on CNN.

Furthermore, there was agreement about what types of partisan figures make news. Upwards of six in ten partisan statements on both networks were attributed to presidential candidates; most of the remainder were ascribed to campaign officials. Partisans not directly associated with a campaign were far less commonplace. These included other elected officials, individuals portrayed as supporters or opponents of a candidate, and interest-group representatives cast in political terms.

The people who speak on the news are the people reporters are in contact with on a routine basis, and their presence on television is a function of the way news is collected. On both networks in 1992, they were political actors either running for office or running campaigns. As the election year progressed, the ranks of the surviving campaigns swelled with aides and assistants (in part to handle the increased demands of media exposure). Consistent with this, the proportion of campaign officials appearing on both networks increased over the summer in proportion to the expansion of the reporter's Rolodex. On both networks, reporters rounded up the usual sources.

Even the few nonpartisans appearing in the news could be said to have a partisan cast. A number of them were former or "nonaligned" elected officials—potentially partisan individuals if portrayed in a different role. The rest were a mixed lot of individuals, usually undifferentiated members of the public who were not portrayed as supporters or opponents of a particular candidate, and the periodic "expert" on politics or policy. But the total numbers of these truly nonpartisan speakers were small. Based on the array of voices assembled to tell the story, the campaign on both networks was related in distinctly political tones.

Topic Themes

The two networks converged not only on who did the speaking but also on what they were speaking about. The campaign was presented as a series of overlapping dramas distinguishable by theme. These themes are ranked in Figure 2.3 according to the attention given them on ABC and CNN. The figure shows that both networks employed the same conceptual model of the campaign, devoting coverage first to the horserace then to the other "miniseries" of 1992: issues, candidate image, the media-campaign process, "nonissues," and other nonthematic campaign topics.[11] Each network devoted a similar percentage of air time to four of the six topics; the exceptions were horserace coverage (which got more attention on CNN) and process coverage (which got slightly more coverage on ABC).

Topic Area

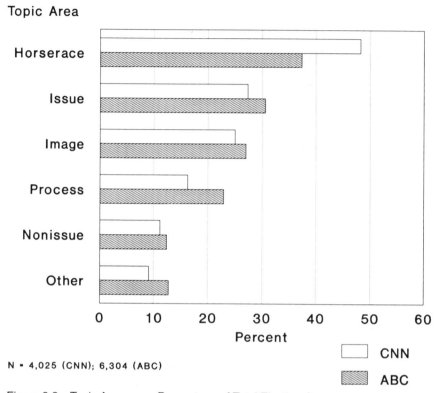

N = 4,025 (CNN); 6,304 (ABC)

Figure 2.3   Topic Areas as a Percentage of Total Election Coverage

Horserace. All told, a bit less than half of CNN's coverage and slightly more than one-third of ABC's campaign report contained some material about the horserace—who's ahead, who's behind, who's catching up, which candidate is using what strategy to perform how well in opinion polls, and other tidbits of a familiar nature to the regular consumer of television news. Given that horserace excitement plays directly to television's need for drama and conflict, we might have expected these figures to be even higher. Multiple topic references were commonly present in single statements, so theoretically *every* statement could have contained something about the horserace. Moreover, television news producers are widely believed to be horserace addicts. One prominent study asserts that the televised picture of the 1988 presidential primary contest was overwhelmingly horserace oriented,[12] and we have already seen that the volume of ABC election coverage shot up as the 1992 horserace intensified. The difference is that, this time around, a more diversified set of topics met both networks' need for exciting, recent, dramatic television.

Issues. Policy issues were at the forefront of those other topics getting a fair share of media attention. This observation disputes the widely regarded con-

ception that television is not interested in matters of substance, a view supported by research into campaigns of America's recent past.[13] In fact, some
researchers have used these studies to argue that the media undermine democratic dialogue and debate.[14] Issue coverage in 1992 did not contradict these
findings entirely. The overwhelming share of references to policy matters
were about the economy, a subject that newsworkers universally agreed was a
matter of great concern to the public. Noneconomic policy concerns (no
doubt of some interest to portions of the audience) were cited far less frequently; foreign policy didn't even make it on the radar screen. Other issues
were covered in 1992 much as they had been covered by television in the past,
which is to say hardly at all.

But the economic situation was a different matter. Conditions were ideal
for this particular policy concern to emerge as a regular television feature.
Economic indicators slumped perpetually downward. Candidates talked in-
cessantly about the recession. Producers collectively believed that the issue
had created an intangible "national mood," a belief reinforced by footage of
unemployed managers in New Hampshire and long lines of prospective employees seeking work at a Chicago hotel. These conditions were self-reinforcing, elevating the issue to the level where it became part of the election saga
and keeping it there. No other issue made the cut because no other issue was
perceived to be relevant enough to a wide enough audience to command the
camera's attention. Nevertheless, past conclusions about television's lack of
interest in issues of any sort need to be revised to permit that newsworkers will
entertain their viewers with an issue in that rare instance when they believe
their attention spans will allow it.

Image and Process. Owing to the economic story, issue coverage was so salient in 1992 that it received roughly the same emphasis as two other topics:
candidate image and the process of covering the campaign. Image coverage
was a running drama about the candidates: their character, their capability to
be president, and—to distinguish substantive references from rhetorical
flourishes—their posturing and positioning on the issues. Process coverage
was where television covered itself, telling the viewer about the spin-doctor-
ing, sound-biting efforts of candidates and their operatives to win favorable
coverage in the various other campaign miniseries. That this topic could constitute a thematic component of coverage comparable in mention to the issue
and image dramas underscores the degree to which both CNN and ABC conceptualized the campaign in the first person and were inclined to pass the details of their own experiences on to the audience.

Nonissues and Other Topics. Nonissues were the most discontinuous of
miniseries, constituting a sequence of unrelated, mostly brief, usually nonre-
curring items about a candidate's background, behavior, or ethics. If they can

at all be considered issues, they are issues with implications for politics but not policy, valuable inasmuch as the voter needs to know whether Jerry Brown smoked pot as governor or Ross Perot got rich from government contracts. Nonissue stories are ideal for television, with their image-rich, conflict-laden themes that often smell of scandal. So it is a bit surprising that nonissues constituted only slightly more than 10 percent of total coverage and were thus the least telecast campaign story.

In past elections, audiences have been treated to a cornucopia of such nonissues. A number of these were explosive enough to become campaign crises temporarily dominating all coverage until they consumed or derailed a candidate. In 1992, the election was noticeably devoid of the sort of illicit trips to the Bimini Islands that rocked previous campaigns. This is not to say there were no crises; indeed, in the weeks before New Hampshire the Bill Clinton scandal-of-the-week club provided enough material to temporarily reduce the campaign to a burlesque parody of all previous nonissues.

On both networks, the early rumors of Clinton's marital infidelity and Vietnam nonparticipation generated a glut of nonissue coverage dense enough to threaten his candidacy. But starting the last week of January, both networks began reporting that Clinton was trying to put allegations about his past behind him.[15] This coverage diminished in February as Clinton remained in contention and dropped permanently below crisis levels once Clinton claimed—and the press granted him—the "comeback" mantle following his performance in New Hampshire. Nonissue stories about Clinton's past would emerge periodically after New Hampshire, but never with such vengeance and intensity that his candidacy was again threatened. After New Hampshire, nonissues surfaced and disappeared with regularity, but no other crisis situation occurred.

The coverage relegated to the "other" category in Figure 2.3 consists of news items that did not fit into any of the previous thematic groupings. These constituted only a small percentage of coverage on both networks. Many were generic references to public attitudes about things other than the horserace, issues, images, processes, or nonissues (often pithy but vapid sound bites, like "I'm a Republican, but I don't know about this year"). Some were references to election procedures, such as how delegates are selected for party conventions or how the electoral college works. Others discussed past campaigns, candidates, and presidents. References such as these were sporadic, nonthematic, and unrelated to the salient topics that constituted the substance of television coverage on both networks.

Topic Coverage over Time. In addition to agreeing on what to cover and how much attention to give each thematic campaign element, the volume of topic coverage tended to rise and fall at the same rate and at the same time on both networks. In Figure 2.4, the number of references on each network to

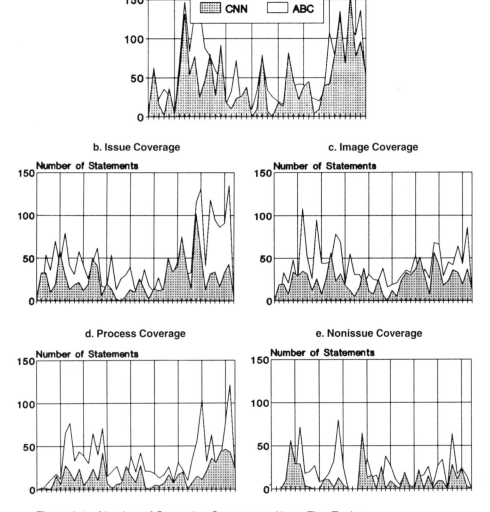

Figure 2.4   Number of Campaign Statements About Five Topics

each topic[16] is portrayed on a time line that encompasses the entire campaign period. Most of the graphs show CNN and ABC coverage escalating and diminishing in tandem as the two networks defined and redefined the campaign in similar if not identical terms.

There was a clear consensus about the ebb and flow of the horserace. Coverage on both networks peaked during New Hampshire and to a lesser extent during Super Tuesday, declined through the late primaries, spiked briefly at the end of the primary season and again during the conventions (with the Democratic convention commanding more horserace interest), and finally rose to a crescendo during the general election campaign. The two networks only deviated in two places where ABC briefly covered the horserace more extensively: during Super Tuesday and two weeks after the New York primary.[17]

Similarly, attention to the issues rose and fell at the same pace on both networks. There was a small peak during the early primaries and a much larger one during the general election, when issues received more attention than at any other time. Here, we can also see the effect of an editorial decision at ABC to create a forum to explore the issues on its "American Agenda" segment, which runs on an occasional basis on "World News." Starting in September and continuing through the election, these segments were dedicated to covering the main candidates' positions on selected topics. During this time, the amount of issue coverage carried by the two networks deviated. The enhanced quantity of issue coverage on ABC likely would not have occurred if the decision to focus on the issues had not been made in advance and if a segment of "World News Tonight" had not already existed to serve as a vehicle for their presentation. The use of the "Agenda" segment to augment issue coverage is discussed in greater detail in chapter 12.

Coverage of image and process items followed the same basic trend on both networks, albeit with a few peaks found only on ABC. For the most part, references to candidate image remained constant throughout the campaign, a staple of election coverage. The amount of attention devoted to process items was more variable, especially on ABC, where the pattern was similar to that of horserace coverage. As the horserace heated up and attention to the election increased, so did the amount of attention television devoted to itself.

A sawtooth pattern was unique to nonissue coverage and consistent with a topic composed of many unrelated, short-term dramas. Each peak represents the brief existence of a particular nonissue, each valley a pause in the screenplay. Both networks related nonissues in this fashion. Where peaks overlap in the graph, agreement existed on the news value of the story. Where they do not, it is because only one network felt a story was worthy of coverage. This finding indicates that the news consensus that nonissues should be a regular part of the election story did not always extend to the particulars.

For instance, both networks covered Gennifer Flowers's allegation that she had an affair with Bill Clinton. But only CNN carried in-depth coverage of

Ross Perot's treatment of his employees, and only ABC pursued the Jerry Brown pot-smoking story. Some nonissues, because of their content or salience, had "obvious" news value and consequently received universal attention. Others were the particular pets of one news organization, the result of editorial decisions to pursue a story (as opposed to waiting for an individual to come forward with an allegation). Unless they were Flowersesque enough to warrant attention by other outlets, nonissues did not necessarily receive wide play.

Issue Versus Horserace. Typically, campaign coverage is dichotomized into issue coverage and horserace coverage. Most critics judge the latter as being the least pertinent to making choices in a democracy but by far the most likely to command the attention of television. We have already seen that in the 1992 campaign, economic issues provided an exception to this rule. This finding raises an interesting question about issue coverage: What conditions are necessary for television to focus on an issue? If 1992 is unusual for the amount of reporting devoted to issues, under what circumstances will issue coverage share the spotlight with the juicier horserace?

One requirement appears to be a slow, confusing, or unresolved horserace. Another is a hot, conflictive policy issue. When horserace coverage is tracked against issue coverage on both networks, as in Figure 2.5, an interesting pattern emerges. At three distinct points in the campaign when competition lagged (see the circled areas in Figure 2.5), both networks devoted more attention to the issues than to the horserace, although television's overall interest in the campaign waned. In other words, coverage of the election moved to the pace of electoral competition, but issues composed a greater portion of television's coverage during times when the competition was slow.

That overall election coverage rose and fell in relation to the way reporters interpreted the horserace is consistent with how broadcast television has covered past elections. As in previous years, horserace coverage drove all election coverage, increasing or decreasing the total amount of interest CNN and ABC paid to the election. In contrast to previous elections, however, the 1992 campaign offered a fairly limited horserace, resulting in a considerable amount of down time. The Republican field offered an incumbent who, though unpopular, was challenged only by a television news commentator. The Democratic field was late to form (by recent standards), and with the advent of the early allegations against Bill Clinton, the candidate viewed by the media to have the best organizational backing and the most experience was badly wounded. Next "in line" was Paul Tsongas, a little-known former senator with limited name recognition, hardly any organization outside of New Hampshire, and a speech impediment. In horserace terms, the field lacked a frontrunner. As a result, the competition seemed unformulated, muddied, unclear.

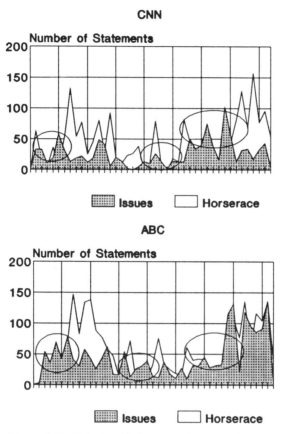

Figure 2.5   Relationship Between Issue and
Horserace References on CNN and ABC, by Week

By the time the New York primary rolled around in early spring, Pat
Buchanan's challenge to George Bush had all but played out and Bill Clinton
had outlived all his opponents except for Jerry Brown, who was far behind in
delegate support and saddled with a reputation for being too existential for
conventional politics. A credible "ABC" movement (Anyone But Clinton)
never developed, leaving the Arkansas governor without strong competition.
From a horserace standpoint, the finish line of the primary stage had been
crossed.

There were peaks of horserace interest later in the spring and summer as the
Ross Perot petition drive gained steam and the Texas billionaire's numbers
rose in opinion polls. And of course there were the party conventions in July
and August. But the horserace was in hiatus from convention time until Labor
Day, which for television news executives traditionally marks the "official

kickoff" of the fall campaign, the cue to saturate the airwaves with horserace matter.

Predictably, during those periods when the horserace was either unformulated, momentarily resolved, or in hiatus, overall election coverage lagged. But surprisingly, during each of these periods and on both networks, the absolute amount of issue coverage surpassed the absolute amount of horserace coverage. In other words, both networks paid more attention to the issues than to the horserace when the horserace was cold. Of course, it helped to have a conflictive economic issue of enduring national concern; without this, it is questionable whether issue coverage would have been prominent even when the horserace was not newsworthy. With a salient, conflict-laden, relevant issue at hand, cable and broadcast television chose to emphasize the issue more than the horserace at these times. And note that "issue" is singular; anything not related to the economy was still largely discounted.

The recipe for issue coverage, then, combines a slow or uncontested horserace with a hot, worrisome policy concern. Under these circumstances, the volume of election coverage—still determined by the horserace—may be at its nadir, but the story will be portrayed in terms of the issue. The reason for the prevailing judgment that television simply is not interested in the issues is that we hadn't seen this combination of conditions since television became the most important linkage between voter and candidate. The 1976 and 1988 elections offered competitive races without a singularly prominent, worrisome policy issue. The economy and America's strength abroad were paramount in 1980, but the race was fiercely contested. The 1984 election offered plentiful references to "morning in America," but neither intense competition nor salient issue.

Low horserace interest with high issue content is an unlikely combination of factors. An issue of great magnitude would normally be expected to generate a large, competitive field of candidates. In 1991, while big-name Democrats were deciding to sit this one out, the economy was in recession but television had not yet begun portraying a depressed "national mood." George Bush wasn't popular by acclamation as he had been during the Persian Gulf War, but he was still perceived in many Washington circles as a war hero who would be reelected without much trouble. The primary field was set by January, and the economic recovery never came. Conditions were in place for the media to pay attention to the economy.

Subject of Coverage

When commonly reported subjects of election coverage are considered along with the thematic topics, it becomes apparent that the election story was cast in terms that interested television personnel: The choices were not only political but *personal* and *nonideological,* with the emphasis on reporter sources, their audience, and themselves. Partisan individuals were overwhelmingly the most frequent subjects of coverage. Most of these individuals were candidates, although coverage of campaign operatives increased somewhat as the months went by. During the primaries, when campaigns were still small and loosely organized, reporters had fairly free and direct access to the candidates.[18] This access, coupled with the reporter's predisposition to conceptualize election news as a story about a race, translated into the strong candidate emphasis apparent in Figure 2.6. In the fall, attention to candidates dropped off on both networks but they remained the predominant subject. This happened as campaign organizations grew larger and the surviving candidates were in greater demand. But on both networks the candidates were still the story.

Even as campaign organizations became more pronounced and layers of campaign workers separated the candidate from the reporter, the campaign as an institution was still rarely mentioned as a subject of election coverage. The campaign is an institution and not a source, and television reporters tend to present information in terms of how it is derived. "The campaign" makes sense as a cognitive structure and was at times used by reporters to stand for the activities it performed and the individuals who performed them. The clear choice, however, was to relate campaign information in the context of who—not what—it came from, and in the process the story of the election became personalized. People, not procedures or processes, were the stuff of the televised election.

They were also the audience for the message. Producers and reporters alike maintain a personalized image of their viewership. Thinking in terms of "the average guy who watches us," newsworkers take an individualized view of the audience for their work that parallels their first-person approach to news sources. Together, these elements define their role: connecting individuals at home with information from (and/or about) individuals involved in some activity. During an election, this means the candidates or their aides.

Interestingly, these individuals—members of the public, the candidates and their operatives, and the reporters who cover them—are exactly the subjects who got the most attention in the story itself in 1992. After candidates and their aides, public citizens were the second most commonplace subjects of election coverage, often anonymously or symbolically portrayed ("Juanita is an unemployed mother of two"). Statements about candidates were still far more commonplace—six times more frequent, to be exact—than statements about citizens.[19] But even marginal attention to the public demonstrates how television defines its mission as a conduit between the political world and the viewer then incorporates that mission into the substance of coverage. The presidential campaign is conceptualized as the interplay between the political sphere and the public. Symbolically, politics is characterized by the candidate, the public by a sound bite of one of its "typical" members.

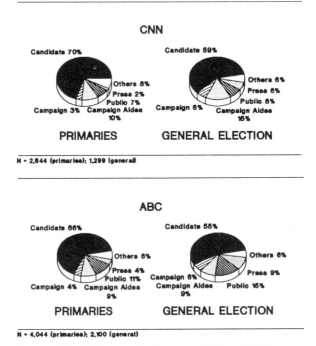

Figure 2.6   Statement Subjects on CNN and ABC

When election coverage is produced, the self-defined role of the media as link between politics and polity is converted into these archetypal forms. The story is portrayed in terms defined by television's place in the process, from television's perspective. Later, when we consider objects (individuals and institutions portrayed in relation to subjects), we will see that the public has a larger role in the campaign story as an object of candidate behavior. And we will see a far more prominent role for the press itself, also as the object of candidate behavior, as we observe how reporters wrote their own experiences into the campaign story.

If candidates, their aides, and generic members of the public constituted the subject matter of campaign coverage, a lot of groups, individuals associated with groups, and institutions were left out. The small slice of Figure 2.6 devoted to "others" combines all statements about individuals or groups either supporting or opposing a candidate as well as nonpartisan groups and the individuals associated with them. This category encompasses a vast array of actors, from the National Rifle Association to the Sierra Club to the American Civil Liberties Union to the Veterans of Foreign Wars to essentially every organized group or interest. It includes the specific portrayal of individuals as members of a socioeconomic group, such as blue collar workers, the wealthy, or the working poor. It extends to portraying individuals in terms of age or gender distinctions (young, female, etc.), racial or ethnic characteristics, or place of residence.

Only 333 of 10,329 statement subjects were about group supporters, opponents, or nonpartisans, and only 476 statement subjects categorized individuals or members of the public in specific socioeconomic or demographic terms. There were only 166 mentions that could even loosely be considered ideological in nature, and most of these could be more accurately described as political references to Republicans or Democrats (there were hardly any references to conservatives or liberals). Both the cable and broadcast portrayal of the election favored the generic over the specific and the partisan or political over the ideological.

With the election represented as a race toward a personal goal, this nonideological perspective makes perfect sense. Elections could be seen as opportunities for philosophical discourse and could thus be cast in ideological terms. It is even conceivable to imagine that elections could be portrayed in terms of the competition between or among ideologies, which would allow television to cover the campaign without abandoning the use of football and baseball analogies. But there is little room for ideological references in a personalized conflict. Even the unusual attention given to economic issues in 1992 tended to be addressed in terms of the candidates' awareness of and proposed solutions to the problem as opposed to, say, their philosophy of governance.

I do not mean to argue that one perspective is qualitatively better than the other. Rather, I am saying that television's is only one of a host of possible perspectives that could be brought to bear on the election and that this outlook is inevitable given television's central location in the course of events and its tendency to personalize the world and talk about itself. For all the discussion of variety afforded by the explosion of cable channels, technology can offer only greater availability, not greater choice. That is up to the programmers, and they are most strongly influenced by consensual assumptions about news.

Just as the heavens appear different depending on what planet you happen to occupy, the election story looks the way it does because of where the media are positioned in the process. Similar sources, similar reporter-source relationships, and similar ideas about what constitutes news cut across whatever format differences may exist between CNN and ABC, yielding a press consensus about election news content. In the next four chapters, we will see how this consensus manifested itself in coverage of the 1992 campaign, putting aside temporarily the cable-broadcast distinction to examine the story that viewers found no matter where they turned.

A principal component of that story was the central role of the media in the electoral process. Tendencies for "me" the reporter to tell "you" the viewer what "I" am experiencing facilitated television's proclivity to portray the election as a story about itself. This leads us to recast Walter Cronkite's signature claim—"That's the way it is"—in the first person, as television reporters essentially say, "That's the way we see it," or, with increasing regularity, "That's the stuff we're interested in," where what we're interested in is quite often little more than our own experience. Nowhere was this more evident than at those times when television election coverage was about the process of creating television election coverage, the subject to which we now turn.

3

Covering the Coverage:
The Self as News

Coverage of the process now threatens to drown it.

—Jeff Greenfield, ABC News[1]

On March 6, 1992, Brit Hume submitted the following account of the Bush campaign to ABC News: "Stung by news stories characterizing Mr. Bush's campaign events as lackluster, Press Secretary Fitzwater ordered the press room loudspeakers turned off, to force reporters—lazy bastards he called them—to go outside and see the cheering crowd for themselves."[2] That very day, Jill Dougherty of CNN reported the same occurrence in almost the same language:

> As President Bush steamrolled through the South, his press secretary was rolling over the national press following Mr. Bush, calling them—quote—lazy bastards, telling them to get out of the press work space and go to a Bush rally to report on it for real. Marlin Fitzwater then cut off the public address system that routinely provides an audio feed of the president's remarks to reporters who must file their stories under tight deadlines.[3]

Conflicts such as the one reported on March 6 between reporters and campaign officials are as old as the free press itself. What makes this exchange—and numerous others like it—so noteworthy is the fact that it was, indeed, reported. Secretary Fitzwater yelled at correspondents so that his actions would affect coverage. Instead, his actions became *the subject* of coverage, as reporters saw the conflict itself as a source of news. True to journalistic convention, both accounts of the incident were written in the third person (he called *them*

35

lazy bastards), but in stark contrast to that same tradition, the group being objectified was the group to which the reporter belonged.

One of the preeminent stories of the 1992 presidential campaign was the reporter's own story: the interactions with candidates; the experiences on the road; the frustrations of covering a national campaign; and other similar items about the process of reporting a presidential election and the place of the press in that process. The experiences themselves were not new, but their appearance in a running miniseries deemed worthy of valuable news time represented a significant development in television's political role.[4] One in five statements about the election included some reference to the media. These statements appeared more frequently on ABC than on CNN, but CNN was not immune to conceptualizing the campaign in reporter's terms.[5] Often, both networks featured behind-the-scenes details of dubious relevance to the election itself and of limited utility to the public.

Consider, for instance, this follow-up to Fitzwater's actions, also contained in the March 6 CNN story:

> Reporters say there's a good reason to have the audio feed to the filing center. [Sound bite of CNN correspondent Charles Bierbauer, identified as the President of the White House Correspondent's Association, saying: "You could have reporters who are in a work area rather than at the event where the president is because that's the only place they can plug in their computers, hook up their microphones, listen to what the president is saying and get their reports done before it's time to jump back on the plane."][6]

Does the public need to know *why* reporters conduct their business as they do? In the best journalistic tradition, the CNN piece attempts to balance its initial quote from the press secretary with an "opposing viewpoint" explaining the set-up he had attacked. But presenting the opposing viewpoint required interviewing and reporting the statement of a fellow journalist and had the effect of advancing the reporter-versus-campaign theme, all the while placing the otherwise hidden world of the reporter on center stage.

Types of Process Coverage

Coverage of coverage took five discernable forms. There were a large number of unspecified references invoking the media in general or television in particular. There were a few behavioral accounts of things candidates did in order to improve their chances of being covered in a favorable light, and a considerable number of statements about the motivation guiding these behaviors. There were frequent mentions of the particulars of the candidate-press relationship. Finally, there were a smattering of technical comments about the mechanics of covering the campaign.

General References

This category accounted for the greatest share of process coverage on both networks, particularly during the general election campaign, as Figure 3.1 indicates. Statements falling into this group tend to be generic, self-conscious references to television or the media, encompassing comments about news reporting, talk shows, even on occasion entertainment programming. Collectively, they reveal the tendency of television decision-makers to talk about the world in which they live; some, like the statement from Jeff Greenfield quoted at the start of this chapter, reveal great self-awareness about the imagined effect of that world. Thus, process coverage is often at once self-referential and self-aware, addressing items that concern the media to the point of speculating about the wisdom of including them in campaign coverage. Invariably, such introspection is reported in the third person, as though the consequences of process coverage are beyond the means of those creating it. In 1992, this practice generated stories with an oddly detached feel, written by reporters who were compelled to cover their role in the campaign and who were aware that doing so might undermine the responsibility they felt to their audience, yet who were somehow unable to do it any other way.

General statements like these were typical:

> The trouble for Clinton [is] the press hounds him about his character; *voters seem more worried about other things.*[7]

> [There is] a feeling among many voters [in New Hampshire] that some of *the press and the public are not necessarily interested in the same things,* and a feeling that much of the press ... is actually cutting the candidates off from the voters.[8]

> [Clinton tries to] get past the press in order to talk to the voters.[9]

The irony of these statements is that their very existence validates their premise. If the press is intent on reporting that the press is keeping a candidate from getting out his message, then the candidate is not getting out his message. Reporting items such as these simply serves to advance their own truth. Notwithstanding the considerable self-awareness contained in such observations, the tendency to report about "the press" as though it were any other third party raises an important question: If the media are aware that as they write themselves into the story they alter its content, why do they keep doing so? To follow the "media-in-the-process" soap opera is to wonder whether reporters cannot resist the desire to put themselves and their interests at the center of their coverage, relying on the occasional self-analysis as a cry for perspective, as if to say: Stop me before I broadcast again.

The answer rests in large part with how "the story" is conceptualized by television personnel, who (as we will see in Part II) invariably believe that such a thing as "the story" exists and that it can be differentiated from things that are simply "not news." It would be impossible for "the story" to originate

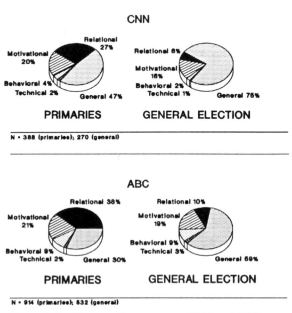

Figure 3.1   Process Coverage on CNN and ABC

from any viewpoint but that of the individual writing it. However, when correspondents personalize the content of their material rather than simply letting their perspective serve as a vantage point for observation, the result is self-referential, self-conscious reporting in the guise of third-person narrative.

A process story broadcast before the Iowa caucuses demonstrates this phenomenon. In 1992, the brief candidacy of Iowa Senator Tom Harkin made the nation's first caucus routine and unsuspenseful—two words hardly in the lexicon of television producers. Accordingly, one could predict the minimal media coverage Iowa received. On January 28, ABC News reported that the press had little interest in Iowa—in its own right, a self-referential process observation. But the network went further, as the main purpose of the report was to inform the viewer that the press was interested in why it wasn't interested: "Iowans have lost the political clout and media attention they used to enjoy. Now the only media interest is in what's not happening."[10]

The story (if it needed to be told at all) could have been readily reported in terms of, say, lost revenue to Iowa business as a result of a noncompetitive caucus. Doing so would have maintained television's first-person vantage point (Iowa to media: Having a good time, wish you were here) without injecting self-conscious insights about why the story made it to the evening news. Instead, as was so often the case with process statements, the reporter talked of "them" but the content said "me."

Campaign Behavior

Sometimes, coverage of the press-campaign relationship focused on gestures made by candidates, campaigns, or campaign operatives to advance their causes in a media-dominated electoral game. This sort of process coverage, which is somewhat more evident on ABC than on CNN, incorporated two particular types of campaign behavior: efforts to construct a public image and attempts to influence media coverage. Both relate the actions of political subjects toward the press.

Image construction came in the form of staging events, running campaign ads, timing activities conveniently for television broadcast, carefully selecting attractive or emotional backdrops for a presentation—anything the campaign did to portray a favorable televised impression. These events became process references when reporters addressed the intent behind the event rather than the event itself. How, for instance, will people in New Hampshire select a candidate? Gene Randall on CNN tells us, "Television figures to play a major role," as "political ads will help a lot of people decide how to vote next month. Accordingly, before long, those ads can be expected to blanket the airwaves much as this day's snow is blanketing the ground."[11] As early as January 9, before most political ads had even been produced, Randall looked at the snowfall and saw in its coat a metaphor for the impending blizzard of campaign commercials. Anticipating (accurately) how candidates would behave as the primary drew near, CNN chose to inform the national audience of this detail long before the fact.

Reports of attempts to influence coverage concentrated on behind-the-scenes activities such as creating and marketing campaign ads, staging rallies for television, and getting a candidate's supporters on the air. Always, the campaign's efforts were explained in terms of how to get noticed by television, often to the point where gaining and holding media attention appeared to be the only functions of the campaign. The most comprehensive example of this sort of process coverage was broadcast on ABC two weeks before the November election. Two stories were devoted exclusively to the efforts of the Bush and Clinton Michigan campaigns to get their messages out to the public. Every behavior relayed in both stories is understood in terms of influencing television coverage. The Bush/Quayle effort was reported first:

> Yesterday, at the first hint of winter, the Republican chairman in Battle Creek was putting out signs to welcome Vice-President Dan Quayle. Window dressing, really, because he had already told all the local radio and television stations that Quayle was coming. And that's the most important thing he can do—use the local media. At a local high school gym, everything was prepared so that when the Vice-President did arrive, there would be a colorful environment for television coverage. Television coverage in all the local markets across the state is what the campaign is after—get the message on television and radio. This did not turn out to be a giant rally, but when the faithful who came only filled up half the school

gym, it still looked like a lot of people on television. ... And last night it was the lead story on television stations in at least three small Michigan cities. ... It will be this way all over the nation for the next 13 days—Republicans will do it and Democrats will do it.[12]

Everything is defined in terms of advertising and packaging the Quayle appearance for television. Other objectives of the Quayle visit are marginalized, including the personal impact of a vice-presidential visit on the citizens who turned out for it. The visit—the entire day—is used to symbolize campaign efforts to influence media coverage; why else would a late October vice-presidential campaign stop in a small midwestern city command national television time? The piece immediately following this one promoted the same theme, using examples from the Clinton/Gore campaign:

Everything is coordinated—radio, television, daily surrogates like Senator Jay Rockefeller at a Detroit hospital, then rallying the troops for Clinton. And even while invitations to another Clinton surrogate's appearance are going out, a local talk radio host plugs his next guest [video of Sen. Rockefeller appearing on talk show]. The questions are soft, the answers familiar. ... At WXYZ [television], a Clinton commercial airs. Enough commercials, the campaign calculates, for every viewer in Michigan to see at least two a day.[13]

Behavioral references do not capture the interplay of the candidate and the press, only the candidate's actions toward the media. They may address the inevitable tension that occurs between media and campaign when the latter attempts to use the former for its own ends, leaving reporters feeling frustrated in the wake of the effort. But reporters always have the last word, and representing the campaign's effort as simply a ploy to influence coverage can be salve for the wound.

This ABC portrayal of candidates in New Hampshire assesses the role of local television coverage in the campaign process: "The secret here [is] getting close to the people—or getting close to a camera that shows you getting close to the people."[14] Any correspondent or political operative will confirm the validity of this statement; it simply details one of the campaign's ongoing media games. In the television age, reaching people electronically replaces reaching people directly, although the secret to doing it effectively requires maintaining the appearance of personal contact and controlling the theme you communicate: at best, putting the campaign in the most favorable light, at worst, manipulating the message. The media are the vehicle for this exercise, but they are not in the business of advancing campaign agendas. So, tension often erupts. From the media standpoint, campaigns are engaging in cynical behavior when they attempt to twist and shape what is reported; the media respond by delivering what they think is an honest but suspicious account of that procedure.

Process references quite often reflect the cynical relationship between reporters and campaign officials, as seen by and related by the reporter, giving the viewer a skeptical look at those who would live in the White House and those who would put them there. Reporters are distrustful of those who want something from them, and when the media cover campaign attempts to influence coverage or portray a particular image, they simply call it as they experience it. But the effect of including these episodes in coverage must not be overlooked. Such stories invariably communicate a contemptuous view of the system. Reporting these activities has not altered or stopped them, but it has compounded their impact by laying bare the acrid components of an acrimonious process to an already distrustful public. Similarly, cynical coverage is commonplace among references to the motivation underlying candidate behavior and the relationship between the campaign and the press.

Candidate Motivation

Taking their story one step beyond what a candidate did in order to receive media play, correspondents in 1992 often related their understanding of the incentive guiding a candidate's actions. Motivational references looked past the actual behavior of the candidates, presenting a theory about why they acted a particular way. Of course, such theorizing invariably placed television in the election's center ring. Why did Bill Clinton toss around a baseball at a Red Sox spring training game before the Florida primary? Not simply to reach voters, but to reach the vehicle necessary to reach voters—as CNN put it, to make "a triple play for media coverage in three Super Tuesday states."[15]

Motivational references usually work backwards from some event involving the media in order to explain the candidate's actions relative to that event. So, it may have been sufficient from a news perspective for ABC to report that President Bush held a news conference on March 11. But the reporters went further, casting the press conference in purely political terms while explaining the singular reason for its occurrence: "As if to show that he considers the Republican race over, the president today did something he hasn't done in nearly two months—he held a formal White House news conference."[16]

Motivational observations such as these constituted one-fifth of all process references reported during the primaries on both networks and on ABC during the general election. Such references invariably propose the same hypothesis: Candidate actions are explainable (only) in terms of political ambition for which media attention is of utmost importance. President Bush, it is implied, would no sooner hold a press conference for nonpolitical reasons than Governor Clinton would attend a spring training game just to reach the voters in attendance (or because he liked the Red Sox). These conclusions are not necessarily inaccurate, but they are the only judgments television will portray. Viewers are not presented alternative perspectives necessary to challenge the reasoning that is obvious to the reporters who tell the story. Consequently, the story about reporting the story further reinforces television's perspective that all campaign actions are political and all political actions are staged for the cameras.

Candidate-Press Relations

So it is as well with relational statements, which address the ties between the press and the candidate or campaign. These references relate a particular set of candidate behaviors involving direct interaction with the press corps. As with behavioral references, the intent of the candidate's actions may well be to influence coverage. Instead of relating indirect activities such as staging rallies or running campaign ads, however, relational references specifically invoke candidate-press interaction.

The story is inevitably related in the third person but from the media's perspective. Often, the viewer is told things of dubious importance to the audience but of great interest to the reporter, such as the frustration or unhappiness the correspondent feels toward the campaign. A July entry on ABC about the first Clinton-Gore bus tour betrayed this perspective. The correspondent first revealed his view of the world by saying that the tour was so effective as to make the campaign "as real to [the public] as television" (an observation worth considering in its own right!). The audience was then told that this effect was the product of the campaign cynically keeping "the cameras focused only on what the campaign sees as helpful to them." And viewers were told by a correspondent, in the third-person voice of a supposed nonparticipant, how this made the press feel and act: "The media were not amused, but they went where they were told anyway, according to the script."[17] The audience learned that the campaign was an act staged by the candidates as all the while reporters were but the extra players in a script they did not write. But, of course, they *do* write the script telling us about the play—the only script heard by millions of viewers each evening.

That script contained a sizable percentage of references to media-candidate interplay of this sort, particularly during the primary campaign, where relational references composed better than one-third of the process references on CNN and ABC. The following account of the second bus tour ran two and a half weeks after the first bus tour story appeared. The tour was still a novelty in the communities it reached, but not for the national press. Note the complaints about life on the bus juxtaposed against the equally caustic account of the sort of kissy local coverage the bus tour sought—and got:

> Like the first bus tour, this one set out to see voters in out of the way places, but the buses also make it easy to get local press coverage. More than 150 journalists are on board, triple the number on Clinton's plane. Local news operations can afford to send reporters on Clinton's bus. The campaign charges only $100 a day, donuts included. Clinton and Gore continue to draw good crowds *but say little the national media has not heard again and again.* [Sound bite of national re-

porter saying: "On this second bus tour, news: zero."] But for journalists from small, midwestern cities, just having the [Clinton/Gore] ticket in town is newsworthy enough. [Sound bite of local reporter: "We go through some pretty blah periods sometimes where you really have to fish for news so this is a story that's pretty big for us."] That's why after a day on the bus, Iowa anchorman Bruce Owney began his newscast with a long story about the bus visit. The local coverage is almost always friendly. Some headlines read like welcome mats, the kind of exposure the campaign couldn't buy with commercials. ... *The national press may be bored* but for Clinton on this trip, local news has been good news in the 15 media markets from St. Louis to Minneapolis.[18]

Once again, the press was the story. ABC related the second bus tour as a story about the number of reporters the bus could accommodate, about the affordability of the bus to local media, about why the bus tour was a big story in small markets, about why the national press believed there was no news substance to the trip, about why they were bored. Anyone who has traveled great distances on a bus that makes frequent stops can understand the sort of frustration that can set in. On ABC, that frustration informed news content. After one trip on a Greyhound, the emphasis quickly shifted from the efforts of the Clinton staff depicted in the first bus tour item to the news needs of local television and the pain and suffering of the national media in a report that all but asked, "Are we there yet?"

Like the skirmish between Marlin Fitzwater and the national press, relational process references usually portray conflict between the press corps and the campaign as it appears from the press's perspective. Sometimes, relations are given a cooperative spin, with the press and campaign operatives shown sharing a mutual experience that is larger than both. This is the implication of Jeff Greenfield's observation about what transpired following a candidate debate: "Just about the instant a presidential debate ends, the candidates and their handlers and the press feverishly gather around each other trying to figure out who won and who lost."[19] But this sort of cooperative portrayal is unusual because the media tend to see themselves as combatants in an ongoing struggle with campaigns rather than as partners in a shared experience.

So, it may have been inevitable that the buildup to the New York primary would take on an intensely competitive, press-oriented perspective in the nation's largest media market. The process miniseries heated up with a barrage of colorful media-as-gladiator references that portrayed the candidate-press relationship in terms that played off the stereotypes of life in the Big Apple commonly seen on television entertainment programs. Jerry Brown, the public was told, "could count on the New York media's appetite for controversy to magnify the daily darts of criticism he throws at Bill Clinton."[20] Clinton, in turn, "got a tiny taste of what to expect [in New York]: an attempted mugging by New York City's big, loud, aggressive press corps. The combative [New York] media market, with five TV stations and six newspapers, is just part of a New York political culture that historically treats the Democratic primary as a kind of blood sport."[21]

There was more. The New York press was called "a meatgrinder that wears TV make-up and carries a poison-tip pen. ... The talk-shows don't just talk, they rage." TV viewers were told how reporters felt about New York politics, that "analysts talk about the New York primary as if it was pollution." They were told that in New York, "the press is like a shadow lurking over the candidate's shoulder every second."[22] Every commercial metaphor for life in New York was brought to bear on a description of the New York media-campaign relationship: noise, pollution, disregard for human feeling, attempted mugging, a shadow behind one's back that portends ill will. These images were certainly not the work of the New York Chamber of Commerce and arguably not germane to election coverage. But ABC could not resist making the lure of the New York media circus into the story about the New York campaign. Reinforced by footage of cameras and lights engulfing Bill Clinton as reporters yelled "Hey guv-nah!" in that most unusual of accents, television made itself the story, effectively telling the national audience, "Just look at how bizarre this election process is; just look at how strange we are."

Technical Matters

More analytical than technical, process coverage incorporated relatively few references to the mechanics of covering the campaign. This is in part because of the narrow way technical references are defined: as specific mentions of insider jargon about how news reports are put together. Whereas thematic references to candidate-press relations might involve numerous individual statements, mentions of technical minutiae such as "sound bites," "spin," or "spin doctors" would be made briefly in passing. The combined number of these isolated references filled only a small portion of election news statements.

I chose to examine these mentions precisely because their meaning needs little explanation for many readers, despite the fact that the terms are peculiar to television. The fact that jargon like "sound bite" and "spin" has found its way into the vernacular is prima facie evidence of television's tendency to cover itself in its own terms. Where else could the viewing audience have heard references to these things if not on television itself? If they heard it on television, it could only be because the people who bring us the evening news have come to incorporate the language of their trade in the product they produce.

For readers who are not familiar with the terms, "spin" refers to the emphasis placed on events in a story. Bill Clinton's second-place finish in the New Hampshire primary could have qualified as "distant," or reporters could have supported his claim to be "the comeback kid"—without any change in the factual basis of the story, such as the candidate's percentage of the vote.

Campaign operatives who vehemently attempt to get reporters to accept their version of the story are called "spin doctors" by the press, and when they go into action, reporters will say they are engaging in "spin control." "Sound bite" is a television term that refers to brief video clips of an individual saying something pithy and pertinent to a story. Typically, television news will contain sound bites in an effort to diversify the presentation of the story so as to hold audience interest. This term has become such an integral part of the television-campaign relationship that candidates routinely talk about sound bites and television has taken to incorporating these references into coverage. Ross Perot even made the term a verb, when he implored the press not to "sound bite" him.

References can be made to these items in mere seconds, and rarely are they the *focus* of coverage; instead, they are related in statements about other things, such as in, "What's the 'spin control' coming out of the other campaigns this evening?"[23] and "In the predawn darkness before most of Detroit gets its wake-up call, local radio stations are getting theirs from this young man: Eric Hoffman offers them 'sound bites' from the Clinton campaign."[24] Relatively speaking, these observations are significant despite the small percentage of process coverage they represent. Specific references to "spin" or "sound bites" made up only 2 percent of the process coverage on CNN and ABC during the campaign. Their importance rests with the fact that they are mentioned at all. Television's belief that no further elaboration on these inside terms is needed beyond their mere mention demonstrates the degree to which the inner workings of the medium have become a commonplace part of its story.

The use of such slang compounds the fact that television coverage incorporates statements about how candidates attempt to control the media. Both Peter Jennings's aforementioned "spin control" comment to Cokie Roberts on the eve of the New Hampshire election and the "sound bite" observation about Clinton's Michigan campaign provide evidence that television addresses the election in its own terms and uses its own terminology in the discussion. The resulting effect is to lay bare the reporter's often distrustful perspective on campaign-media relations in phrases once reserved for newsroom discourse. "Spin control" brings to mind a military operation where press and campaign field workers are opponents, and "spin doctor," a hospital where reporter/patients lie helplessly under anesthesia as the physician "corrects" the story to reflect the doctor's perspective. These metaphors, mixed though they may be, capture how reporters often express their relationship to campaign operatives whose mission to portray their candidate in the most favorable light is vastly different from the reporter's goal to tell a story. The fact that this conflict is incorporated into the story, and that correspondents sense no need to clarify or explain their own backstage terminology, underscores the extent to which television has fixed its sights on itself: The story of the campaign is the story of the media in the campaign.

Television on Television

Consistent with this practice of covering the coverage, the story about telling the story is replete with images of reporters and references made by reporters. The main actors are the correspondents themselves and the candidates. The action is personal and, although impartial to particular candidates, it is generally cynical.

Compared to the total picture of election coverage, a greater percentage of process references were attributed to reporters and a smaller percentage of comments were made in sound bites. Sixty-six percent of the process statements on both networks were made by correspondents, whereas only 14 percent appeared as sound bites of individuals; this compares with 60 percent and 25 percent overall.[25] On CNN, an additional one in ten process statements were made by reporters, commentators, or analysts during the course of on-screen discussions of the process with one another. In other words, the media miniseries was predictably delivered in the reporter's voice.

Visual images associated with these statements underscored this emphasis. On both networks, when process statements were being made, better than 40 percent of the time the viewer saw pictures of reporters talking about the media: nothing fancy or even particularly interesting, simply a "talking head" (to use a television term) with a microphone. This was the most frequently portrayed image in the process drama, the reporter as instructor offering insights into his or her experience covering the campaign. Candidates, without whom process coverage would be impossible, shared the screen with reporters. Together, the two groups constituted the bulk of the imagery telecast by CNN and ABC during the process miniseries.

Images that did not appear may be even more instructive. Process coverage scantly included pictures of singular individuals (representatives of the so-called public), people in crowds, staged campaign events, campaign ads, or even of campaign operatives, running mates, and the like. Such images rarely occurred because the process story was simply not about them. There was no direct connection with the public (the story was told "to" us, yet it was not "about" us). Rather, viewers heard the reporter's personal account of life on the road with the candidate.

Thus it is largely uninteresting footage that accompanied the process story. Even the pictures of candidates tended to be of the talking head variety, with few crowd shots or interesting backdrops. Sometimes, as Figure 3.2 indicates, on-screen graphics supplemented talking heads, adding visual variety to a story that did not naturally generate interesting or colorful pictures. These made-for-television frames spiced up the presentation of topics lacking the

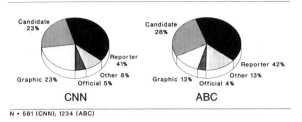

N = 581 (CNN); 1234 (ABC)

Figure 3.2   Visual Images Associated with Process
Coverage on CNN and ABC

draw of frequent sound bites and conveyed information central to the thematic nature of process coverage in order to underscore the main points of the story for the viewer.

But the story-about-the-story maintained a regular presence on both networks despite the rather limited and uninteresting series of pictures accompanying the words. In a medium widely believed to be driven by the availability of good pictures, this is noteworthy. The accessibility or choice of videotape cannot account for the consistent presence of process news as a regular feature of election coverage. Instead, the content of the material prevailed despite the lack of interesting video. News value was found in the appeal of a story line with natural and obvious concern to those who were reporting it.

Between CNN and ABC, the particulars of that story varied somewhat even as the constant themes of candidate-media relations, candidate motivation, and candidate behavior did not. In its process coverage, ABC devoted equal attention to the major party nominees during the primaries and the general election campaign, relegating process coverage of Ross Perot to an extended footnote. CNN discussed President Bush more than Governor Clinton in process terms, while its process coverage of Perot commanded about twice the percentage of coverage found on ABC. And, as Figure 3.3 relates, CNN coverage of Perot's general election campaign was the basis for far more process coverage than either of his competitors received during this stage. On CNN, "Perot II" was an integral part of the process story; on ABC, neither the first Perot effort nor the sequel made for much process drama. As one might expect, the primary candidates who were winnowed out of the process simply were not the focus of much of this sort of discussion. Tsongas, Brown, Harkin, Kerrey, and Buchanan combined received less than one-fifth the process coverage of the three surviving candidates.

These differences were a matter of editorial choice—we have already seen that ABC simply paid less attention than CNN to the Perot campaign. But they are differences in emphasis more than content. If the CNN process miniseries emphasized the Perot effort more than the Bush reelection drive, it nonetheless discussed the same media-oriented topics found in ABC's process play.

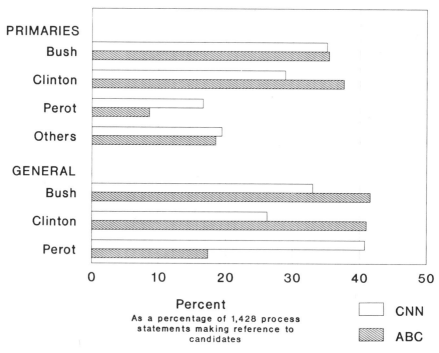

Figure 3.3   Percentage of Process Statements About Select Candidates on CNN and ABC

Substantive similarities extended as well to the nonevaluative nature of process coverage. The theme of the story might have been self-referential and cynical, but candidates were portrayed in a balanced, impartial way on both networks. Combined, 78 percent of statements about the process were neutral; that is, they contained no obvious bias for or against a candidate or campaign. An additional 11 percent were "mixed" or balanced, containing both a positive and a negative assessment of an individual or campaign. The remaining few statements split evenly between those clearly favorable or positive toward a political actor and those undoubtedly negative.[26] Thus, process coverage was without noticeable bias toward any of the political combatants.

Considering the inward focus of the story line, this is not surprising. Fundamentally, reporters were talking about themselves and evaluating their experiences, which were not political in nature and did not expressly invoke the political outcome of the campaign. It could even be argued that this entire line of coverage—the whole process miniseries—was astride the campaign, neither related to its content nor necessary to its outcome. The information related would not help the viewer reach an informed vote choice as much as it would instruct the viewer as to the peculiarities of generating all the other coverage that constituted the election story. Detached from the evening news, these process items would make an interesting documentary about covering a campaign, or even a good made-for-television movie (provided more compelling visual images could be found). But they were of dubious value to the consumer of election news.

They were far more useful to the reporter than to the viewer, for as we will see in Part II, they enabled him to vent frustration, alleviate boredom, find new quirks in redundant experiences, and address the familiar in a medium that required storytelling. As an outlet for correspondents under pressure, telling the story-about-telling-the-story was an obvious and helpful way to get the job done. That is why coverage of the process marbleized television's year-long account of the election.

4

Issues and Nonissues: Bread and Circuses

The economy and politics—these days, it's impossible to separate the two.

—Peter Jennings, ABC News[1]

[The Gennifer Flowers press conference] was a media circus of the highest—some might say lowest—order.

—Charles Feldman, CNN[2]

Television is not supposed to be interested in campaign issues; they are dry, technical in nature, and do not lend themselves to the sort of action footage or crisp quips believed to keep the viewer watching. Those who have studied past campaigns have consistently resolved that issue content is outdueled for television time by the horserace and personality items.[3] The 1992 election marked a dramatic departure from this conclusion. This time, issues received a great deal of attention—or, more accurately, *one issue* did. Conditions were such that the story of the economy became one of the ongoing thematic components of coverage on both cable and network television. This chapter will examine the makeup of issue coverage in the 1992 campaign and assess the conditions that brought the economy to the fore.

This emphasis on a serious issue in 1992 did not come at the expense of the more traditional soap-opera features of campaign coverage. There were still the allegations or rumors about candidates, their illicit or unethical behavior, serious illnesses, questionable judgment, and other matters that television calls "issues" but that bear no relationship to policy matters. I call them "nonissues," not because they have no substance but because their substance is derived more from the campaign's carnival side than from its serious side. In this chapter I will also look at the top nonissues of the 1992 campaign and consider how they came to occupy the considerable space they claimed on the television screen.

Issues: The Economy, Stupid

In 1984, Ronald Reagan's advisers were confident that their opposition could not run a successful campaign against the mounting federal deficit, in large part because a deficit is abstract, complex, technical, dry—just the sort of thing that would not play on television. By 1992, times had changed. With public opinion polls showing large numbers of Americans feeling burdened by economic conditions, and with the media believing this to be the case, the economy nudged its way into the campaign headlines, spearheading a surge of issue-oriented coverage unparalleled in recent elections. The discussion was oriented to the mass audience and tended toward the generic, but it was ongoing and intensive. Three in ten statements on CNN and ABC contained issue references, nearly half of which were about the economy.[4]

On both networks, interest in the issues peaked twice: once during the early primaries and again during the general election. Figure 4.1 shows that during both these phases, coverage of the economy was the singularly most discussed issue, with a host of other domestic and foreign policy topics following suit. In fact, the issue miniseries is best understood by addressing two questions: What received saturation coverage, and what received only passing attention? The answer to the first question is the economy. The answer to the second question is everything else.

The fabled admonition posted in the Clinton campaign war room, "The economy, stupid," could just as easily have been television's election coverage motto as the Democrat's campaign theme. Statements about unemployment and taxes led the parade of references to the economy. This is in part because unemployment is easily symbolized on videotape by long lines at the unemployment office or at a prospective employer's doorstep, in part because taxation is a traditional topic of economic and political discourse. Taxes in particular were widely discussed by candidates in this post–"read my lips" election year, and there is a widespread sense among media personnel that taxes concern a broad audience. All of these factors contributed to the high degree of attention given the subject on the evening news.

When the assumption of ample audience appeal is lifted, media attention diminishes, even for economic topics dear to the hearts of the candidates. Talk of unemployment or taxation was five times as likely to appear on either CNN or ABC broadcasts as mentions of either social security or trade policy, items of interest to smaller segments of the viewing audience.[5] More technical matters received even less attention. The two networks offered only a smattering of references to such things as industrial policy, interest rates, and infrastruc-

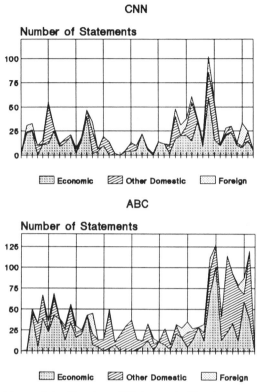

Figure 4.1 Number of Statements About
Domestic and Foreign Policy on CNN and ABC,
by Week

ture, regardless of how often Governor Clinton may have delved into the minutiae of these topics. For all its newfound attention to economic interests,
the evening news still did not present itself as a forum for detailed discussion
of issue particulars.

Beyond these bread-and-butter matters, television's attention fell off
quickly. Figure 4.2 details the share of issue coverage devoted to various domestic and foreign policy issues. A broad range of noneconomic subjects were
discussed, but coverage of each was shallow. Health care, which could arguably be classified as an economic topic given the link between health costs and
deficit reduction, heads the list of second-tier issues. It was given some attention on both networks prior to the New Hampshire primary and before the
departure of Nebraska Senator Robert Kerrey, who had made health care his
central campaign theme. Following New Hampshire, health care was only
sporadically addressed until the general election campaign, when Clinton and
Bush engaged in a brief dialogue about the subject.

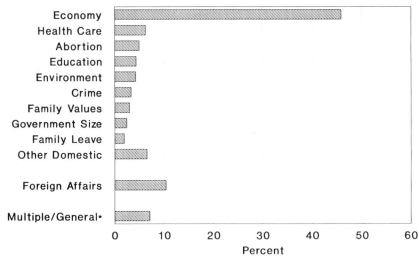

Domestic or foreign policy items

N • 3,028

Figure 4.2   Percentage of Attention Devoted to Select Issues, CNN and ABC Combined

Following health care are seven less salient domestic issues, each of which received between 2 and 5 percent of issue coverage. The abortion issue was on television's back burner throughout the primaries but suddenly became a hot topic during the convention phase. This flare-up was due to the threatened floor fight at the Republican convention over strict antiabortion language in the platform. Once this conflict passed, the subject all but vanished, receiving only three more references on CNN and ABC evening news during the general election period. The conflict inherent in the abortion issue, although great, was not sufficient to elevate it to a premier topic of discussion. It took the high degree of *political* controversy native to the convention fight *about* abortion to make it an issue worthy of discussion on the evening news.

Television also didn't get very excited about education or the environment, notwithstanding claims by George Bush to be both the "education" and the "environmental" president. These issues were featured during the general campaign and, along with government management, were offered as matters of concern to the West Coast audience during the California primary stage. Both were emphasized more by ABC than by CNN. The issue of crime also received more attention on ABC, most of it during the general election. "Family values" straddles the line between issue and ideology, addressing a philosophy of governance as much as a set of specific policies. ABC treated it as an issue late in the election campaign, once President Bush and Vice President Quayle started talking about family values at their rallies. No mention of the topic was made before the California primary stage, because none of the candidates had yet brought it up. Family leave, in contrast to family values, is a clear policy issue; it was mentioned in passing by both ABC and CNN during the general election campaign, when Congress sent President Bush family leave legislation that he did not support.

Most of the references to these noneconomic matters were made on ABC's "American Agenda" segment, the regular feature of "World News Tonight" that focuses on American problems and policy. As mentioned in chapter 2, ABC News had decided prior to the fall campaign to use "Agenda" segments to devote attention to candidate positions. This feature accounts for the relative lack of attention given by CNN to topics like education, the environment, crime, and family leave and explains the general election bulge in ABC noneconomic issue coverage evident in Figure 4.1. Because of the subject-by-subject format, the result was a few stories on each issue, hardly enough to compete with the attention television was giving to the economy but enough to diversify somewhat the range of issues addressed on ABC and silence critics who claimed television news had few substantive interests.

To underscore the point, one need only consider the liberal number of issues garnering no more than a handful of mentions on either network *all year*. These topics either were not addressed beyond the "American Agenda" series or were overlooked almost entirely by both networks.[6] Collectively, twelve domestic issues made up only 7 percent of the entire issue drama: energy, agriculture, drugs, civil rights, poverty and homelessness, government ethics, congressional term limits, child care, school prayer, pornography, AIDS, and cable television regulation. An eclectic assortment of concerns, these topics speak to a wealth of items germane to an election supposedly about domestic matters. Any of them easily could have been the focus of more television coverage and certainly would have been of interest to some portion of the audience. Instead, they were relegated to third-tier status, behind the economy and a few select domestic concerns.

If we consider the relatively minor amount of attention paid to most domestic topics, it becomes clear that aside from the economy, television's treatment of the issues was business as usual. ABC's intermittent efforts to highlight certain issues helped matters, but in truth television stomped on the economic material and treaded lightly on everything else. The issue story of this election was the story of the economy.

Nowhere is this more apparent than in foreign policy coverage, traditionally a key component of presidential elections. In 1992, foreign affairs was the policy orphan of the campaign, so ignored that it barely registered as a newsworthy topic. On both networks' evening news shows over ten months, there were only a combined 314 references to specific foreign policy matters—less than the 329 statements about Bill Clinton's draft history! Moreover, one-fifth of these were about American defense spending—arguably a domestic economic concern.

It was as if the rest of the world had gone away. The anticipated flood of references to the Persian Gulf War, once expected to be a sound bite staple of the campaign, simply never materialized (only 100 statements were made about Iraq). The Soviet Union was gone as a political entity and as an election topic; it was mentioned only 55 times on CNN and ABC combined and not once during the general election. There were only four statements about arms control. In a post–Cold War election, before American troops were sent to Somalia and before the media became aware of Bosnia, foreign policy was a story about the past. The Persian Gulf, Russia, nuclear weapons—these were battles resolved, far less pressing than the future-oriented domestic economic concerns that dominated issue coverage.

Of course, the world hadn't gone away—it only felt like it had to those making the editorial decisions about what to broadcast. Theoretically, Iraq or Russia or nuclear weapons could have been included on "American Agenda" reports, but as we will see in Part II, "Agenda" reporters were typically assigned to domestic issues. Furthermore, television newsmakers simply did not consider foreign policy to be part of the story in 1992. The prevailing belief was that the public was not interested in it and candidates were not talking about it—an attitude reinforced by opinion polls and by the self-fulfilling fact that candidates rarely answer questions they are not asked.

*   *   *

Unlike stories about the process of covering the campaign, which were dominated by reporter statements about the press, issue stories contained a large share of partisan references by and to the individuals being covered. This was evident in the percentage and content of sound bites associated with issue references. Sound bites composed almost one-third of the issue story, compared to one-quarter of overall election coverage.[7] They were dominated by political individuals—candidates, their operatives, and other elected officials— talking about the issues or someone's position on the issues.

The greater concentration of sound bites in the issue arena showed that both networks saw issue coverage as a story driven by the candidates and constructed the news accordingly. Whereas the process story originated with the correspondent's own interests and experiences, the issue story emanated from sources—in particular, political sources. Reporters gave shape and direction to the story through the questions they asked the candidates and through the footage they selected to use. But the emergence of the issue story was heavily dependent on the candidates and their surrogates discussing the issues, either of their own volition or in response to reporter questions. Correspondents, of course, elaborated on what candidates said (better than half the issue statements were spoken by reporters), but the story was built around the words and exploits of political figures rather than the immediate experiences or interests of reporters. In fact, correspondents expressed little first-person curiosity about the issue theme and engaged in hardly any on-air dialogue with one another about issue concerns. Only twenty-three issue observations were made during the course of discussion between anchor and reporter or reporter and expert, and rarely did an analyst appear on camera to discuss issue matters.[8]

Given this emphasis, it is scarcely surprising that issue stories focused on candidates almost to the exclusion of all other participants. Candidates were the featured subjects of nearly seven in ten domestic and foreign policy statements, as Figure 4.3 demonstrates. This finding holds for CNN and ABC, with the former emphasizing candidate subjects a bit more strongly. The mass public was given a far more limited role. Where private citizens were portrayed, it was invariably in response to the economic climate. People were described as unemployed, lacking health care, seeking government assistance, and the like. They were rarely presented as the subject of issue stories, even though poor economic conditions, not to mention other policy matters, ostensibly addressed public circumstances.

Instead, as we will see in chapter 6, the public was portrayed in relation to the candidates and their positions on the issues; they were seen as the *objects* of a *political* battle about policy direction rather than the featured *subjects* of a *policy* discussion about public concerns. Policy discourse was presented as a partisan dialogue involving presidential contenders; the public was depicted largely in relation to them. People responded to what candidates said but did not act as premier players in a policy discussion where they stood to win or lose.

If the public had a limited role in the domestic issue story, it had essentially no place in the minor foreign policy drama that meandered its way through campaign coverage. No public function was offered because television did not seek footage of individuals talking about international matters the way it gathered sound bites of people worried about putting bread on the table. The role of the public in the miniseries went the way of worries about nuclear weapons and the former Soviet Union, to name two prominent television favorites from the "old" days. As the public was perceived to be unconcerned about foreign policy matters (an assumption supported by opinion polls and reinforced by reporters not asking foreign policy questions of candidates), how could they be portrayed as subjects of coverage? This assumption relegated foreign policy to a short story about candidates and their operatives in which citizens had no apparent interest and were therefore not assigned a role. Candidates, to the degree they were depicted discussing foreign policy at all, were effectively talking to themselves.

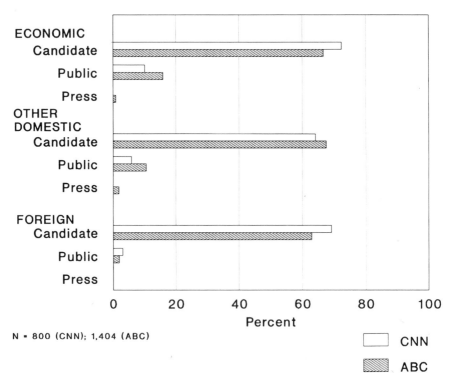

Figure 4.3   Subjects of Economic, Other Domestic, and Foreign Policy Stories on CNN and ABC

They certainly were not portrayed as talking to reporters, because the media wrote themselves out of the story as well. In contrast to process coverage, issue references were almost never about the press. In both foreign and domestic matters, correspondents highlighted the candidate orientation of the story by removing themselves as subjects of discussion. Neither did they present themselves as objects of coverage, as individuals with whom candidates were engaged in an issue dialogue.[9] Rather, they were silent. Television saw issue matters as a story about the office-seekers and dutifully stepped aside.

The pictures on the screen told the story. Issue references were accompanied on both CNN and ABC by a similar set of pictures, starting with a heavy dose of candidate "talking heads." Almost four of ten issue statements left the studio accompanied by candidate images, as Figure 4.4 attests. Another 5 percent included pictures of campaign personnel. These were generally dry, generic videotapes of familiar faces, not the staged, photo-opportunity, "candidate-portrayed-against-the-Statue-of-Liberty" shots designed to foster a political image. Mostly, candidates were shown talking about their or their opponent's position on an issue or serving as a pictorial prop while a cor-

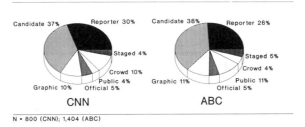

N = 800 (CNN); 1,404 (ABC)

Figure 4.4   Visual Images Associated with Issue
Coverage on CNN and ABC

respondent talked about them. Reporters themselves were depicted far less than in the process story.

In keeping with how the issue story was told, the public appeared infrequently. Between crowd and individual shots, the public was portrayed in 14 percent of CNN's coverage and 15 percent of ABC's. On ABC, the public was more likely to be symbolized by individuals rather than presented as an undifferentiated mass. This is in part because of an editorial decision, akin to using the "American Agenda" series, to videotape focus groups of individuals in several regions of the country talking about, among other things, campaign issues. During the general election campaign, "World News Tonight" was lightly peppered with excerpts from these groups—"typical" Americans sitting around a table discussing the election with Peter Jennings. Even though focus group footage did not constitute a large percentage of election coverage, its presence explains the disparity between the two networks in the amount of attention given individuals.

If the issue drama was a saga about those who would be president, it was one in which the participants were addressed unequally. In particular, it was a tale of two candidates—Bush and Clinton. Foreign policy matters, divorced as they were from the story of electoral competition, were almost exclusively portrayed as the domain of President Bush. A lesser role was given to his primary opponent Patrick Buchanan and to his Democratic challengers, including Bill Clinton. On front-burner economic matters and other domestic policy concerns, the news also highlighted the incumbent, but it allowed a somewhat larger role for Clinton than he received in the foreign policy arena. These findings pertain to both subject and object references, the latter being where a campaign actor was the target of a comment from an opponent. By this measure, President Bush was either the subject or object of two-thirds of the foreign policy coverage and better than half the economic coverage mentioning the presidential candidates.[10]

Largely hidden is Ross Perot, whose independent candidacy emerged (and reemerged) precisely because he argued that the major contenders were not discussing the issues. For reasons we will address in Part II, Perot was a negligible contributor to the election's issue component. His absence was most glaring in the economic arena, where he was either subject or object of no more than 6 percent of the stories that mentioned presidential candidates. This is especially consequential given the amount of televised attention devoted to the economy, particularly as an ingredient of the political race. Perot may have made an electoral splash, but despite his rhetoric he was a nonfactor in the televised economic play as it was shown on the evening news. In retrospect, this may have been a blessing for the independent, who went on to claim 19 percent of the vote on November 3, inasmuch as a good share of coverage about the economy was negative. For the length of the campaign, CNN and ABC portrayed the economy in unfavorable terms, combining fact-based reports of declining economic indicators with impressionistic pieces about how the ongoing recession (a negative phrase in its own right) had depressed something called the "national mood."

This observation is based on a detailed appraisal of the statements contained in economic stories. Each statement was assessed to determine whether it made judgments about the state of the economy. Evaluations could be negative (raising doubts, say, about the health of the economy or the likelihood that a candidate's plan would help much); positive (providing encouraging economic statistics or indicating a change in the perceived public psychological recession); or mixed (containing both positive and negative information in a single statement, such as in, "Unemployment claims were down last week, but the labor department calls this a short-term anomaly"). Comments about the condition of the economy and assessments of the candidates' economic policies and positions were considered. Depending on the context of the statement, the evaluation could be the newscaster's own comment or the words of a campaign actor relayed via sound bite.

Doris Graber argues that unfavorable news coverage may take two forms: the communication of displeasing information and the communication of information in an unfavorable way.[11] Both forms describe coverage of the economy in 1992. The big loser was George Bush, who, as the incumbent, was portrayed far more often than his opponents in the context of the bad economy. Television news said that it was, in effect, his economy; he was responsible for it. Figure 4.5 shows the extent of this negative association. Omitting neutral statements, which accounted for slightly less than half the references to Bush and just under two-thirds of the references to Clinton, the evening news linked Bush to the economy on 223 occasions over the course of the campaign—three times as often as Bill Clinton.[12] The economic picture contained few positive words for anyone. But it was most negative for the president, who was specifically linked to pessimistic economic news 233 times, or 71 percent of the total.[13]

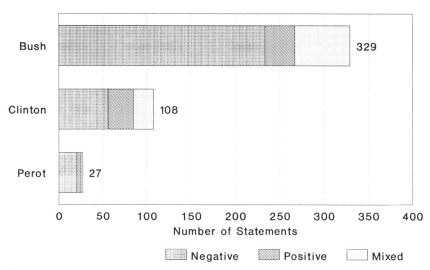

Figure 4.5 Evaluation of Statements About Major Candidates and the Economy, CNN and ABC Combined

Distinctly positive observations were far less frequent. Only 34 statements about Bush and the economy fell into this category, most of them accounts of the president's own cheerful words about the subject. And the volume of coverage was overwhelming; the 233 negative statements associated with the president were more than *all* the evaluated references to Governor Clinton and the economy, which *combined* totaled only 108.

So, President Bush was associated with the sour economy in absolute terms more frequently than his opposition was, and the percentage of acrid references connecting Bush and the economy was also higher. Even Bush's own favorable incantations didn't help him much,[14] although CNN and ABC did report them. Neither was he aided by positive imagery to counterbalance the dampening effect of negative fiscal assessments. We have already seen that most economic footage simply showed candidates or correspondents with their lips moving, with few staged backdrops of the sort campaigns love for portraying a positive feeling to the audience. It was a striking contrast to 1984, where Graber finds myriad negative words associated with coverage of Ronald Reagan's reelection effort but also the powerful appeal of favorable visual messages. George Bush suffered from negative text that was either reinforced by pictures of unemployment lines and closed shops or simply not challenged because of a dearth of engaging imagery.[15]

This trend began literally on day one and persisted until immediately before election day. Throughout the campaign, there was a negative cast to a particular type of economic coverage—Bush's strategic efforts to grapple with the issue. In late January 1992, ABC reported on the president's efforts to convince the public he had an economic program with this lukewarm assessment: "'It will work' may not seem the catchiest sales pitch, but remember, until this week all the president has had to say about the economy was that it was in a free-fall and that he cared about it."[16]

This statement could just as easily have appeared in October. Its emphasis on economic free-fall reinforced the message that the Bush administration was unable to get a handle on the matter. So it was with coverage of Bush's economic strategy for the better part of ten months.

And so it was for each major contender with policy matters of all sorts; between candidate allegations and reporter observations, issue coverage was decidedly negative. On noneconomic domestic policy issues, as with the economy, the major presidential contenders received bad press overall. This fact is simply but effectively illustrated when all negative comments about an issue are totaled and subtracted from all positive statements for each candidate. Negative results represent net negative coverage over the course of the election; large negative numbers indicate very negative coverage.

Figure 4.6 confirms that President Bush received worse press than his opponents, not just on economic matters but on all policy concerns. When the negatives are subtracted from the positives, the incumbent is left with a deficit of 144 negative statements about his involvement with noneconomic issue matters. Between negative evaluations of his record and charges from opponents that he had failed, television coverage left the distinct impression that Bush was a president who did not excel at domestic policy. Many of these negative evaluations referred to problems the nation faced that the Bush administration had not solved or addressed. Issues such as health care, crime, AIDS, and the string of items portrayed on "American Agenda" reports often focused on lingering or worsening domestic situations.

Coverage of the Clinton agenda, in contrast, included statements about what the candidate promised to do alongside critical evaluations of his Arkansas record or his proposals. The coverage generally pointed out where his assumptions were unrealistic or where his dollar estimates did not add up. This combination made the tenor of Clinton's coverage less severe than Bush's; consideration of future promises about unresolved problems almost nullified the impact of comments questioning his performance as governor. And Clinton simply wasn't as big a part of the domestic issue story.

If President Bush was inextricably bound to a poor economy, he at least held claim to being a strong foreign policy president. But coverage on this front offered only slightly less bad news than what befell him on the domestic side. Like the restaurant patron who complains that the food is bad *and* the portions are small, Bush received little attention from television in his purported strong suit, and when he did, the news wasn't very encouraging. There were 28 more negative than positive statements about the president and foreign policy, which is quite a large disparity for a matter that received little at-

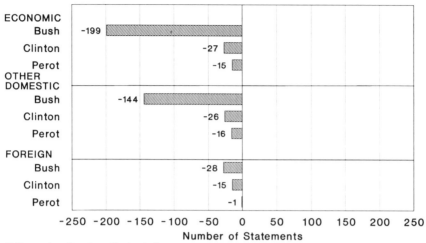

Figure 4.6   Number of Negative Evaluations Subtracted from Positive Evaluations of Candidate Statements About Select Policy Issues

tention (there were only 58 evaluated references to Bush and foreign policy during the entire campaign).

Most of the comments in this small pool were about the Persian Gulf War. The event that George Bush would otherwise point to in triumph was rarely a topic of television coverage and was treated critically when it appeared. Much of the negative coverage followed Saddam Hussein's renewed saber rattling during the general election campaign, which generated a flurry of stories about how Operation Desert Storm had failed to remove the Iraqi leader from power.

One final way of examining issue coverage is to distinguish substantive references to programs, platforms, approaches, statistics, and the like from that subset of issue references composed of catchy campaign phrases designed more to posture than to inform. All candidates posture, and posturing is often conveyed in the made-for-television sound bite, so one would expect issue posturing to be a sizable component of campaign coverage.[17] Often, posturing takes the form of candidates saying positive things about themselves or negative things about their opponents. Television, of course, has the choice of portraying the positive ("I'll cut the deficit in half in four years"), the negative ("We can't stand another four years of neglect"), or, of course, ignoring the matter entirely.

Not surprisingly, the issue posturing shown on both CNN and ABC was more often negative than positive. This finding is consistent with the overall negative tone of issue coverage in 1992 and underscores television's predilection for conflict. Verbal assaults, especially if communicated crisply, can be interesting and entertaining, and the candidates did not disappoint. Even before President Bush resorted to describing Senator Gore as "ozone man," all contenders were using colorful language to portray their opponent's policy positions.

Statements categorized as issue posturing were also evaluated according to their negative, positive, or mixed content. On both networks, evaluations of issue posturing closely reflected the findings on substantive issue mentions. Again, Bush received a greater share of negatives than his opponents. Part of this negative posturing was a result of Bush's own approach to the economy, which at times involved acknowledging that things could be better or that he should have reacted more quickly; essentially, negative posturing about himself. Of course, given the president's floundering on the issue, there were few choices available to him.

It was hard for candidates not to be swallowed up by the economic story in 1992 because there were so many ways that being associated with the story could hurt. Between being affiliated with negative details about the recession, to being the recipient of an opponent's charges, to drawing scrutiny about campaign promises or being caught in the negative reflections of reporters, candidates—especially the incumbent—found the economic story problematic. Even Bill Clinton needed to elevate his rhetoric and promises to fit the apocalyptic tone of recession coverage, a fact that may not have hurt him so much on the campaign trail as it dogs him in the White House. The real winner may well have been the person not caught in the crossfire, who managed to convince a large share of the population that he was a policy hero without being mentioned in the policy debate: that "issue" candidate, Ross Perot.

Nonissues: Pot Smoke and Mirrors

Paul Tsongas's health. George Bush's health. What Jerry Brown smoked, and what Bill Clinton didn't. Ross Perot's behavior toward gays, POWs, government contracts, former employees. Two spellings of Gennifer. From start to finish, "nonissues" such as these littered the electoral landscape. Nonissues are items with no bearing on policy that for a (usually brief) period become topics of obsessive discussion in the television campaign. They need not lack substance, although they often do. They tend to be about allegations of a candidate's wrongdoing or questionable judgment or about potentially hazardous conditions that could in theory influence a candidate's ability to perform the job. At best they allow the voter to extrapolate possible presidential performance from candidate behavior. At worst, they are irrelevant, silly, distracting, and harmful to candidates—pointless save for the conflict they generate and the fact that their (sometimes literally) sexy subject matter makes irresistibly good television.

There were twenty-four distinct nonissues broadcast on CNN and/or ABC during the 1992 campaign,[18] mostly of brief duration but ever-present nonetheless. Rarely would multiple nonissues overlap, but seldom would a week go by without one; nonissue coverage thus took on the stalactite pattern discussed in chapter 2. On both networks, a nonissue would burst onto the scene, dominate coverage for a period of hours or days, then disappear, leaving valuable air time free for the next one. Each its own story, nonissues were less a miniseries than they were a sequence of network specials, often complete with the type of audience hook that would make them ready for prime time. Specific plots changed rapidly, but collectively, references to nonissues composed better than one in ten campaign statements.[19]

It seemed as if no subject was too personal to merit coverage. There was sex (Bill Clinton's alleged affair with Gennifer Flowers and George Bush's with Jennifer Fitzgerald). There were drugs (Jerry Brown's alleged California pot parties and Bill Clinton's infamous noninhaling). And, of course, there was television: a protracted dialogue between the vice president of the United States and sit-com newscaster Murphy Brown over the ethics of having a fictional baby out of fictional wedlock. Perhaps the most surreal episode of 1992, this nonissue included political coverage of the Emmy Awards and the vice president sending a real gift to the new fictional baby, then recording a real promotional advertisement for the program in which he mocked his earlier distaste for it.[20] All deemed newsworthy, all part of the story of the 1992 campaign.

Table 4.1 details the ten most heavily reported nonissues of the election. This list reveals that Bill Clinton and Ross Perot were the staples of nonissue coverage. Clinton was the subject of four of the ten nonissues, including the two premier stories, and Perot was the subject of three. Jerry Brown, Dan Quayle, and Paul Tsongas rounded out the top ten.

A number of nonissue stories questioning Perot's past actions made a staccato presence during both the spring and fall Perot campaigns: Has Perot told the truth about his past? Has he told accurate and complete details about his renowned effort to reclaim Vietnam POW/MIAs? Has he been investigating President Bush, and has President Bush been investigating him?

The Clinton stories cast doubts on the Democrat's ethics. A rather complex nonissue about possible conflicts of interest between Hillary Rodham Clinton's law firm and the government of Arkansas received coverage during two weeks in March. It finished seventh on the list, tied with an October nonissue alleging that the governor engaged in subversive activities while a student abroad. This nonissue included stories about the federal government's examination of Clinton's records and "momgate" allegations that the Bush administration was looking for evidence of subversive behavior on the part of the governor's mother.

TABLE 4.1   Ten Most Heavily Reported 1992 Campaign Nonissues

Rank	Number of Statements	Dates	Topic	Candidates
1	329	2/6–10/27	Vietnam draft*	Clinton
2	117	1/24–1/29	Gennifer Flowers*	Clinton
3	103	4/9–4/15	Pot smoking while governor	Brown
4	76	5/14–7/2	Perot's past	Perot
5	62	5/20–8/31	Murphy Brown's baby	Quayle
6	55	6/4–10/22	Vietnam POWs/MIAs	Perot
7	53	3/11–3/27	Hillary Rodham Clinton's law firm	Clinton
	53	10/5–10/22	Alleged subversive activities	Clinton
9	36	2/13–3/9	Cancer history	Tsongas
	36	6/22–6/24	Mutual investigations	Perot, Bush

*Also considered a campaign crisis

The two most heavily reported nonissues, though, haunted Clinton throughout the campaign, at times threatening his political viability. In this regard, they precipitated a campaign crisis for the Clinton people. Questions about the candidate's Vietnam draft record—whether he used influence to avoid the draft and whether he was honest and consistent in his public explanations of what he did—constituted the campaign's longest-running nonissue. It was mentioned almost three times as much as the second-ranking nonissue, Gennifer Flowers. Unlike most other coverage of this sort, the matter surfaced early and stayed around; the first report of Clinton's Vietnam history broke before the New Hampshire primary on February 6, the last appeared just days before the election on October 27. These references reinforced the many generic questions raised about Clinton's "character," discussed as "image" references in chapter 5.

In sharp contrast to the Vietnam nonissue, the circus that featured Gennifer Flowers's allegations of adultery in Arkansas was in town only a week. First mentioned on January 24, by January 29 the Flowers story had disappeared as a nonissue in its own right. But during that one week, there were 117 separate references to it saturating the airwaves and dominating the campaign's early moments. One week later the draft story emerged, reinforcing then replacing the Flowers story as nonissue du jour. Memory tends to exaggerate the amount of coverage the Flowers nonissue received, perhaps because by February, questions of Clinton's extramarital behavior had been raised and abandoned but never fully resolved. The legacy of doubt, the extent and timing of the coverage, and similar ethical questions evoked by other nonissues continued to blanket the Clinton campaign even as Gennifer Flowers herself was relegated from network star to the tabloid *Star.*

Likewise, Bill Clinton's admonition that he tried marijuana but "never inhaled" remains one of the most well remembered moments of the campaign. But as a nonissue, it was just that: a moment receiving tremendous play during so many pot "roasts" on the "Tonight Show" while hardly ever appearing on "World News Tonight." Among the twenty-four nonissues, the question of whether Bill Clinton smoked pot finished dead last, with only eleven distinct statements about it on CNN and ABC combined. In contrast, allegations about whether Jerry Brown inhaled merited 103 references in mid-April, when he was the only Democrat still challenging Governor Clinton, enough for third place among nonissues. And allegations of President Bush's affair with Jennifer Fitzgerald placed eighteenth on the list with fifteen mentions, a far cry from the saturation coverage given Gennifer with a "G."

Why do some nonissue stories endure while others flounder? The reason involves more than their inherent television appeal. Sometimes the answer lies in the circumstances needed to keep the nonissue alive, at other times in how it emerged. Take the two alleged affairs. An item from ABC, in the best tradition of self-referential process coverage, explained how the Jennifer Fitzgerald story evolved: "It began as a footnote in a book about Washington influence peddling. ... But today, the story appeared on the front page of the New York *Post*. The story opened the way to a direct question of the president during his press conference this morning. ... The president's comment in turn opened the way to local news and radio talk shows.[21] Likewise, the Gennifer Flowers story originated as a front-page headline, albeit in a tabloid that graces supermarket checkout lines. Similarly, the Flowers story advanced with a press conference, staged in this case by Flowers herself, which also opened the way to press coverage of all kinds. Like President Bush, Governor Clinton denied the allegations. But before it was all over, CNN and ABC had made 102 more statements about Flowers than about Fitzgerald.

The difference rests with the circumstances surrounding each event. The Bush allegations were not new to reporters; they had surfaced during the 1988 campaign, at which time there was not enough material to support protracted coverage. The same thing happened in 1992. Fitzgerald herself did not come forward with the allegations, nor did the original source of the nonissue (the aforementioned book on Washington influence peddling) contribute additional corroborating evidence. Under the circumstances, the president's denial ended the matter as far as television was concerned, no matter how much of a ratings grabber reports of a presidential affair would have been.

Ultimately, the same thing happened with the Flowers allegations. Members of the ABC election news unit interviewed for this book claimed that personnel in Little Rock investigated the story, and when nothing deemed newsworthy was found, the network dropped it. They said that they never really covered the Flowers affair at all, an assertion supported by the short duration of the nonissue but challenged by the intensity of that week's coverage. In Flowers's case, unlike Fitzgerald's, the charge was both new and firsthand; it took a few days for the press to examine its validity. During that time, the story remained in the news, crossing over into the realm of process coverage where television's interest seems never to wane. For the brief period while it was unresolved, the Clinton-Flowers fiasco moved from a nonissue about alleged infidelity to a nonissue about the media problems caused by the nonissue.

Having reported the original accusation, television magnified its impact. One report, for example, said that "Clinton's campaign now has to answer unsubstantiated charges of extramarital affairs, the latest in a supermarket tabloid."[22] It was reported that "it's fairly clear" (probably to reporters, although no reference was given) that "Governor Clinton must start all over again"[23] and that the candidate struggled with the press "as if Clinton were tangled in barbed wire, trying to free himself from the issue, but not quite able to do it."[24] It is true that coverage of the affair itself did not advance beyond the initial allegations, which when unsubstantiated were dropped from coverage by both cable and broadcast television. It is also true that until such verification was finalized, the story became one of media relations, a nonissue posing as a process item.

In general, the nonissue firestorm will burn if it produces a media conflict that invites process coverage, if fueled by new allegations or new facts substantiating old charges, or if not overpowered by the emergence of a different (read: interesting) nonissue. On this latter point, the Gennifer Flowers matter was inevitably drowned out by the Vietnam draft item (a fact that provided little solace to the embattled candidate), and other nonissues later followed suit. The May excursion into Perot's past was derailed by Murphy Brown's baby, and the Jennifer Fitzgerald story was followed rapidly by questions about the president's health.

The other way to understand the emergence and endurance of nonissues is to look at how they are initiated. Nonissues, like all stories, are generated when source is united with reporter. Some begin as comments made by candidates, by one campaign leaking information to the press about another, or when someone like Gennifer Flowers comes forth with an allegation. When the comment, information, or allegation gets reported somewhere, a nonissue is born. This is how the Clinton marijuana story began: The candidate made a comment in response to a question about pot smoking. His explanation included the tortuous assertions that he didn't break drug laws because he wasn't in this country when he was exposed to the substance and that he didn't even inhale it. Anything about drug use automatically qualifies as interesting television, and the convoluted form of the statement made it intriguing if not entertaining. Hence, Clinton's drug history briefly became a campaign nonissue.

The Jerry Brown marijuana nonissue had greater longevity. Like other stories, it began as a tip from a source. However, in this instance, the press played an aggressive role in investigating the matter. In particular, this was ABC's story. ABC highlighted the report and gave it prominence on the evening news just two days after the New York primary, when Brown was the only Democrat still challenging Bill Clinton. CNN, in contrast, mentioned the situation only briefly, emphasizing the candidate's angry denunciation of the allegation rather than the particulars of the charge.

This nonissue survived for a week largely because ABC had a vested interest in it and, once challenged, an interest in justifying its initial report. Ultimately, doubts were raised about the validity of the original claims, ABC stopped pursuing the matter, and it faded away (along with Jerry Brown, but for different reasons). Had not ABC decided to persevere, the matter probably would not have ranked third among campaign nonissues. The investigation and the decision to pursue the story were the result of choices made by ABC.

Every news organization has its topics or candidates of interest, which explains why some nonissues tend to be featured on one network but not the other. CNN may have had little interest in Jerry Brown's pot use, but it had great interest in Ross Perot, whose candidacy was born on the network's "Larry King Live." Nonissues about Perot's past, about his attitude toward gays, and about how he treated his employees were spearheaded by CNN, which conducted investigations similar to the ABC probe of Jerry Brown. In each case, the network's interest in the topic delivered it to the evening news. ABC, in keeping with its low-level concern for the Perot campaign, did not pick up these items.

The Clinton marijuana story was different, a consensus piece reported on both networks without the necessity of an initial investigation. Some nonissues fell easily into this category because they were obviously newsworthy to reporters. The Gennifer Flowers press conference, questions about Clinton's draft record, Paul Tsongas's cancer history—all were easily recognized as items about potential wrongdoing, questionable judgment, or hazardous conditions, and all were accordingly reported in the appropriate nonissue format. Provided new information was forthcoming or additional questions were raised, they continued to be universally reported. Thus, Gennifer Flowers made a brief splash, but the draft story lingered forever.

The consistency with which nonissues emerged during the campaign spoke to television's requirement that there be something of this nature to report. If a campaign does not generate them spontaneously, the media will do its part to cultivate them. Items resulting from investigations will reflect the editorial preferences of the organizations initiating them and may not get picked up elsewhere. Thus, there will be some deviation between the networks on which nonissues they report. Beyond the consensus stories, the networks are in accord about the relative amount of attention given nonissues in campaign coverage, but they differ on some of the particulars.

When networks foster the reporting of nonissues, they act within the boundaries of journalistic responsibility even as they exercise a larger role for themselves in the process of determining how the campaign evolves. By deciding to pursue whatever sources they had on the Brown marijuana story, and by deciding to feature the story prominently on "World News Tonight," ABC made a decision that had the potential to alter the trajectory of the campaign. The allegations emanated from the network's reporting, and they came at a time when no other nonissues were being discussed. The decision to pursue this story can be defended as a responsible news judgment, but it should also be noted that producers and news executives more than political figures brought it to the fore.

Sometimes allegations are newsworthy simply because of who makes them; other times, the press makes a conscious decision to investigate first. When the press pursues them, it effectively becomes an actor in the campaign, seeking out forums for aggressively applying the news values that inform all nonissue coverage. Given television's constant need for this sort of story, had Jerry Brown's accusers not existed, it was likely just a matter of time before television found something to placate the need for nonissue coverage.

*   *   *

Between issues and nonissues, cable and broadcast television provided the home audience with a consistent set of messages about what was important. The serious impact of the lingering recession played in peculiar contrast to the sometimes trivial, sometimes amusing nonissues chosen by the major networks for our consumption, creating a cacophony in coverage that could confound the careful viewer. The issue miniseries reminded us almost daily of the serious political ramifications of our national economic woes, as all the while the networks bombarded us with a set of nonissues whose common denominator was the personal tribulations of the candidates.

Depending on when they tuned in, viewers would be correct to conclude from this portrayal that something was seriously (or, in some cases, comically) wrong with the nation or its major presidential candidates. But it would not matter where they turned. Even though CNN and ABC chose to emphasize different nonissues, the difference was akin to deciphering which Amy Fisher movie to watch. The fact is, both networks ran a nonissue miniseries, and whereas the content varied, the impression left by the presentation was the same.

It could be argued that the attention paid to economic matters constitutes the brighter side of these partly cloudy conditions. It is true that, because of an unusual confluence of political and economic circumstances, cable and broadcast television paid attention to domestic issues in a manner not witnessed in recent years. Even if issue coverage was largely equated with economic concerns, it still falls under the rubric of substance in a way that nonissues do not. But it should be remembered that it took a weak horserace as well as a weak economy to turn television's attention away from the political racetrack and that this combination is rare. The challenge to those at both networks who equate issues with substance would be, if not to reconceptualize how elections are portrayed, then to continue to focus on the issues in future years when these conditions are different. This may not be easy, for as we will see in chapter 5, even with circumstances as they were in 1992, matters pertaining to winners and losers continued as in the past to consume a hefty share of television's attention.

5

Horserace and Image: Waiting for Perot

Indiana, North Carolina, and the District of Columbia hold primaries today, but there is virtually no suspense.[1]

—Diane Sawyer, ABC News

With no suspense comes no coverage; by the time in early May when the Indiana, North Carolina, and District of Columbia primaries were held, ABC had already reported that the campaign was "losing steam" because "many" believed the Democratic nomination had been decided.[2] The unspecified multitudes responsible for this conclusion were, of course, affiliated with the media, who each election cycle look to the competitive qualities of the campaign to sustain coverage. The 1992 election was no exception; the horserace was the most covered topic of the campaign because of its natural interest to political reporters.[3] However, the field this time garnered a different mix of horserace attention, with less interest in frontrunners and longshots, momentum and expectations than in previous years[4] and more attention to organizational benchmarks in the primaries, debates in the general election, and polls and strategies throughout.

Complementing the horserace story was an ongoing drama about candidate image and imagery. This element of campaign coverage portrays candidates posturing on the issues and sloganeering. It depicts them emphasizing their capabilities, defending their characters, and attacking others on these grounds or being attacked themselves. The image and horserace stories are complementary. Both involve judgments of how the candidates are received and evaluated by one another, the public, and the press. Both rely heavily on personal, political assessments. Both presume competition, expressed explicitly in the win/lose terminology of the horserace, implicitly in the posturing and jockeying of imagery.

But they are stories told from different perspectives about different candidates. The horserace is a story told by reporters, whereas image references are made largely in the candidates' own words. Horserace references tend to be declarative and descriptive; image references are usually evaluative. The horserace and image stories in 1992 both showcased challengers, albeit different ones.

Ross Perot starred in the horserace miniseries—the only place in the campaign where he made his presence felt. Image coverage portrayed a two-person race and played to Bill Clinton's strengths by emphasizing issue positions and campaign promises over concerns about character and capability.

Theoretically, the intense horserace emphasis could have helped George Bush by deflecting attention away from his record.[5] However, the incumbent did not measure up to his rivals on the key benchmarks employed by the media to assess progress, such as poll standings and debate performance. And we have already seen that posturing about the issues linked Bush more than his opponents to the sour economy. Consequently, Bush found little advantage in television's ravenous interest in the horserace or stump images.

In this chapter, I will explore the campaign-as-competition and campaign-as-imagery themes by looking at the reference points against which the race was evaluated: benchmark measures, poll standings, debate performance, and strategic planning and results. I will then examine three distinct image concerns: posturing on the issues, candidate character, and professional capability. Finally, I will contrast the horserace and issue stories, looking at their different perspectives and methods of presentation.

Primary Concerns: Ups and Downs

Despite its gargantuan presence on the television screen, the 1992 horserace lacked that raciest of qualities: competition. Typically, television covers the presidential contest as if it were the National Football League season, filtering out a primary field of would-be star contenders with ongoing accounts of wins and losses, delegates earned and momentum gained, frontrunners swapping position with main challengers, and longshots trying to beat the odds. These assessments generally continue throughout the fall playoff season, contributing a sense of excitement building to November's main event.

In 1992, accounts of candidate ups and downs tallied little more than 10 percent of all horserace references, as indicated in Figure 5.1. These items have all but defined the horserace in the past, forcing presidential hopefuls to campaign on the media's own terms. Expectations generated by the media have become the standards against which the press evaluates the candidates, assesses wins and losses, and thereby winnows the primary field. Resources have disappeared when candidates have failed to generate the appearance of momentum by meeting or besting press-induced standards in a world where

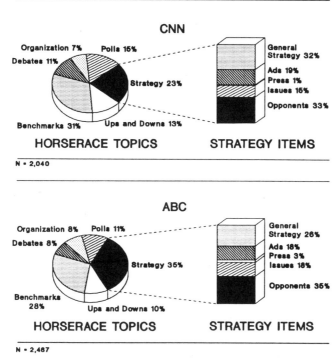

CNN

Organization 7%   Polls 15%

Debates 11%

Strategy 23%

General Strategy 32%

Ads 19%
Press 1%
Issues 15%

Opponents 33%

Benchmarks 31%   Ups and Downs 13%

HORSERACE TOPICS   **STRATEGY ITEMS**

N = 2,040

ABC

Organization 8%   Polls 11%

Debates 8%

Strategy 35%

General Strategy 26%

Ads 18%
Press 3%
Issues 18%

Opponents 35%

Benchmarks 28%   Ups and Downs 10%

HORSERACE TOPICS   **STRATEGY ITEMS**

N = 2,467

Figure 5.1   Horserace Coverage on CNN and ABC

finishing an "unexpected second" pays dividends, but finishing a "disappointing" second means disaster.

The process did work this way in 1992, but there was far less *coverage* of it because it was over so quickly. Neither cable nor broadcast television reported the Republican contest between George Bush and Pat Buchanan as a real race because no one in the media believed that Buchanan, a commentator and speech writer, would seriously threaten the incumbent's renomination. Buchanan got some attention for making a dent in Bush's New Hampshire primary margin, but it did not endure.

On the Democratic side, there were no household names. Following some pre-horserace "Will Mario run?" coverage centering on the presidential musings of New York's mercurial governor, Mario Cuomo,[6] the field assumed its final form: Virginia governor Douglas Wilder; Iowa senator Tom Harkin; Nebraska senator Robert Kerrey; former California governor Jerry Brown; former Massachusetts senator Paul Tsongas; and Arkansas governor Bill Clinton. Wilder withdrew almost immediately and was barely ever mentioned in coverage of the presidential competition. Harkin and Kerrey were cast as longshots based on their placement in the New Hampshire polls; they never bested their low expectations and were out by Super Tuesday. Brown lingered but was rarely taken seriously; his campaign was even described on ABC as "a boutique" that traveled by train and lacked purpose.[7]

This process of elimination left Tsongas and Clinton, two perceived lightweights, to compete for the heavyweight championship. Because these contenders lacked the credibility to be cast in an all-out competition for the big prize, television largely downplayed the most competitive elements of the horserace story. ABC even ran an item on February 11 questioning the "electability" of the Democratic challengers, wondering aloud if any of them could win in November.

But television still wielded great power in shaping the race. Once it became clear that one of these individuals was probably going to be the Democratic nominee, the medium focused its attention on which of them it was most likely to be. The decision to concentrate on Bill Clinton came early; some newsworkers at ABC even suggested it was an editorial decision made before New Hampshire. Of course, much of the attention was not positive, especially during the early crises surrounding Gennifer Flowers and the Vietnam draft. The fact that Clinton warranted the kind of scrutiny he got, however, is indicative of television's decision to take him seriously.

Bill Clinton received most of the attention that CNN and ABC paid to horserace ups and downs. Much of this type of coverage occurred between the New Hampshire and Super Tuesday campaign stages. Overall, only 67 mentions were made of all candidates' positions in the race.[8] Three-fourths of them were made before Super Tuesday; Bill Clinton was named in 30 of these, almost always as the "frontrunner." There were only a sprinkling of references to "main challengers" or "longshots." Despite his New Hampshire primary win, Paul Tsongas was only briefly portrayed as the field's frontrunner, and then always with a question mark after his name.

Without a field of would-be presidents to rank, television did not play the expectations game. The issue was raised only 60 times, with 46 references coming before Super Tuesday. Nineteen of these involved the New Hampshire Republican race, whereby television attempted to assess whether Bush had performed up to "presidential" standards.[9] Most of the rest were about candidates failing to meet expectations, usually a barometer of impending withdrawal announcements.

Likewise, assessments of momentum were hardly useful because there was no one against whom the two eventual nominees could be measured. CNN and ABC discussed candidate momentum 117 times;[10] 58 of these references invoked the two eventual primary victors. Paul Tsongas was reported to have momentum 20 times, and Pat Buchanan, 15 times. The remaining few references were scattered among the other hopefuls.

Given the lack of competition, there was little need to address the wins and losses usually attributed to the presence or absence of momentum, although with 194 references this most basic element of competition was also the most discussed. References to "winning" and "losing" typically followed primary voting, but there was little of the anxious anticipation that in 1980 George Bush had called "Tuesday night fever." Primary victories were noted even after the field had been completely winnowed; among the eight candidates competing for the two nominations, Clinton and Bush combined for more than half the references to primary wins, most of these pro forma. In contrast, delegate vote totals were mentioned less frequently,[11] an indication that the real primary competition had been concluded early.

What television found lacking in the primary campaign it compensated for with the emergence of Ross Perot as a viable political actor. Perot offered television what the established parties did not: an unexpected dose of excitement and drama, a sense of the unlikely tempered by just a hint of the possible. His "what if" candidacy, born on CNN's "Larry King Live" and driven initially by public response to his television persona, contrasted sharply with a contest that played like a B-movie. The horserace miniseries would have been a flop without him.

Consequently, horserace attention was heaped upon Perot. Figure 5.2 shows where he first made his presence felt: between the New York and California primaries, just as the last remnants of the Democratic contest were disappearing and weeks after horserace excitement had left the Republican side. He commanded the racetrack until his sudden departure from the contest during the Democratic National Convention only to reemerge more prominently than ever during the last weeks of the campaign. His stardom in this miniseries was in sharp contrast to the role he played in other facets of the campaign story. Ross Perot, the "issues" candidate, received minimal issue coverage. As we will soon see, he was not a part of the image story, either. In fact, Perot did not appear as a major player in any of the other campaign topics. He was exclusively a horserace phenomenon.

Perot was perceived to be different from conventional presidential candidates and was covered accordingly. Relieved of the procedural yoke that political parties require of their candidates, Perot was free to run as he wished provided he could get his name on the ballot. Media attention fixed on his state-by-state effort and the grassroots activity that fueled it. Perot was framed as a populist, as an individual whose campaign status derived from the spontaneous outpouring of public support, even as television granted him the tools he needed to cultivate it. Coverage of Perot II maintained this extrasystemic perspective even though his reentrance to the race was clearly more managed and manipulated than his initial emergence had been.

Perot's momentum was evaluated against a unique set of standards. Rarely was he mentioned in the context of traditional "up" or "down" measures. Instead, Perot consumed one-fifth of the general benchmark references made during the campaign—an especially large proportion considering that his

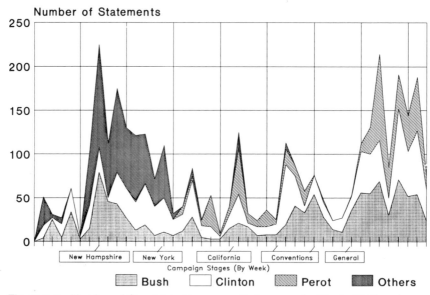

Figure 5.2   Number of Candidate Horserace References by Week, CNN and ABC Combined

campaign was a limited engagement.[12] Many of these references involved speculation about whether he would run (and later, run again); others assessed his strength in various parts of the country; still others evaluated him against previous political mavericks.

Perot was everything the rest of the field was not: colorful, fresh, interesting, different—newsworthy. He was the splash of hot sauce television badly needed. A man without a party but replete with political connections, he was the outsider by horserace standards only, the three-billion-dollar populist. And he knew how to keep his name in the news by playing the horserace game.

Perot was also invariably included in horserace references assessing the strength of candidate organizations. Of interest to television largely during the primaries, organizational benchmarks typically used to gauge candidate viability primarily include endorsements and campaign contributions. In Perot's case, they were mainly accounts of petitions signed and ballot space attained.

Although money and endorsements are just as important to a campaign's health in October as in February, organizational benchmarks were predominately mentioned during the primary campaign as a way of understanding the horserace. Between CNN and ABC, almost nine in ten organizational references were made before Labor Day.[13] Some took the pulse of the eventual also-rans, but there were few such references because these candidates were in such bad political health. On both networks, organizational benchmarks were the standard used to assess the status of the Perot effort; on ABC, they also served to track Bill Clinton's progress toward the Democratic nomination.

General Concerns: The Great Debate

Debate coverage was to the fall campaign what organizational benchmarks were to the primaries—and more, especially on CNN, where debate references comprised 11 percent of the horserace story. Although relatively new to the presidential contest, televised debates have become a quadrennial fall staple, appearing as regularly as the Olympics ever since Gerald Ford and Jimmy Carter squared off in 1976. Debate coverage is significant in light of evidence suggesting that the televised forums heighten public awareness of the election and have, in some instances, altered the course of public discussion about the candidates.[14] Often little more than joint press conferences, rarely addressed by reporters in terms of their issue content, debates are a horserace story of the first order, giving television a late-season opportunity to appraise who "won" and who "lost." In 1992, there were four debates, including one among the vice presidential candidates, which played to audiences of record size.[15]

On the evening news, debate coverage formed something of a drama within a drama, a self-contained horserace saga. Actually, much of the coverage did not center on the debates at all but rather on the debate about the debates: whether the candidates could resolve differences about when to have them, where to have them, how to stage them, and how many to hold. This conflict played out for a stretch of two weeks in early October, much to the delight of the media. Television was fully cognizant of the central role it played in negotiations about maximizing audience share (would the debates be scheduled opposite the World Series?) and format issues (would the debates resemble "Meet the Press" or "The Phil Donahue Show"?) and willingly passed this information along to the viewing audience. The "debate debate" provided a forum for a horserace event to bleed into process coverage.

Peter Jennings of ABC was well aware of this when he told viewers, "You may not think this debate business has an amusing side to it and that we in the media are all too carried away with whether George Bush or Bill Clinton and whether, yes, Ross Perot will ever debate."[16] But that didn't stop him from recounting an item about television's quintessential influence on the debate drama: that Bill Clinton invited George Bush to debate on an edition of "Larry King Live," to which the president had already accepted an invitation. Continued Jennings: "CNN said right away they'd be delighted to make it happen but minutes after that the president's press secretary said that's not possible. The president is actually taping the broadcast in the afternoon and a live debate with viewers about to call in would not be possible."[17] CNN also covered this exchange, albeit more modestly.

Eventually, differences between the Bush and Clinton campaigns were resolved, with the two agreeing to include Ross Perot in a series of debates featuring a variety of formats. One arrangement had never been attempted before. It called for the candidates to field questions, filtered by a moderator, from a live studio audience, in the fashion of so many daytime television talk shows. The debate debate may have been resolved, but the unusual, Donahue-inspired format provided new opportunities for television to remain self-interested. In a discussion with Peter Jennings, ABC's Jeff Greenfield said of the new approach, "It's the most unusual format I have ever seen in any presidential debate by far," and in a nod to what interests the television news community, added, "It will dominate the coverage tomorrow."[18] He was correct, of course, as cable and broadcast television continued to address the infiltration of alternative media in the debate arena.

Having indulged in the process implications of presidential debates, coverage eventually centered on the more traditional competitive aspects of debate performance: who won and who lost. The standard of judgment was not debating points but horserace criteria: Did a candidate do better than expected, or hold to his agenda, or look "presidential," or—most important—avoid making any gaffes? Considering the volume of references made to the horserace during the campaign, the number of these evaluations was quite low—only 85 in all—partly because no one was adjudged to have made the kind of serious mistake that could dominate coverage for days.

Among these assessments, CNN was slightly more positive than ABC was about the performance of all three candidates, but the same pecking order emerged on both networks. Figure 5.3 portrays the combined debate evaluations of the three contenders as the net result of subtracting negative statements from positive statements, just as issue evaluations were addressed in the previous chapter. Bill Clinton and Ross Perot made out well, the former because he was perceived not to have lost any ground, the latter because the media really didn't know what to expect of him. George Bush was the big loser, rating particularly negative reviews on ABC.

The consensus was not that Bush was a poor debater but that he had not helped his underdog campaign because he hadn't done anything dramatic enough to warrant positive spin. Therefore, he lost because he did not win. In contrast, Ross Perot appeared direct, crisp, and for someone blessed with low expectations, surprisingly prepared. He had won because his performance was good television. If that left Bill Clinton somewhere in the middle, it was good enough because he was leading the pack going into the event. At least, this is how his debate performance was evaluated by the great mentioners.

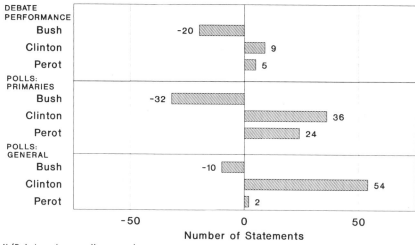

DEBATE PERFORMANCE
Bush -20
Clinton 9
Perot 5

POLLS: PRIMARIES
Bush -32
Clinton 36
Perot 24

POLLS: GENERAL
Bush -10
Clinton 54
Perot 2

-50 0 50

Number of Statements

N (Debate, primary polls, general polls) - Bush, 42, 64, 34; Clinton, 23, 54, 80; Perot, 13, 34, 32.

Figure 5.3   Number of Negative Evaluations Subtracted from Positive Evaluations of Debate Performance and Opinion Poll Ratings

Constant Concerns: Polls and Strategy

There was a time when television depended on the calendar to give it primaries, conventions, and similar benchmarks with which to assess the horserace. No longer. Today the gap between scheduled events is packed with polling data, providing instant gratification for those who wish to know how the candidates are doing and especially for those who feel compelled to tell us. Surveys are a constant of the contemporary horserace, guaranteed a large role in coverage because the networks commission them, putting a substantial monetary commitment behind the news judgment that it is essential to have benchmark capability at their command.

The 1992 campaign was a poll orgy. So much survey data emerged from New Hampshire that it was hard to imagine anyone living in the tiny state who had not been contacted by a pollster. There were polls in other key primary states, and following important primaries the networks would present poll data that assessed which demographic groups supported each candidate and why. There were delegate surveys prior to the conventions. Following Labor Day, the national polls began in earnest; by mid-October, ABC reported survey results regularly. CNN reported them every day. There were tracking polls, indicating whether the candidates were picking up support or losing ground. In late October, ABC presented a fifty-state poll assessing which candidate was ahead in the electoral vote contest. By the end of the race, networks were actually reporting *each other's* poll results; the CNN tracking poll in particular became a subject of coverage elsewhere when it showed the race narrowing to a statistical dead heat just days before the election.[19] When election day finally arrived, what better way to interpret what happened than with data from exit polls, reported dutifully by both networks along with figures from the vote that—viewers were told—was the only one that counted.

On both networks, the amount of attention paid to polls outdistanced all other benchmark categories save for generic benchmark mentions. The networks realized a return on their investment. But the ubiquity of polls exaggerated their importance. By the end of the campaign, mind-numbing doses of survey data were viewed by analysts as influencing late decision making. When Bill Clinton's long-standing double-digit lead began to weaken in October, analysts widely attributed the decline in Clinton's support to people having second thoughts about what the polls said was an inevitable outcome. In other words, previous poll numbers caused present poll numbers. Surveys were not simply reflecting the horserace; they were shaping it.

In such an environment, it doesn't always help to hold the lead, as the above example indicates. But it doesn't hurt either. For most of the contest, the sure-loser image of George Bush was reinforced by polls (accurately) showing him well behind. This was neither a reflection of bias against Bush nor a case of bad "spin"; it was simply a sign of public opinion, reported over and over again. In light of the networks' commitment to survey data, they would have thoroughly reported whatever the polls said, no matter whom they profited. In 1992, the beneficiary was Bill Clinton, as Figure 5.3 attests. Accounts of poll results about Clinton were, overall, quite positive—the flip side to Bush's negative figures. In fact, there was little change in the disparity between Bush and Clinton in poll results reported throughout the campaign. During the primaries, Bush was far behind; he caught up during the fall months only to face a blizzard of data showing Clinton still maintaining a slim lead.

Like polls, references to candidate strategy constituted a major, enduring element of the horserace story. More prominent on ABC than on CNN, strategic references came in the five varieties portrayed in Figure 5.1. Strategy toward opponents is the quintessential horserace story: what candidates are doing in order to get the upper hand in the effort to win votes. Strategy toward the press recounts campaign maneuvering of "free media" coverage in the effort to portray a particular image in newspapers and on television. References to campaign ads address the "paid media" component of the campaign's efforts. Strategy toward issues involves how campaigns approach, ignore, or shape their responses to particular issues for the purpose of controlling public debate. General strategy references are undifferentiated comments about strategy that do not fit into these other categories.

Given the vast amount of attention paid by television to economic issues and to its own role in covering the campaign, it is a bit surprising that references to strategies involving the issues and the press received the least notice of the five strategy categories. Neither CNN nor ABC conceptualized the strategic portion of the horserace in either personal or issue terms.

Of the two, the dearth of strategic references about the press was the more curious, especially in light of the fact that process reporting filtered into such far-ranging areas as issue stories and debate coverage. It suggested an imbalanced approach to the role of the press in the election. The correspondent's impact on the campaign was given more attention than the candidate's bearing on the press, at least as far as horserace strategy was concerned. It was as if there was an inward direction to media-oriented coverage, making campaign news not only self-referential and self-conscious but self-oriented as well.

Coverage of strategic maneuvering by candidates toward their opponents is a more conventional strategic category and attracted a larger share of attention than strategies involving the issues or the press. On CNN and ABC, most of these references were about the Bush campaign's strategies toward its various opponents: Pat Buchanan during the early primaries, Ross Perot in the early summer, Bill Clinton in the fall.

Clinton was the only other candidate to receive much attention in this category. Although Clinton's strategic maneuvering was not covered as thoroughly as Bush's, references to it built over time as he established his electoral viability and as his primary opponents dropped out. Ross Perot, in contrast, was virtually never addressed in terms of his strategy toward opponents; he simply was not depicted in terms of his adversaries.[20] Both Perot campaigns were portrayed in isolation, apart from the competition of the Bush-Clinton event.

Underscoring this portrayal was the amount of attention paid to Perot's television ad campaign, which until the final days of the fall campaign was aimed at generating support for himself rather than at tearing down Bush and Clinton. During the general election, one-third of ABC coverage of campaign ads was about Perot; on CNN, 91 percent was about the independent.[21] This finding is significant because Perot II *was* an ad campaign. Largely devoid of press conferences, free of public appearances save for the campaign's final moments, the second coming of Ross Perot transpired in a television studio. Bankrolled by a personal account that puts public financing to shame, Perot was able to set the standards for his campaign. He chose to operate in isolation, away from press scrutiny, producing and broadcasting informative commercials, or "infomercials," of up to thirty minutes in length that rotated with shorter, conventional ads on CNN, ABC, and the other networks.

Consistent with the logic of election coverage, which places a premium on anything associated with television, these devices were treated as though they were campaign events by CNN and ABC. In late October, ABC assessed the effectiveness of Perot's commercial effort ("He's drawing surprisingly big audiences") and even explained the term "infomercial" to the audience (calling them "half-hour blocks of TV time paid for by the purveyors of juice extractors, or electronic dehydrators, or home haircut kits" that "you're likely to find on cable channels or very late at night."[22]) Evening news broadcasts carried regular accounts of the latest Perot infomercial, complete with sound bites of that night's offering, providing for free what otherwise costs millions. Coverage of the Perot ad campaign segued directly from references to the other candidates' public events, placing the independent's commercials in the same context as the flesh-pressing exercises of traditional campaigns:

> Ross Perot will be hitting the airwaves again. He has three thirty-minute television commercials planned for this week.[23]

> Perot hopes to build on [his success in the first presidential debate] with a new series of 60-second commercials. Perot is also finishing up work on two more lengthy political commercials. He's bought a half-hour of network television time Friday night to present his economic game plan, and he'll be back Saturday night with an hour-long broadcast.[24]

> Ross Perot will continue to keep a low profile on the campaign trail, but on television it's another matter. Perot is planning a TV blitz in coming days to try to convince voters he has a chance to win.[25]

> Mr. Perot has spent a very large amount of money—at least $37 million now—to promote himself on television, as many of you have seen, and for the most part, not with the usual 30- or 60-second commercials.[26]

Perhaps more valuable than the extra visibility was the priceless legitimacy conferred by television on the Perot campaign as a result of the decision to treat his commercials as campaign events. A different news judgment would have given the Perot effort the same sporadic attention paid to other candidates' ad campaigns, leaving the Perot camp wanting for free media exposure. Without the sort of public and press events that typically command television coverage, Perot could have become a television news sidebar, someone who was not treated to the same degree of coverage as his opponents—implicitly, not a real contender. Instead, by treating his ad blitz as "an event," television elevated him to coequal status with his rivals. Ross Perot was assured continued evening news coverage without having to venture out of the television studio.

Several factors worked to Perot's advantage. His television ad campaign was unprecedented in scope and cost, so its unique nature contributed to its news value. The networks had already made a commitment to cover Perot beginning with his spring campaign; he was already perceived to be a factor in the race when his infomercial campaign began. His participation in the fall presidential debates further underscored his position as a presidential contender. He had significant support in public opinion polls, and despite the fact that he consistently ran a distant third and did not appear likely to win any electoral votes, experts to whom reporters listen could not be sure that he would not tip the balance of electoral power in November. And, of course, by spending so much money on broadcasts he was frolicking in television's playground; it would have been too much for television to restrain itself and not publicly discuss the man who was paying so much attention to the medium.

These factors were self-reinforcing. By acknowledging Perot on evening news broadcasts, television legitimated the impression that he was a player in the race and not a sideshow. Voters confronted with the conundrum of whether they were wasting their vote on a third candidate were assured of his viability. Moreover, Perot could continue to campaign from a television studio knowing that he would still get coverage on the evening news; he could reach "the people" while avoiding interpersonal contact.

Images and Imagery

Throughout the campaign, a stream of charges, countercharges, allegations, and assertions provided the content of the image story, a counterpoint to the horserace production. Candidates were portrayed jockeying for position with one another on who had the best solutions to America's problems, whose character was most befitting of the presidency, who was most capable of managing the chief executive's enormous burdens. On horserace matters, competition was depicted as the method by which candidates attained specific electoral goals. On matters of imagery, the contest was about which candidate could most convincingly present himself in a favorable light.

In a year when economic concerns received unusual play on the evening news, it was not surprising that most image references on CNN and ABC involved issue posturing, as discussed in Chapter 4. On both networks, posturing accounted for six of every ten image statements, as Figure 5.4 attests. Issue posturing was about rhetoric and campaign promises. It included candidate claims about what benefits they would bring if elected and charges about what harm the opposition would engender. Posturing at times was presented in first-person sound bites, such as this Bush attack on Clinton at a Georgia campaign stop in late October: "It's flip-flops, it's on the right-to-work laws, it's on free trade, it was on the war itself, it was on term limits—you cannot be all things to all people. You can't say one day, 'I'm for the Blue Jays, but maybe I'll be for the Atlanta Braves.' I'm for the Braves, and that's the way it is."[27]

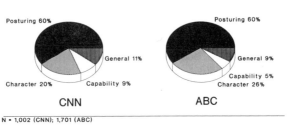

CNN   ABC

N = 1,002 (CNN); 1,701 (ABC)

Figure 5.4   Image Coverage on CNN and ABC

Some issue posturing involved dueling sound bites, as with this Clinton-Bush exchange about health care. First, Clinton: "There's not a country in the world that's been able to control health care costs and provide basic health care to everybody unless the national government took the lead in controlling costs."[28] George Bush "responded" in a separate sound bite: "Who wants health care with the efficiency of the House Post Office and the compassion of the KGB?"[29]

Issue posturing was also portrayed through reporters paraphrasing the main players:

[Bill Clinton] was campaigning in Wisconsin and Illinois today, talking about the economy and accusing Mr. Bush of distorting his position on taxes.[30]

Once again the presidential candidates are exchanging long-distance barbs over the economy. During a campaign stop in Delaware today, George Bush took aim at Bill Clinton's stance on the North American Free Trade Agreement.[31]

Devoid of policy content (how *is* Bill Clinton going to get the national government to control health care costs?), issue posturing is covered as a competitive game, in terms of the claims and charges a candidate makes in the quest to garner political advantage. As the campaign progressed, issue posturing became a greater component of the election's march of imagery. In the early days of the primary campaign, issue posturing constituted slightly more than one-third of the image references portrayed on CNN and ABC. As Figure 5.5 shows, by the general election campaign the figure had bulged to around 70 percent. As the months passed, posturing steadily became a more paramount element of the image story, edging out statements about character and capability for attention on the evening news. The persistent growth of television's attention to issue posturing mirrors the year-long dip in American consumer confidence and George Bush's descent in public opinion polls. The faltering economy provided an obvious rationale for portraying images of what the candidates had to say about it.

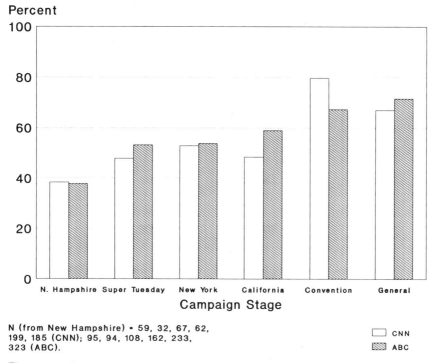

Percent

N (from New Hampshire) = 59, 32, 67, 62,
199, 185 (CNN); 95, 94, 108, 162, 233,
323 (ABC).

☐ CNN
▨ ABC

Figure 5.5   Increase over Time in Issue Posturing as a Percentage of Image
References

This trend twice worked to the advantage of Governor Clinton. At a time when the public was unhappy with the economy, the Democratic challenger benefited from the intense war of words. Even though Bush and Clinton were each portrayed attacking the other, and coverage on both networks consistently balanced the words of the two candidates, it was not the incumbent's issue. We have already seen how George Bush was linked to the economy far more often than any of his challengers were. Attention to issue posturing reinforced the impression that the economy was Bush's problem and focused public opinion on something widely perceived as a presidential failure.

It also helped Clinton that mounting attention to issue posturing meant less coverage of character and capability, two areas where he was vulnerable to attack. George Bush tried to deflect discussion away from the economy and toward his opponent's perceived shortcomings, but save for a few brief weeks after Labor Day, he never effectively controlled the agenda. In fact, character references peaked in absolute and relative terms during the New Hampshire primary, when they constituted 34 percent of image coverage on CNN, 42 percent on ABC.[32] Much of this coverage was fallout from the Gennifer Flowers–Vietnam draft nonissues of the New Hampshire stage.

Following the New York primary, there was a sharp drop-off in the amount of attention both networks gave to questions of character. Figure 5.6 shows the number of character references aired on each network on a weekly basis over the course of the campaign. Even though questions about Clinton's Vietnam history lingered through Election Day, it proved to be a low-grade fever rather than a life-threatening condition. Public opinion polls consistently said people had doubts about whether they could trust him, but Clinton's character never reemerged as the type of front-burner issue it had been initially. A small late-campaign bump in the number of character references represents the best efforts of the Bush campaign to reignite the matter.

One final indication of the Bush campaign's inability to seize the image agenda lay in the amount and kind of attention television devoted to matters of presidential capability. An incumbent president running against a little-known small-state governor could be expected to make his experience a matter of discussion. But, in fact, references to capability constituted the smallest share of image statements. As with character references, capability peaked as an agenda item during the New Hampshire primary on both CNN and ABC.[33]

Furthermore, the coverage Bush received was not favorable. When net assessments of the president's capability are contrasted with overall appraisals of candidate capability, on the whole, the president's performance was brought into question. During the primary phase, 32 statements about the incumbent's capability were critical or negative, while only 5 were positive. This was not the case with his opponents. Taken collectively, negative assessments of all other primary contenders, including Bill Clinton,[34] were balanced by an equal number of positive observations.

Bush did not fare as well as his opponents because his handling of the economy raised questions about his leadership capability. Coming as this did just one year after his public approval ratings hovered around 90 percent, Bush clearly lost the initiative on an image matter that he otherwise would have offered as a central campaign theme.

Two Different Miniseries

The horserace and image miniseries complement each other because collectively they draw attention to the political wherewithal reporters find critical to the creation of a president. But they are distinct stories about different players told in dissimilar voices. The horserace is the reporter's story about the candidates, related in the reporter's words from the reporter's perspective. The image saga derives more from what television elects to present of what the candidates say.

Number of Statements

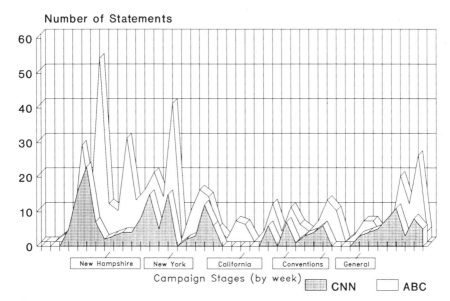

Figure 5.6   Number of Character References on CNN and ABC, by Week

Nowhere was this difference more evident in 1992 than in the proportion of each story told by political actors in their own words. Image stories were driven by sound bites: Almost 40 percent of the campaign's issue posturing, character references, and claims about capability were made directly by political contenders.[35] The horserace story, in contrast, was told by reporters; only 16 percent of horserace statements appeared in sound bite form.[36] In addition, reporters much preferred publicly discussing the horserace to publicly discussing the images. Between CNN and ABC, 259 comments were made about the horserace during the course of anchor-reporter dialogue or on-air discussion between anchors and political experts. There were only 37 such statements about images and imagery.

The contrast was evident in the visual images accompanying each topic. Horserace statements, as Figure 5.7 demonstrates, were more often affiliated with pictures of reporters than with pictures of candidates. Image statements were exactly the reverse. Thus, pictures of reporters often accompanied reporter interpretations of the horserace: who won a debate, who was behind in the polls, who was up and who was down. They commonly segued into a graphic image reinforcing the reporter's words, particularly if the statement was about an opinion poll. Image statements coincided with footage of candidates making charges or defending themselves in their own words. The reporter's influence was felt through the selection of the sound bite; the words were the candidates' own, and the interpretation was left to the viewer.

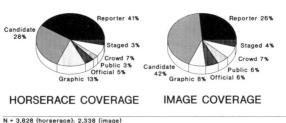

N • 3,828 (horserace); 2,338 (image)

Figure 5.7   Visual Images Associated with Horserace
and Image Coverage, CNN and ABC Combined

Subject portrayals in both story lines reflected the same set of sources: Candidates, and as the year went on, campaign officials dominated the image and horserace stories. But different candidates starred in the two dramas. The horserace story emerged around the lines of competition. Throughout the primaries, Clinton was the subject of more horserace statements than any of his opponents, save for a brief moment following Tsongas's New Hampshire victory. As candidates withered, those left standing claimed a greater share of the horserace story. In the general campaign, CNN split its attention evenly among Clinton, Bush, and Perot; ABC split evenly between Clinton and Bush, paying half as much interest to Perot.

Although Perot was written into the horserace story, he was not a character in the image script. That was a story about George Bush, much of it involving his posturing about the economy, with a sidebar about his leadership capability. Bush was mentioned more often than his opponents on these matters during the general election campaign: that is, more often than Clinton and far more often than Perot. Between the two networks, 328 image references during the general campaign were about Bush, compared with 210 about Clinton and only 81 about Perot. The independent was perceived by reporters as a player in the horserace competition, but his portrayal in the dance of imagery was quite limited.

Throughout the campaign, Perot was treated differently from the more conventional party candidates. He was the only candidate on television to be portrayed in terms of the people who back him, and these supporters themselves frequently appeared as the subject of horserace stories.[37] Otherwise, he was portrayed on his own, a single figure without an organization taking on the political establishment, a candidate only in the competitive sense.

In this regard, Perot was symbolic of the overall approach television takes to campaigns even as he was an anomaly. As it did with Perot, television personalizes and politicizes campaigns, emphasizing the individual over institutions, partisanship over ideological discourse, competition over all else. In 1992, these tendencies were most clear in the horserace and image stories. Perot was a godsend to a medium in need of sprucing up a lackluster primary race and fit in nicely with a campaign script that placed a premium on competition.

Once again, this dynamic applied as readily to cable coverage of the campaign as it did to traditional broadcast news. On CNN and ABC, the same mixture of individuals and partisan themes characterized horserace and image coverage. Even though ABC paid less attention than CNN did to the Perot campaign, both networks turned to Perot to add excitement to the competitive aspect of coverage. Both told the horserace and image stories from similar perspectives, presenting the former largely with the first-person observations of reporters, the latter with candidate sound bites. Both were more declarative in their portrayal of the horserace and more evaluative in their treatment of candidate imagery.

Such similar conceptions of the 1992 presidential contest applied as well to the portrayal of individuals, institutions, and the relationships among them. These are the items we will address in the next chapter, the last one to chronicle similarities in the CNN and ABC portrayals of the campaign.

6

Individuals, Institutions, and Relationships: Stuck in Concrete

What the home audience comes to know as "the election campaign" is a product of the judgments made by correspondents and producers regarding what a "campaign" is. Raise the issue of what a campaign looks like with anyone who has trudged through the New Hampshire snow bearing the weight of a minicam or a tight deadline, and you're likely to hear it described in less than placid terms: hectic, confusing, rushed, chaotic. Nonetheless, a striking consensus about the campaign *story* manages to arise from this bewilderment. This consensus reflects the common frame of reference employed by those charged with designating events, activities, and individuals as either wheat or chaff—that is, with selecting what to air on the evening news. It indicates a common point of view or perspective, an approach that enables those involved, as Erving Goffman says, to distinguish whether "what is actually happening is plainly a joke, or a dream, or an accident, or a mistake, or a misunderstanding, or a deception, or a theatrical performance, and so forth."[1]

In this instance, what is actually happening is called a political campaign, from which is derived a product called television coverage of a political campaign. The components of coverage are quite specific. Depending on one's perspective, a large number of activities, individuals, and institutions may be perceived to be associated with the campaign. Still, only a select few become part of the experience of coverage. This fact alone is neither good nor bad but rather is offered as an observation of a process; my aim is to illuminate the content of campaign coverage by approaching it as the outgrowth of choice rather than as a foregone conclusion. We have already explored the primary activities involved in campaign reporting by examining the major topics of coverage, and we have seen how these topics are fundamentally the same on cable and broadcast television. Here, we will look at those individuals and institutions included in—and excluded from—the television story, individually and in relationship with one another.

People in the News

Both CNN and ABC emphasized political personae in their portrayals of the 1992 election. Presidential candidates and their associates garnered the bulk of coverage; institutions, like political parties and campaign organizations, warranted far less. The latter, as Martin Wattenberg points out, are abstractions, which are much harder to convey through the visual medium.[2] It is difficult to get a good graphic image of a political party; videotaping a candidate is far easier. Institutions are also not sources, and reporters tend to conceptualize the campaign experience in terms of the individuals from whom they get their information.

Figure 6.1 portrays the share of attention granted to the most frequently covered types of individuals and institutions in 1992, either as subjects or as objects of statements about the election.[3] There was a clear consensus between CNN and ABC regarding who merited the most consideration. On both networks, individuals were favored over groups, the political over the nonpartisan, and political individuals most of all.

Foremost among these were the presidential candidates. The meat and potatoes of election coverage, they appeared in the news far more than any other individual or institution. They drove the action in the campaign story, providing the substance for and serving as symbol of the competition that had such a prominent place in television's conceptualization of the event. CNN emphasized both nation and process by calling its election coverage "Campaign USA '92," and ABC stressed the role of the public in its label, "The '92 Vote." But the audience was told through the overwhelming presence of candidates that the story of the election was really about the men who would be king.

Both networks went to great lengths to "balance" their coverage of the candidates, and by their own standards they did a good job. No partisan bias was evident in the amount of exposure given the main contenders, and equitable attention was given to the survivors of the primary race.[4] Although Ross Perot got less notice than Bush and Clinton on ABC, both networks devoted a comparable proportion of coverage to the major party figures.

However, if partisan bias was not a factor in candidate coverage, two subtle consequences of choice were apparent. First, aside from Perot, hardly any attention was conferred upon presidential candidates operating outside the mainstream party system. As we will shortly see, this choice was consistent with the nonideological nature of television election coverage.

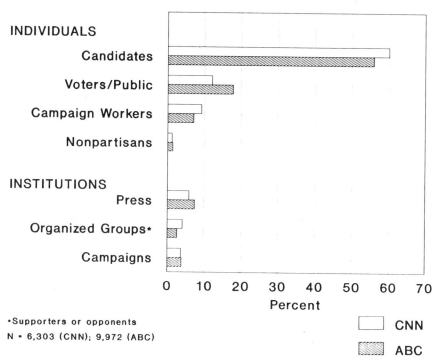

INDIVIDUALS
Candidates
Voters/Public
Campaign Workers
Nonpartisans

INSTITUTIONS
Press
Organized Groups*
Campaigns

0 10 20 30 40 50 60 70

Percent

*Supporters or opponents
N = 6,303 (CNN); 9,972 (ABC)

☐ CNN
▨ ABC

Figure 6.1   Portrayal of Select Individuals and Institutions as Subjects or Objects of Campaign Coverage on CNN and ABC

Second, the extraordinary emphasis on candidates in general derived from the assumption that a campaign is effectively a race for political power among a few individuals. Most if not all television personnel would consider this observation to be self-evident, perhaps ridiculously so. Political units are expressly organized to cover the candidates, reporters are assigned to candidates, polls track support for the candidates: Coverage is enmeshed in the actions and fortunes of the people seeking the presidency. Save for process coverage, where the press itself provides the point of departure for the story, candidates are the vehicle for the discussion of election topics.

By the titles they give their election reports, however, the networks themselves suggest other ways news coverage could be fashioned. Could not "The '92 Vote" revolve around public attitudes and opinions toward politics and policy, issues of voter motivation, or the actions and interests of organized groups? Would it not be consistent for "Campaign USA '92" to emphasize the national nature of the election, perhaps through comprehensive regional reporting? Each of these conceptualizations could include the topics the networks already cover, although from a different perspective and with a different emphasis than reporters are accustomed to at present; which could permit the inclusion of additional material. Candidate references would of course still be a part of coverage, perhaps still a central part. But they need not automatically be the dominant part; that is a function of choice.

To an extent, each of these items is a component of campaign coverage already, although none of them stand out in a story dominated by candidates and some appear in only trace amounts. Voters or undifferentiated members of the mass public did appear regularly as either story subjects or objects, but not nearly as much as candidates. On CNN, they encompassed 12 percent of the story line, compared with the candidates' 60 percent share. On ABC, the public appeared slightly more and candidates appeared slightly less, but there was still a 38 percentage point differential between the two. And nonpartisans barely registered on either network, composing slightly better than 1 percent of the subject or object references in election news.

Institutions and Their Representatives

Overall, individuals received far more attention than groups, which are much more difficult to portray on television. Some institutions cannot be depicted symbolically with images or readily represented by a spokesperson, which renders their visibility quite low. "Campaigns" are the institutional equivalent of candidates, yet, it's hard to get a picture of a campaign and impossible to use it as a source. Indeed, campaign sources are candidates and aides, and individuals in these select groups were given ample personal exposure on television.

Campaigns were never addressed as abstractions or portrayed in terms of their internal workings but rather were mentioned exclusively by reporters as a synonym for "candidate." Consequently, campaigns tended to be personified. Correspondents on both networks would offer "the Bush campaign said today" or say that "the Clinton campaign feels" a particular way. This style was entirely consistent with a personalized approach to the election story, despite the fact that "campaign" evokes an organization and "candidate" an individual.

Abstract groups were the hardest to portray and got the least attention; organizations lacking the ability to be personified were mentioned even less frequently on television than political campaigns were. Political parties, for instance, were rarely addressed, as they did not lend themselves to easy visual representation and had few spokespersons. Their most natural representatives, the national party chairs, were seen speaking effectively for themselves or on behalf of candidates, but not as symbols of the political parties.

At the other end of the spectrum, the most commonly portrayed institution was the medium itself, which is readily represented by the reporter's first-person presentation. Media personnel worked themselves into coverage in two main ways. At times, political reporters or television analysts appeared on screen or were addressed by others in sound bites. At other points, correspondents made reference to "the press," "the media," or "television" in the course of a report.

This should not be surprising. To those who constitute it, "the media" is a personal entity, experienced close-up in terms of individuals and routines rather than abstractly from a distance. This intimate knowledge renders it more personal than institutional in nature to those charged with reporting about it and other campaign actors. From a technical standpoint, television is easy to portray in concrete terms because the medium is readily symbolized by the individual telling the story. And, of course, correspondents and producers are effortlessly motivated to discuss the media because of their natural interest in what they do. Consequently, there were more references to the media than to other institutions, even in cases when others offered at least some of these advantages.

Groups supporting or opposing a candidate, for instance, were mentioned slightly less often than the mass media. Of the references to such groups that did appear, some were to Ross Perot's supporters, often called "volunteers," who were loosely organized under the Perot banner.[5] Others were references to organized interest groups. In these cases, the groups were generally symbolized by a spokesperson or invoked by a reporter. When symbolic portrayal is available through the presence of sources and the political relationship between group and candidate is clear, television personnel have both the means and potential motivation to cover these groups without deviating from broadly defined election themes.

Yet in 1992 they received limited attention. This is partly because group supporters and opponents are umbrella headings encompassing a multitude of individual organizations and their myriad sources. Unlike the ubiquitous presence of the mass media, groups surfaced only when "the story" came around to them. As the story was conceived in terms of candidate competition, groups were peripheral except at those moments when they were included in the debate. These moments were typically brief, and when they passed, so did coverage. It was not unusual, for instance, for coverage to focus momentarily, say, on prochoice groups opposing President Bush. This story might generate a statement or two about their position. But once the protest ended, the news value of the group would diminish and it would once again be relegated to lesser status. Attention paid to group supporters and opponents is the sum total of many fleeting individual references.

This practice tended to limit coverage of those groups that were neither easily personified nor overtly political, particularly interest groups that could be perceived to play an important role in a different conception of the campaign. Certainly, interest-group activity and the flow of PAC money has a place in the election. Yet this possibility is not evident from television's account.

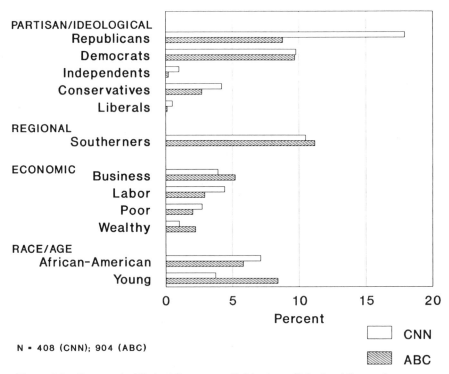

N = 408 (CNN); 904 (ABC)

Figure 6.2   Portrayal of Select Groups as Subjects or Objects of Campaign
Coverage on CNN and ABC

Figure 6.2 portrays the groups receiving the most attention on the two networks as a percentage of group coverage.[6] They compose a fairly mainstream
gathering. Controversial interest groups were rarely featured despite their assumed natural television appeal. Salient and contentious interests, such as
prolife groups (6 references) and prochoice groups (23 references), were as
absent from the campaign dialogue as the issue of abortion itself. Despite the
contention early in the Clinton administration surrounding the new president's pledge to end discrimination against gays in the military, there were
only 22 campaign references to gay or lesbian groups on CNN and ABC combined.

Other organizations received even less attention. Veterans, AIDS activists,
law enforcement associations, education groups, and the handicapped received no more than a few references each. Civil rights groups received virtually no attention. Farmers were mentioned only briefly during the primary
campaign. Even lawyers were only mentioned 12 times. And despite the presence of Al Gore on the Democratic ticket, environmentalists were barely more
than an afterthought in campaign coverage.

Ideological groups of the right and left and individuals who could not maintain viability in the electoral competition were also absent from the television story. American politics was portrayed as a game about power, played by people with an interest in "laying claim to the White House." Policy agendas were implied and sometimes stated, but the contest was not portrayed as a clash of ideologies. Such discussions, and the divisions they suggest, would be antithetical to the concept of America as a singular unit with a common purpose, an entity portrayed as cohesively facing down recurrent threats from within and without.[7] Ideological cleavages could threaten the inevitability of this perspective. Herbert Gans finds that television adjudges ideology relevant only at the political extremes: "In the news, ideology is defined as a deliberately thought-out, consistent, integrated, and inflexible set of explicit political values, which is a determinant of political decisions. ... Given that definition, most American political groups are thought not to be ideological."[8] Political competition, in contrast, is usually experienced as an event that validates the nation. No matter how competitive the campaign, the culmination is a vote in which losers and winners accept the outcome—a process inevitably leading to a national reunion on inauguration day.

In keeping with this theory, references to the partisan political tags "Democrat" and "Republican" outnumbered even the most bland ideological labels, such as "liberal" and "conservative." Party labels were attributed 281 times to groups or individuals symbolically presented to portray a group ("Martha is a Republican"). The terms "liberal" and "conservative" were used only 44 times, as shown in Figure 6.2. Other ideological terminology was not used at all. There were no references to groups such as "libertarians," "communists," or "socialists," even though each could claim representation on the ballot. Neither did television address classifications germane to a more focused ideological discourse, and that readily surface in news magazines, such as "neoliberal" and "classical conservative."

The absence of ideology in the televised election story complements the limited fashion in which political competition is typically portrayed on the screen. There is little room for anyone other than Democrats and Republicans. "Independents," defined as those not affiliated with a major political organization, appeared a total of six times over the course of the campaign. Even with a third candidate in the race, little attention was paid to alternative partisanship or nonpartisanship. Ross Perot neither formed a political party nor espoused a particular ideology, enabling television to portray his followers in personal rather than partisan or ideological terms.[9] Moreover, Perot's presence was not utilized as a forum for addressing alternative political options under the rubric of "dissatisfaction" with the party system. There were no references on either network to individuals claiming to be affiliated with any other American political party besides the Republicans or Democrats. In those rare circumstances when Perot supporters were characterized in partisan terms, they were typically described in narrow, conventional ways—as wayward Republicans or Democrats unhappy with their choices in 1992.

The common justification given by reporters for not covering other parties was political and practical: Those parties had no chance of winning an electoral college victory, and hard choices needed to be made about allocating scarce television time. This explanation was undermined by the amount of broadcast attention given Perot, a candidate television personnel openly felt had no chance of winning. Rather, television coverage favored circumscribed partisanship and emphasized hot but safe competition for an electoral prize. Perot added life to a limp horserace but posed no real threat to a narrowly constituted American ideological discourse because he made no pretenses about engaging in it. Had a grassroots effort emerged around a candidate of the ideological left or right—say, a national equivalent of David Duke's politically viable attempt to become Louisiana governor—television would have faced an editorial challenge about how and how much to cover this event. Perot was easy; cast as an alternative rather than as a threat, he enlivened the dance of sound bites without forcing television to deviate from its portrayal of the campaign as a battle between Republicans and Democrats, discontented though some may have been.

Demographic and Socioeconomic Groups

The extent to which partisan imagery saturated campaign coverage was evident in the degree to which groups were designated by familiar political symbols. Even the limited number of references to organized groups or symbolic portrayals of the mass public were most likely to be identified in partisan terms. None of the standard socioeconomic or demographic categories generated as much attention; references to economic status, race, age, gender, and regional identification each commanded a small to insignificant share of coverage.

Regional references predominated among these groups, again for reasons of political competition. Better than one in ten group references identified an individual or groups of individuals as "southerners," making the South the only part of the country to warrant this much attention. It came during two distinct campaign phases. The first was during Super Tuesday, reported by both networks as a regional contest focused on a slate of mostly southern primaries. The second was during the general election campaign, when ABC chose to emphasize the South as a "battleground" region in which a ticket of two southern Democrats fought for votes in a Republican stronghold. The network offered a series of reports about the South, featuring focus groups of symbolic southerners and stories about "Reagan Democrats," who were identified in neutral fashion by their region more often than by their race (mostly white) or gender (generally male).

Thus, "the South" served to symbolize two of the thematic devices of the horserace: the regional strategy of the Super Tuesday set-up, designed as it were to produce moderate southern candidates, and the question of shifting political alliances, which might ultimately land a Democrat in the White House. No other primary stage was defined in regional terms, and consequently no other region was portrayed as frequently or as singularly as the South.

Aside from Democrats, Republicans, and southerners, few other demographic categorizations appeared on either network in significant numbers. Like ideological references, socioeconomic designations were hard to find. Only two such groups, African-Americans and young people, appeared with any frequency during the long campaign, and the number of references to each fell short of the frequency with which southerners appeared in television's version of the election.

Once again, political criteria can explain the (minor) role of African-Americans and young people in the election story. Questions about whether Bill Clinton could expect support or interference from Jesse Jackson were raised by both networks during the primary campaign when it became evident that the Arkansas governor was going to be his party's nominee. These considerations were reported as horserace benchmark measures assessing the relationship between Jackson and Clinton in which poor relations were interpreted as problematic for the nominee, something akin to losing an important endorsement.

The situation was reported against the backdrop of what it implied about political relations between Clinton and the African-American community, specifically, what effect a strained Clinton-Jackson relationship might have on African-American voter turnout. African-Americans as a group appeared in the election story largely in this partisan context. Most of the speculation, and concurrently, most references to African-Americans as a group, occurred prior to the general election campaign. During the autumn months, the Jackson-Clinton relationship failed to have an impact on the horserace and the number of references to African-Americans declined accordingly.[10]

The role of young people in the campaign was not as singularly linked to political criteria; stories about education and family leave, for instance, invoked the image of the twenty-something generation when discussing some of the difficulties Americans "typically" face in these areas. Still, much of television's interest derived from the twin political conditions of a young presidential and vice-presidential nominee on the Democratic ticket and a high-visibility drive to turn out the youth vote. The two circumstances reinforced each other and collectively boosted the attention paid to young people as a group.

Efforts to reach young voters attracted television coverage because the promoters relied so heavily on the medium to reach their targets. Television was naturally drawn to attempts by the Clinton campaign to use the medium to project a young impression, including a saxophone-playing appearance by the candidate, in shades, on the late-night "Arsenio Hall Show." The "Rock the Vote" campaign telecast video messages imploring young people to exercise the franchise; MTV carried an ongoing series of election-oriented programming. When Bill Clinton appeared on an MTV forum, the twinning of youthful candidate and youth-oriented public service message was complete. Television news coverage picked up the images, and young people became a minor component of the election story.

Neither the Jackson-Clinton benchmark contest nor the MTV/Clinton images were widely covered aspects of the campaign. Consequently, neither African-Americans nor young people were frequently portrayed as actors in the 1992 election. One can only speculate about how many more African-American portrayals there might have been had Jesse Jackson and Bill Clinton engaged in a full-fledged political battle. It is noteworthy that with even a small political hook, these groups appeared in measurable quantities, whereas numerous socioeconomic groups lacking a political connection to the story hardly received notice.

Among economic groups, business and labor are generally the most visible categorizations, and these are best understood as interest groups: References to them in 1992 were usually to business "leaders" and "organized" labor. Income groups were more scarce. Despite the amount of attention lavished on the economy, there were few mentions of "the poor" or "the wealthy," "blue-collar workers," or even "the middle class." These economic categorizations suggesting social class status evoke an ideological approach to economic conditions. Rather than portray the economic story in this fashion, television relied on more familiar political terminology and focused on the dispute among candidates over economic issues. To the degree that the rest of us were involved, television generally made reference to a simple, undifferentiated public. The televised version of economic circumstances was a political story evoking the economy—rather than an economic struggle impacting specific social groups—which played out against the backdrop of an election campaign.

A wide assortment of other groups, any of which could be expected to be cast in a wider role in television's rendition of the presidential election, received at most a handful of mentions. These groups included the elderly (10 references), women (21 references), men (2 references), Jews (28 references), Catholics (5 references), born-again Christians (4 references), and Hispanics (3 references). Native Americans and Asian-Americans received no measurable coverage in the news stories examined for this project. Neither did Protestants. They were, like most others, footnotes in a tale about partisan political competition, portrayed in personal fashion by a visual medium.

Relationships Among Campaign Actors

Reporters may depict campaign actors relating to one another in any number of ways. Candidates may address other candidates or talk about their supporters or detractors; members of the public may express their opinions about a candidate; the press may question a candidate's motivation or behavior, explore public opinion, or question its own role in the process of covering the campaign. The mix of relationships is limited only by the number of characters in the play. For the viewer, knowing how the characters relate to each other provides a key to understanding the dynamics of the story.

It also adds insight into how the election was conceptualized by those who reported it. As with fiction, understanding plot lines and character can reveal a lot about the author. Did reporters and producers portray candidates in relation to one another or in relation to other campaign actors? In particular, how did they perceive candidates relative to the voters and to the press? On those occasions when the press wrote itself into the story, how did reporters depict themselves relative to candidates or members of the public?

These questions may be answered by examining the relationships between the subjects and objects of campaign statements. Subjects and objects imply precisely what they would in any sentence. For instance, should George Bush attack Bill Clinton's character in a sound bite, Bush would be the subject of the statement and Clinton would be the object. Should a reporter say she spent many hours waiting for a response to a question she had posed to Ross Perot, the reporter would be the subject and Perot would be the object.[11]

In the aggregate, in 1992 television showed political actors and institutions (candidates, campaigns, and campaign workers) relating most often to each other, secondarily to the public, and least to the press (see Figure 6.3b). Consistent with television's tendency to personalize and politicize coverage, candidates were paired with one another—that is, they appeared as both subject and object of a statement—more than one-third of the time. Abstract references to "campaigns" were few, as we have seen, but when they did occur they were linked most frequently with candidates (through statements like, "The Bush campaign [subject] feels the president [object] is picking up momentum"). Better than half the statements about campaign workers paired them with a candidate.

Political actors were linked secondarily with the public. In particular, campaign workers, who themselves were not seeking election, and "campaigns" as institutions were infrequently portrayed in relation to public citizens. Candidates themselves were also less likely to be paired with the voters than with each other. And among all statements involving political actors and the public, the political actors were the subjects as opposed to the objects in almost three of every four. Thus, television more often portrayed lines of communi-

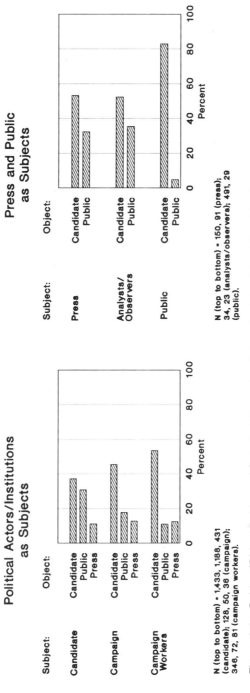

Figure 6.3 Subject/Object Pairings of Selected Campaign Actors, CNN and ABC Combined

cation flowing from the top down, from campaign to voter, than the other way around.

Similarly, political actors were infrequently portrayed in relation to the press. But, as objects of statements reporters made about themselves, candidates were the item of choice. As Figure 6.3b indicates, reporters betrayed the first-person perspective of their experiences on the campaign trail by casting themselves in relation to the candidates more than in relation to any other actor. The content of these pairings typically involved discussion of the reporter's daily concerns as he or she engaged in, and reported on, the daily struggle with the candidate over the shape of the news agenda.

Overall, subject-object pairings revealed the two central dynamics of campaign coverage to be candidate competition (with the public serving as spectators on the sidelines) and reporter-candidate sparring (as told from the reporter's perspective). A look at specific candidate pairs shows the story's political silhouette. Candidates were quite often coupled with their main horserace opponents, although there were important exceptions, as Table 6.1 notes.[12] Even when he was one of several contenders for the Democratic nomination, Bill Clinton was already paired by the press with George Bush. During both the primary and the general election campaign, Clinton was linked to Bush more than to any other candidate, both in his own statements and in things correspondents said about him. However, Clinton's main primary opponents, Paul Tsongas and Jerry Brown, were matched primarily with Clinton. This tendency created a nonreciprocal portrayal of candidate dynamics that marginalized Tsongas and Brown as opponents of a man who was already perceived to be running against the Republican nominee. To be sure, the effect was inflated by including data from the convention stage in the primary period; nonetheless, Brown remained an active candidate through the spring and summer months, during which time Clinton's main antagonist was already perceived by the press to be President Bush.

The Clinton-Bush pairing did not work in both directions until the general election stage. Throughout the primaries, Bush was portrayed more in terms of himself—his own campaign or his own operatives—than in terms of anyone else. Only secondarily was he linked with Governor Clinton or with his primary opponent, Pat Buchanan. This tendency resulted in part from Bush's strategy of remaining above politics and acting presidential and thus engaging in limited acknowledgment of his opponents. However, the strategy backfired, working to isolate the president from other actors in the election story until around Labor Day and thus reinforcing the impression that George Bush was out of touch.

The same sort of isolation occurred with Ross Perot, who was characterized as a loner from the first day of his first campaign through November 3. We have already noted how Perot was the only candidate portrayed in terms of the people who endorsed him, his volunteers or grassroots supporters. It is ap-

TABLE 6.1   Subject/Object Candidate Pairings, CNN and ABC Combined

Candidate	Primary Referral	Secondary Referral
Primaries		
Bush	Self	Clinton/Buchanan
Clinton	Bush	Self
Perot	Self	Bush
Buchanan	Bush	
Brown	Clinton	
Tsongas	Clinton	
General		
Bush	Clinton	
Clinton	Bush	
Perot	Self	

parent from Table 6.1 that he did not attempt to connect himself with other candidates. In the general election campaign, the fundamental dynamics were between Bush and Clinton; each was invoked in terms of the other more than either was portrayed in terms of Perot. The independent was described as a "phenomenon" from start to finish, playing by his own rules, almost in a separate political game.

These are the broad outlines of how the main characters were portrayed in the cable and broadcast versions of election news. Intercandidate relationships and political-press-public pairings deviated somewhat by topic, however, giving the various miniseries their own distinct cast of characters with their own interpersonal dynamics.

For instance, the horserace story could but rarely did depict a public dialogue between the candidates and the voters who eventually decided their fate. Political actors were paired with members of the public about half as often as with other political actors. Furthermore, television was far more likely to present the candidate as subject in relationship to the public than the other way around: Five hundred and fifty-nine horserace statements were about the candidate making reference to the public, compared with 156 statements about members of the public discussing candidates. This top-down version of the relationship involved candidates invoking the public through their rhetoric rather than the public addressing political figures with questions and comments. Even in a year when afternoon talk programs provided a forum for unprecedented direct public scrutiny of office-seekers, and despite the fact that the public was paired more with candidates than with any other actor in the story, the evening news version of the horserace was largely politics as usual, depicting candidates attempting to win the support of the public with an "I need your vote" monologue rather than a dialogue.

The candidates themselves were paired off in a similar fashion in the horserace as in the overall election story, with Clinton referring mostly to Bush over the course of the campaign, Bush waiting until the general election to reciprocate, and Perot remaining his own man throughout. But as these relationships are developed a bit further, an interesting set of political dynamics emerge that say a lot about the undercurrents of the race. For horserace matters, George Bush did engage Pat Buchanan during the primaries, or at least was paired with him by the media more than with any other political figure. But he paid far less political attention to Bill Clinton and was linked with the Democrat even less than with his own campaign through the summer of 1992.

Clinton, in turn, was twinned with Bush from the early days. On horserace considerations, he was linked foremost to Bush, then to his own primary campaign. His early opponents warranted the smallest share of his attention, with the longer lasting (and more colorful) Jerry Brown receiving a few more mentions than Paul Tsongas, despite the longshot nature of the Brown campaign. During the general election, it was Clinton against Bush, with Perot filling a secondary role in relation to the Arkansan's campaign.

Perot, meanwhile, responded in kind, making fewer references to Clinton than to any other candidate. Whereas Perot was fundamentally depicted as running in his own race, there was a political subtext that pitted him against George Bush in a match that the incumbent did not enjoin. During the primaries and the general election, there was a secondary link between Perot and Bush, whom the independent addressed more frequently than he invoked their mutual rival. President Bush was portrayed as not responding to the independent, which was consistent with the incumbent's strategy of trying not to alienate Perot supporters. On television, this looked like a one-way attack, absent a White House rejoinder.

As the focus shifted to other thematic components of the election story, these dynamics changed. Issue coverage, for instance, assumed an entirely different set of relationships. The domestic issue story was about the candidate and the public. It derived from the widely held impression at both networks that the public was deeply concerned about the issues, primarily the economy. However, as with horserace references, the story was far more often about candidates telling the public what they would do for them than about the public telling the candidates what they wanted done. In this regard, it was more monologue than dialogue, more candidate assessment than public concern, more campaign promise than voter wish. Despite the fact that most statements from the public about the economy were directed at the presidential candidates, these were outnumbered better than four-to-one by political figures addressing voters.

In process stories, the press itself tended to serve as the subject. The press was the subject of 16 percent of paired process statements—a far bigger percentage than in any other type of story. Most of the time members of the press talked about the candidates, who in turn talked about the press more than they talked about any other actor. Candidates were paired with the press in 45 percent of the process items—a much higher frequency than in any other story line. Only with process coverage did political actors address the press more than they invoked anyone else.

The different ways in which these three miniseries incorporated the public were indicative of how newsworkers linked the audience to the thematic content of the different dramas. The public was included in the issue story and to a degree in the horserace story as participants in the political decision-making process (or, at least, as objects of proposals made by political figures). But they were largely excluded from the media-candidate relationships of the process story. This is because the process saga is a tale of how the press covers the candidate and how the candidate is covered by the press. The twinning of these two actors forms a distinct pattern of coverage found only in this story line about the role of the media in the campaign.

Of course, issue and horserace stories incorporate material germane to classical political decision making. They describe what the candidates are saying about topics of concern to the public and how well they are competing with each other. The voter needs to know this material in order to make a choice; thus, the public was directly involved as story participant. But process stories, while containing information that could inform the vote, speak more to things that concern media personnel. These stories may be interesting to the audience—they certainly are interesting to the media—but the public was disengaged from the story line and treated strictly as an aside.

* * *

The manner in which individuals and institutions are portrayed testifies to the personal, political, nonideological nature of television campaign coverage. The relationships among these individuals further affirms the candidate-centered, media-oriented manner in which cable and broadcast television conceptualize election news. These portrayals are in keeping with the way in which the thematic miniseries are presented and underscore the common approach to campaign coverage at CNN and ABC.

In the next chapter, I will explore the one area in which coverage patterns were different on the two networks—the degree to which the reporting was analytical in nature. On this matter, which approaches the significant issue of how much television reporters mediate the story for the audience, we will find that the effects of covering the story for cable television combine with contemporary journalistic ethics to influence how the story is interpreted.

7

Analysis and Description: "A Philosophical Difference"

This plan may not give Americans all the medical coverage they need, but it might just give the president the political coverage he needs.[1]

—Brit Hume, ABC News

Even the most casual television news consumer is familiar with the sort of observation quoted above. The event in question is an announcement of health care objectives offered by President Bush in advance of the New Hampshire primary. Brit Hume has already addressed some of the details—the proposal comes from the president, the president made an announcement about the plan, the plan contains a list of policy particulars: In short, he has answered the "who," "what," "when," and "where" questions that are as central to traditional journalism as pictures are to television. In this sentence, however, he does something more. He assesses the viability of the proposal while telling the viewer *why* the president made the announcement. This is an analytical observation, a judgment of the correspondent's choosing that places the story in a particular context. In this instance, as was usually the case, the context is political. Question: Is the plan sound and substantive? Answer: Probably not. Question: Why, then, was it offered? Answer: The president needs political help in New Hampshire, and this tentative nod to health care needs may do the trick.

Analytical coverage differs from descriptive coverage inasmuch as it tells the viewer why something has happened. The correspondent takes the liberty both to raise and answer a question about an event, framing it in the manner of his or her choosing. Unlike descriptive statements, analytical items elaborate upon or qualify the action. "President Bush today unveiled a health care plan" is descriptive. Add a brief qualifying statement, and it becomes analytical: "President Bush, seeking to make up some lost ground in New Hampshire's vital primary, today unveiled a health care plan."

Analytical assertions of this sort permeated every topic of coverage on both networks. The statement quoted above took an item about an issue and gave it a distinctly political cast. This approach was quite commonplace and had the effect of blurring the line between issue and horserace coverage. For instance, just days before the Bush health care piece aired, ABC ran a story assessing the economic ideas of the Democratic primary candidates. Its conclusion: "No one message seems to have more resonance than another, and [New Hampshire] voters may simply have to make their choice ... on their instincts and intuition about the candidates."[2] With this sentence, the correspondent placed an economic dialogue in a political framework by directly connecting economic ideas to the New Hampshire vote and offered his conclusions on how voters would decide as a result of *his own* impressions of how people would decipher, rank, and weight the economic messages. Furthermore, the home audience, most of which does not reside in New Hampshire, was treated to an analysis that had no bearing on their personal behavior but that did highlight the idea that political candidates talk about the economy primarily for electoral gain.

Given the political nature of election coverage, horserace and image statements are, not surprisingly, a great reservoir of analytical reporting. Portraying President Bush in late July as "passive" was arguably a descriptive reference derived from political correspondents' judgments about the expected level of campaign activity. But an ABC report went further, clearly entering the realm of analysis by calling the incumbent "oddly passive" for a man down by twenty points in public opinion polls.[3] Similarly, a late-September challenge by President Bush to debate his two main opponents was called "unexpected" by the correspondent who was taken off guard by the announcement; after all, we were told, "The president was about to deliver his fourth standard speech to the fourth rally of the day" at the time.[4] This observation established the framework for a political explanation of why the "surprise" announcement was made, thereby serving as the analytical set-up for the report.

Process coverage, given its self-interested nature, was analyzed as heavily as the horserace was. Statements about covering the coverage generally included some reference to why things worked a certain way. Invariably, the media provided the motivation for a candidate's actions or explained why something didn't turn out as expected for a political figure:

> The different approach to the media by Clinton [i.e.: playing saxophone on the "Arsenio Hall Show"] has a lot to do with the media success of Ross Perot. Even as Clinton clinched the nomination, he had all but disappeared from the media radar screen. Except when reporters would ask Clinton about Perot. That so frus-

trated his aides, they limited news media access to Clinton and looked for friendlier outlets.[5]

Governor Clinton wanted to concentrate as he does almost every day on the economy and for the most part he managed. But the president set a different agenda and as often happens in the battle for media coverage, that's the one that prevailed today.[6]

In these and other like instances, the candidate's behavior was analyzed in terms of his media needs or media relations. The media portrayed themselves simultaneously as a distant third party to the experience and as residents of the political sphere. In their analysis of their own political role, they were at once outside themselves looking inward at their political importance and in the center of the action, relating with authority to the viewer why they could not be budged.

This manner of coverage had its roots in past campaigns. Television's analytical tendencies have been known for some time, particularly where campaign news is concerned. Thomas Patterson found television coverage of the 1976 election to assume an interpretive form that contrasted with the descriptive "string of related facts" he found in newspaper accounts.[7] Michael J. Robinson and Margaret A. Sheehan determined the same to be true of the 1980 campaign, with CBS television churning out nearly three times as many analytical pieces as the UPI newswire.[8] In 1992, both CNN and ABC offered analysis as a routine element of election coverage, by all indications far more so than in 1980, when Robinson and Sheehan found almost two-thirds of television news stories to be descriptive.

Placing News in Context

To assess the extent of analytical coverage in 1992, I coded each statement by correspondents or anchors as either analytical or descriptive,[9] depending on whether it interpreted the material it presented. As Figure 7.1 illustrates, subject matter was interpreted for the audience in almost half the election statements appearing on CNN's "PrimeNews" and in nearly two of three statements on ABC's "World News Tonight." More than in past elections, television actively and aggressively translated the story for the viewer, casting it in the reporter's chosen perspective.

This was the case for each major election topic, although some were more thoroughly analytical than others. On both networks, process and horserace statements were most heavily analyzed, followed by image statements and issue statements. Analysis of issues, in particular, tended to be offset by a sizable proportion of declarative statements about policy positions that lacked mention of their validity, utility, or applicability. It was within the realm of the reporter's self-assessed role to comment on the political motivation behind the

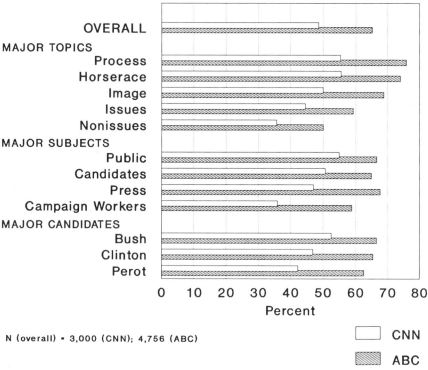

Figure 7.1   Percentage of Analytical References Attributed to Correspondents for Selected Topics, Subjects, and Candidates on CNN and ABC

timing of President Bush's health care proposal but out of bounds to question the policy value of the proposal (say, by calling it "thin," "half-baked," "ill-reasoned," or the like). Consequently, issue coverage included a higher proportion of fact-based comments than the other topics did; even the analytical remark that the Bush plan "may not give Americans all the medical coverage they need" assesses the details of the proposal against the reporter's conception of American health care demands without patently decrying the plan.

Nonissue items were the least analyzed topic, largely because of how they are structured. Nonissues are ever-changing short stories about a host of subjects. As with any story, introductions were necessary to familiarize the viewer with the action. Background statements performed this function, and new ones accompanied every new nonissue drama. Every Gennifer Flowers experience, every allegation of drug use, every health concern requires explanation. Accordingly, a large proportion of nonissue coverage involved declarative statements designed to place the multitude of nonissue stories in context.

In contrast, horserace, economy, and even process stories became familiar to the viewer rather quickly. The audience knew that several candidates were competing with one another to become president, that the economy was in recession and the candidates were talking about it, even that candidates had to interact with the media to get their message out (a theme particularly familiar to regular viewers of ABC News). Once these frameworks were established, television correspondents no longer needed to refer to them. The context for individual stories, then, became how the reporter interpreted what had happened beyond the basics we were already assumed to know. This task required analysis. Of course, President Bush was competing in New Hampshire; that had long ago been determined. Given this, the reporter provided context by analyzing the motivation behind the timing of the Bush health care announcement, which (in his view) furnished the frame of reference necessary to make sense of the event. For ongoing topics of election coverage, being analytical was a strategy for contextualizing experiences in a manner that made them appear at once new and familiar, the clever wrinkle in an enduring story.

Newsworkers at both ABC and CNN see analysis this way. Reporters and producers share the belief that providing the viewer with analysis is a suitable way to place an event in perspective. Said one correspondent, "The facts have to be put into some context, and that's the analysis."[10] Another added, "Analysis is a reporter's job. We're not just supposed to recite who, what, where, and how, but we're supposed to put it into context." A CNN producer agreed: "You always try to put everything into context and you try to put analysis into the story, such that if the president said something on Wednesday that differs from what he said on Monday you'd have to point that out. We do that as well as anyone else."

Correspondents and producers readily distinguish analysis from opinion and feel they are capable of interpreting events while maintaining the well-established value of journalistic objectivity. Much as objectivity is justified through procedures that require the construction of stories from carefully gathered facts,[11] analysis is regularly couched in a political framework that, like the election itself, is readily attributed to the natural order of electoral events. As we will see in Part II, political reporters subscribe to a common understanding of what constitutes election news. Provided a story is reported from within the accepted framework, it may be attributed to "the way things happen in the campaign" rather than to the ideas of the reporter, who functions as mediator between the electoral world and the audience. This approach permits the correspondent to relate a story in arguably subjective fashion without undermining professional standards that eschew subjectivity. Analysis becomes simply one strategy for doing news work.

For this reason, viewers saw a high proportion of analytical references in both networks' election coverage in 1992. However, they also saw a consistently more concentrated analytical message on ABC than on CNN. For every major topic, subject, and candidate, ABC routinely turned in a higher proportion of analytical material than its cable counterpart. The difference was most pronounced in horserace and process stories, and the percentage of analytical references about the press was twenty points greater on ABC than on CNN. But why was there such a consistent analytical disparity between the networks, and why was ABC inclined to treat the press more analytically than CNN in its version of events?

In short, if analysis provides a convenient strategy for explaining an election, why did two networks that otherwise offered similar portraits of the campaign differ on such a significant matter of presentation? Patterson says that analytical coverage is a natural derivative of the video format; in order to focus the story the correspondent "must assume a more active role" than is required of the print reporter.[12] If this is the case, one might not expect to find such a disparity between the networks.

Form Follows Function

The answer rests with the different requirements of the two organizations and the corresponding assessments of each network's mission. As an around-the-clock news service, CNN has a nearly insatiable demand for news content, requiring its correspondents to file early and often. ABC, in the words of correspondent Jeff Greenfield, has "essentially two shots—'World News Tonight' and 'Nightline.'" Its need for news is far more limited, its deadlines for political stories are later in the day, and its correspondents are not required to continually update their material for subsequent broadcasts. Consequently, CNN reporters have less time to contextualize their stories and will downplay analysis for the sake of meeting their deadlines.

Members of each organization tend to be familiar with—and sympathetic to—the concerns and requirements of the other. This CNN field producer expressed the commonly held perception that frequent deadlines at his network restrict the reporter's ability to reflect on coverage the way a reporter on the other three networks might: "If I'm ABC and I'm going to turn two pieces this week on Bill Clinton, I've got a little more room for analysis. Whereas, if I'm CNN, and I'm Gene Randall, and I'm turning two pieces a day on Bill Clinton, I don't have nearly the amount of leeway to really interpret."

An ABC producer who had observed his CNN counterparts related almost the same account of the situation at the all-news network:

> You're spending so much energy just amassing stuff to feed this twenty-four-hour animal that your time for analysis is limited. Whereas, the people who work for the other networks tend to have a little more time, they have a whole day to concentrate on one story. Poor Gene Randall who's been covering Governor Clinton. He's got to pump these things out constantly. When you're skating that fast it's kind of hard to slow down and be analytical. He tries, but that's a very difficult thing to do.

Often a CNN reporter will handle the frequent deadlines by tacking an analytical assessment to the end of a report. According to the CNN field producer, the strategy is "to just present what happened, and maybe in the standup [at the conclusion of the piece] do a little analysis." In fact, this is a fairly accurate account of the typical CNN political report, which in 1992 was more likely to present an analytical summary at the end than weave a theme throughout. ABC reports, in contrast, were more likely to be tailored to an analytical perspective, which accounts for the difference in the proportion of interpretive statements found in the two networks' political coverage. Analysis entails a more time-consuming effort than plain factual reporting, and employees of both networks recognize that the time constraints affecting reporters determine the outcome.

Even though it is valued by newsworkers, analytical coverage is hard to do and is at times viewed as a necessary evil required by television's restrictive format. From this standpoint, CNN correspondents are free to trade off the confining demands of contextualizing coverage for a more direct manner of presentation. ABC correspondent Mike Von Fremd admitted, "CNN has a great luxury, and that's the luxury of broadcast time. I'm jealous of it. CNN with their dual channels throughout the day can really afford almost not to be as analytical because they can let the candidates speak more and more for themselves. I'm not trying to be so much of an analyst, I'm just trying to be a reporter, but when I have to condense it, it comes out that way."

Sentiment such as this demonstrates the complex attitudes held by news personnel toward analytical coverage. Others at ABC shared Von Fremd's sentiment, whereas some at CNN reacted uneasily to the observation that stories broadcast on their network tended toward the descriptive. Several people at CNN equated less analysis with less polish and sophistication and insisted that a concerted effort was under way to correct what they assumed to be flaws in their presentation.

Despite this overlap, a sense of two distinct corporate philosophies toward news dissemination emerged from discussions of analytical coverage with CNN and ABC personnel. Each approach is clearly consistent with the primary purpose of the network. CNN strives to present a first draft of events through the manner and volume of its presentation in a form intended to allow viewers to make up their minds about the news they are consuming. ABC seeks to process the draft, to decipher events for the audience in the brief, encapsulated stories familiar to network viewers.

A CNN producer took note of what he called a "philosophical difference" between the networks, saying that CNN flatly does not seek analytical coverage from its field reporters. The reason, he said, "is sort of imbedded in the corporate culture of CNN. It's not a policy directive. But I think that there's an understanding on the part of our reporters that their job is to constantly inform and update our viewers as to the very latest thing that has happened." A

CNN executive producer agreed, calling the observation that CNN is more descriptive than ABC "a great compliment." She added, "I think it gives you the freedom to really look at (the news), to make your own judgment and draw your conclusions. I do think that is something where we differ with the other three networks."

ABC employees addressed their purpose quite differently. The sense that ABC News intentionally uses its reporters as analysts was repeated by numerous employees of the network. One ABC producer cited a "deliberate intention to be analytical," noting, "We set our course that way." When asked if network executives sought analytical coverage, ABC correspondent Chris Bury was emphatic: "Oh, no question about it. More than anything else, I think, the producers of 'World News Tonight' did not want the campaign to dictate the backdrop. So they were very careful about daily stories."

Analytical coverage, then, is the prescribed antidote to candidates providing what reporters consider a self-serving context imbedded in unprocessed campaign news. It is the reporter's understood role as well as ABC's mission to provide its own assessment of the day's events based on commonly held assumptions about the reasons why campaign events occurred. Thus, analysis and objectivity are to coexist as self-defined network goals.

These views represent not only a difference in corporate philosophy toward analysis but a rare divergence in the approach to presenting the election story resulting from the networks' different formats. In stories about the election on the evening news, CNN's efforts to describe rather than explain are apparent. However, newsworkers at both networks commented, as one CNN producer put it, that "there are other vehicles on CNN [besides reporters] who try to give perspective." Owing to its twenty-four-hour capability, CNN is able to offer large segments of time for analysis by professional political commentators. "In their regular cycles they're going to do straight news," noted one observer at ABC, "because they have all this time set aside for analytical approaches: 'Crossfire,' 'The Capital Gang,' 'Evans and Novak,' 'Newsmaker Saturday,' 'Newsmaker Sunday.'"

CNN correspondent Mary Tillotson concurred, pointing in particular to the centerpiece of CNN's political coverage, the daily afternoon broadcast "Inside Politics."

> ABC, so far as I know, did not air a half-hour daily show devoted exclusively to the campaign. I think if you look at the totality of CNN's coverage, you would find many persons during that half-hour offering some analysis. For example, [analysts] William Schneider and Ken Bode. If you know they're going to a Bill Schneider or Ken Bode doing analysis coming out of a spot from the road with Bush or Clinton, they will assume a rather more straightforward tale would suffice for the correspondent's piece.

These are the stories that generally filtered down to the evening reports like "PrimeNews," absent the analysis that followed. In other words, CNN offered analysis—and lots of it—to its specialty audience while providing material of a more descriptive nature to its general viewers. Either interspersed with reporters on "Inside Politics" or alone on one of CNN's many talk programs, analysts functioned to tell the viewer why something was happening and to do so in a protracted fashion. This analysis *of* an election story was provided by observers who utilized a distinct platform and might thereby differentiate themselves to the audience. But viewers had to watch one of these specialty programs to experience it.

On ABC, where analysis provided the set-up for the correspondent's account of events, the audience was sent a different message. ABC News offered far more analysis *in* the election story through the commingling of analysis and description. Like a chemical reaction, analysis transformed election events into thematic accounts bearing the network's unmistakable mark. CNN's "PrimeNews" audience was more likely to get a statement of election experiences unaccompanied by the sort of elaboration or explanation that could be had elsewhere on CNN. ABC's "World News" viewer was more apt to get a theory of why certain events took place. Each method of presentation satisfied its respective network's goals for analytical coverage, and each underscored the widely held value television news organizations place on analytical coverage.

So, viewing patterns establish how much context an individual gets. Viewers who watch "Inside Politics" or other analysis-oriented offerings are left with explicit ideas about what individuals billed as experts think about the election. However, those who consume "PrimeNews" the way others watch ABC's "World News Tonight"—that is, on a casual basis—have far less exposure to the massive amount of expert commentary produced by CNN for use with a more distinctly political audience.

* * *

The "PrimeNews" format stems from the interplay of corporate, procedural, and normative forces at work at CNN. Likewise, these factors explain the numerous substantive similarities between "PrimeNews" and "World News Tonight" that have been documented in these first seven chapters. Despite philosophical differences between the networks toward analytical coverage, and regardless of the obvious dissimilarity in the services each provides, election coverage appearing on the two networks on any given evening suggests a strong genetic connection. We turn now to an explanation of why this is.

PART II

The 1992 Campaign: Pictures of Television

8

The Newsroom, the Field,
and the Campaign

Why does television campaign coverage look the way it does? In Part I, we examined the tapestry of items emphasized in the evening news version of the election on cable and broadcast television. We saw how, despite the potential for variety offered by cable television, CNN and ABC similarly portray the campaign as a nonideological, partisan, political contest. Both downplay institutions while highlighting individuals, especially presidential candidates. We explored how thematically the two networks share an interest in the horserace but under certain circumstances will address economic issues; how they have a similar appetite for a sustained quantity of nonissue coverage; how they are both keenly interested in themselves. In Part II, we will explore the common threads that create this fabric.

Television news is a product. That is to say, it is created by people and marketed to an audience. Like automobiles, movies, or any commercial item, it is conceptualized, designed, and crafted by individuals in a workplace. Its form and function are dictated by the type of item it is. Network objectives circumscribe the possibilities for what may be created, and those who make this product unite around an identifiable production goal. Newsworkers out to produce election coverage would no sooner create a movie or a documentary than they would a radio or a refrigerator. But within the broad outline of form rests great discretion about content, and the producers of the product are open to a wide range of possibilities.

News as a Consumer Product

To understand this concept, take the example of an automobile. Conceptualized in an office, designed in a drafting room, and built in a factory, it results from the labor of many people at work on different parts of the product who are united by the common goal of creating a car. Although no one individual is involved in every aspect of development, everyone understands the item to be a car because of its particular form and function: headlights in front to illuminate dark roads; an engine powerful enough to accelerate rapidly to sixty (but not, say, five hundred and sixty) miles per hour; seats to carry passengers. Aside from the prerequisites, great discretion exists as to the particulars of its shape, capabilities, and features. It may be a two-door convertible, a four-door compact, a recreational vehicle, or a station wagon; it may have sharp angles, smooth curves, or rear fins. It may accelerate quickly or slowly, perform well at high speeds, or act sluggish climbing hills. It may have air conditioning, a cassette player, fog lights, some of these things, or none of them. It is nonetheless recognizable as a car.

So it is with election news. Conceptualized in executive offices, designed in the newsroom, built by correspondents, camerapersons, and producers in the field collaborating with producers, technicians, and executives in the office, election coverage is the common product and shared goal of people working on its various components. No one works on every aspect of development, but everyone understands the product to be television election news because of its particular form and function: correspondents talking into microphones about the election; camerapersons videotaping election imagery that is subsequently edited and aired; graphic artists designing logos to key an audience to the fact that news material is about "Campaign USA '92" or "The '92 Vote." Aside from these prerequisites, great discretion exists as to the particulars of the shape, content, and features of coverage. What the correspondents talk about, the adjectives they use, and the images selected for air time are discretionary matters. They may emphasize major or minor presidential candidates, interest groups, political parties, voters or nonvoters, foreign dignitaries or citizens. They may address who's ahead and who's catching up in the polls, or which candidates favor wheat subsidies, or where campaign funding comes from, or who smoked marijuana and when. They may address some of these subjects in great quantities, others little or not at all. It is nonetheless recognizable as election news.

For cars and television coverage, several factors may guide the discretionary aspects of production. Again, take the example of the automobile. Perhaps the most obvious impact on whether General Motors or Honda produces a two-door roadster or a four-door sedan is economic: It involves making judgments about the perceived demand for the product and the cost to the company to build it. The decision may be influenced by organizational factors such as technological capability, time necessary to develop the product, and the logistical constraints of production. Viewed from a different perspective, executive-level decision making, the structure of assembly-line manufacturing, and other internal procedures could influence the type of automobile the company is set up to produce. A third approach might consider how the shared attitudes, values, beliefs, or expectations of those producing the car shape the product. The view of automobile as economical transportation, automobile as source of freedom, and automobile as energy saver could lead to the development of different product lines.

These perspectives are obviously interrelated and their relationships complex. The orientations held by automobile producers about what their product should be may be formed by market research about what the public wants, or public attitudes about cars may be shaped by what's produced and promoted. How work is performed may reflect a company's financial situation or contribute to its economic circumstances. Assessing cause and effect is a difficult venture.

Again, the same may be said of election news. The organizational, procedural, and individual explanations posed here about automobile production have been applied elsewhere to the development of television news and why it assumes the form it does. Richard Davis summarizes them nicely.[1] Organizational factors encompass economic pressures, audience demands, deadlines, and the interests of ownership. Procedures include the routine ways news is gathered, such as the requirement of regular, daily reporting and the assignment of reporters to beats. Individual influences encompass a host of professional norms and values about what constitutes a news story and the complementary matter of what generates "good television."

There are different schools of thought about which of these factors is the most influential. Some argue for the dominant influence of economics and organizational structure in shaping television news coverage;[2] others find the strongest influence to be the routinization of news gathering;[3] still others maintain that values and attitudes matter above all else.[4] But, of course, all these items are interrelated. So a more appropriate question for us to ask is: How do they interact to determine the content of the news we see?

Although this is a difficult question to answer, this study provides an appropriate vantage point for such an examination. Looking only at television election news provides a manageable framework for analysis, and examining two networks operating in different commercial environments provides an interesting basis for comparison. The discussion of CNN and ABC News election coverage in Part I uncovered few content differences between the two networks and only limited variations in form, regardless of the different audiences served by cable and broadcast television. Now, it is possible to work backwards from these observations, explore the mix of organizational, procedural, and personal factors in play at both networks, and assess how they combined to create the coverage examined in Part I.

Making the News: An Interplay of Factors

We will find that CNN and ABC are organized differently, each in keeping with the particular mission it performs, and that these differences can explain the deviations in form between the two election news products. There are important differences in how the two organizations are structured, but these differences have only a marginal impact on the routines of newswork—how election news is assessed, gathered, and assembled. Rather, the way in which the election is covered at the two networks has more to do with the commonly shared requirements of television news than with the particular requirements of cable or broadcast.

Routines are dictated more by the environment of the newsroom and the campaign field than by the economic or technological concerns of the network. These settings strongly affect how newsworkers do their jobs. The desk, or the newsroom, serves as the command center where production comes together and large-scale coverage decisions are made. Only those at the desk can maintain an overview of what's happening everywhere else. The field is the domain of correspondents, producers, and crew as they collectively cover the multiple candidates for president and the activities of their operatives engaged in the business of electoral politics. Here, newsworkers are keenly aware of the nuances and particulars of their candidate and largely unaware of the most fundamental occurrences at the other campaigns. As they cover the campaign, they become a part of the campaign environment. They live with the candidate and the candidate's operatives for long weeks containing long days, without exposure to outside influences and without escape. They are invariably sucked in by the campaign's gravitational pull, ever struggling with the loss of perspective that threatens to portray campaign news with a refracting lens.

Inevitably, this tendency becomes a personal matter. Correspondents struggle to maintain professional distance from the campaign personnel they share their lives with. Neither they, nor for that matter their counterparts back at the desk, are positioned to see the whole picture of the campaign *and* its most detailed elements. So they must work together, guided by a common set of assumptions: their values, attitudes, and expectations about what election news is. It is through these common orientations that CNN and ABC come to share similar viewpoints that defy differences in organizational structures and differences in stated missions.

Orientations are commonly held—and constantly tested. Those who create the product viewers see on the two networks speak of their experience on the campaign trail as life in a bubble, defined by the distinctly abnormal world of the campaign. Endless days on the road dedicated to the same pursuit, spent with the same people, bind together media and campaign personnel in a common community of suspended belief. Within this environment, newsworkers must rely on an internalized sense of what is news in order to perform their functions. Orientations about television election coverage are the inner compass guiding their work, without which decisions and choices would be impossible to make.

Although never intended this way by newsworkers, the bubble metaphor is equally applicable to those who work in the offices back in Washington, New

York, and Atlanta. Because they depend on the judgments of the field workers, because they, too, experience relentlessly long days devoted to a single purpose, they partake in the same set of tensions. In light of unyielding pressure and absent the opportunity to step back and reflect, they also depend on their orientations about what is news—the very same orientations held by those in the field—to guide them through the haste and confusion of the newsroom and get the product on the air. What are these orientations? To find out, we must venture inside the bubble, to assess how newsworkers navigate their worlds.

We will do so in the following fashion. In chapter 9, we will examine the unique organizational attributes of the two networks together with the logistical, technical, and economic characteristics they share. Chapter 10 will explore how, despite differences in these structural considerations, the routines performed by newsworkers engaged in getting the election story are quite similar at the two networks. The twin environments of the news organization and the campaign, each of which presents newsworkers at CNN and ABC with constraints to be overcome, will also be examined. The similar way the newsworkers approach these environments leads to the common product they produce; chapter 11 will address the orientations shared by the television news community that inform their basic assumptions about newswork and the desired shape of election coverage—in short, what they create and how they construct it. Evidence of the hold that newsworker orientations have over their product is further addressed in chapter 12, which presents two cases from the 1992 campaign in which the operating assumptions about how to cover an election were violated. In one instance, the network itself tried to alter how the campaign was covered; in the other, the Perot operation refused to behave in the manner with which newsworkers are familiar. But the pull of established perspectives proved stronger than either unorthodox phenomenon.

One note before we proceed. The material presented in Part II comes from interviews that I conducted with members of the CNN and ABC News political units. These were free-ranging discussions about how the political story is covered, the obstacles that make it difficult to get the story, and newsworkers' beliefs about why election news looks the way it does. Overall, 44 persons affiliated with the two networks were interviewed in two stages, one preceding and one following the fall campaign. Some interviews were granted in confidence, and this is reflected in the judicious attribution of direct quotes in Part II. Further details about the interviews may be found in the appendix.

9

News Structures:
"I'm Too Old for This!"

One of my first jobs at CNN, I was one of the producers for the "Newsmaker" shows. We all operated out of the same room in Washington. I still laugh about it, still think about it a lot. After I booked guests, they'd come into the newsroom, I'd hang up their coat and get coffee from a mug I had at home, because we couldn't afford mugs. I brought them in, gave them their copy, and put their make-up on with my little make-up kit. Then I would put them in the seat, mic them, and then go into the control room, and then produce the show, and then say "thank you very much," get their coat, and let them leave. It was the "Chicken Noodle Network," it certainly was.

—Wendy Walker, CNN White House Executive Producer

Times change, and institutions grow. Through the 1980s, as CNN developed its organizational structures, its capacity for broader and more complicated coverage grew. Producing television news is not a basement hobby, even though it may have seemed that way in the early days of CNN. Structure is vital to the successful production of news.

Some have argued that organization does more than just make television coverage possible. One school of thought holds that the way news production is organized directly affects news content. Advocates of this view, most notably Edward Jay Epstein,[1] assert that coverage is shaped by the organizational form of the news operation, economic constraints, political considerations, technological limitations, logistical issues, and related structural matters. Thus, the form of the newsroom is said to fashion the product.

Comparing CNN and ABC News enables us to examine this thesis. Both networks utilize television to reach large numbers of viewers in diverse locations, relying on domestic and overseas bureaus staffed by a full roster of correspondents and producers. Yet, as an international network serving a cable clientele on a twenty-four-hour basis, CNN is organized to perform a different function from the entertainment-oriented, free-radiated ABC. Thus, one would expect to find differences in their organizational arrangements. Several salient structural differences are apparent in the manner in which election news items are originated and produced, ranging from the relationship between the political unit and the network, to the diversification and distribution of tasks among employees, to the nature and amount of competition for air time.

Despite these differences in how news coverage is conceptualized and developed, however, there are far more similarities than differences in the election story on the two networks. As we saw in Part I, election content on the two networks is remarkable for its consistency *despite* differences in the news structures in place at the two networks. This observation points to the handiwork of something common to television as a community that transcends differences in the way a particular network is established, and it suggests a marginal role for organizational forces in fashioning what viewers see.

The impact of structural factors on the news product is more evident in matters of form than of content. Structure can influence the polish and appearance of a story. It can facilitate or retard the coverage of events occurring early in the day. It can affect the rapidity with which the news is covered and enhance the versatility of coverage. Finally, it can determine the analytical nature of the story, as discussed in chapter 7. Despite these impacts, most elements of content are affected more by common assumptions about what constitutes newsworthy events than by how personnel are dispatched to cover them.

The remainder of this chapter will compare CNN and ABC news structures. I will examine five differences in the way the two networks are organized to report political news: These involve programming approaches, staff size and complexity, methods for selling stories, competition for air time, and deadlines. Each is the sort of item that Epstein suggested had a large impact on news content. I will also explore the repercussions of three structural factors for which few differences may be found between the two networks: logistics, technology, and economics.

Different Kinds of Chaos

A network that intends to provide television news coverage all the time obviously has to structure its organization differently from one that provides a series of news programs for an entertainment medium. This most fundamental distinction manifests itself in several key operational distinctions between CNN and ABC. The former is designed with an eye toward quantity, absorbing and processing news material the way a whale eats krill. The latter is structured more like a funnel; a large amount of information may enter, but only a small quantity will survive through to the narrow opposite end.

Program Versus Network Approach

ABC News is organized on a program-by-program basis. Correspondents and producers are responsible primarily to a particular broadcast, of which there are only a few. "World News Tonight" with Peter Jennings, the evening show, is the network's flagship broadcast and the destination point for a large quantity of ABC election reporting, although election stories also appeared regularly on "Nightline" and "Good Morning America," on weekend and overnight broadcasts, and occasionally as background pieces on the network's several news magazine/talk show programs, like "Prime Time Live" and "This Week with David Brinkley."

Campaign stories are assigned to correspondents by a political unit that works closely with senior "World News" producers. Story ideas are developed within the context of particular programs and crafted to meet the news need of the broadcast for which they are produced. One constant concern is story length. Items produced for "World News" are generally shorter (ninety seconds to two minutes) than background pieces for "Nightline," so election stories developed for the evening news program are conceptualized specifically for an abridged time slot. Another concern involves overall program content. If a story idea approximates something that has recently appeared on the program, it is unlikely to be commissioned. The availability and content of other news items will affect a program producer's degree of interest in a story.

CNN is different. Except in rare instances, stories are developed for the general use of the network rather than for specific programs. There are clear distinctions between the newsgathering and production sides of the organization. As with most broadcast news operations, the newsgathering side encompasses domestic and foreign assignment desks—and specialty desks such as the political unit—which are organized topically. Accordingly, in 1992 the political unit placed correspondents in the field and was the generating force for campaign coverage on a daily basis.

The production side of CNN is organized by program. It includes producers for the many news shows that cycle throughout the day on CNN—with names like "The World Today," "EarlyPrime," "Newsnight," and "Prime-News"—and for CNN's specialty shows, such as "Inside Politics." Whereas newsgathering assigns and develops stories, production selects among them for use on air. Unlike ABC, CNN rarely develops material with the needs of a specific program in mind. The production side will have input into how stories are covered, and specialty shows will have a voice in the selection process, but news shows as a rule will not lobby for specific coverage.

Because their stories are shared, CNN producers need to take into account the interests of general news programs like "PrimeNews," the twenty-four-hour CNN Headline News channel, and specialty programs like "Inside Politics." Thus the specialized needs of "Inside Politics" must be satisfied without straying from the network's primary concern of providing general coverage to a broad audience. This task requires close and regular contact among the political unit, the producers of "Inside Politics," and supervisors at CNN's Atlanta and Washington bureaus. If the needs of the specialty and general news programs differ, an effort is made to reconcile them; if this proves impossible and time allows, multiple stories are filed.

Ultimately, each program is responsible for its own content. Each is staffed with an executive producer and a line producer who determine the form and content of the program. They are charged with being aware of the stories available to them and making the selections for their program. Just as "World News" is the premier news broadcast on ABC, "PrimeNews" at CNN, featuring the all-news network's star anchors, is treated to an early pick of material produced by the network on a daily basis. But unlike "World News," "PrimeNews" does not air reports produced exclusively for its use. Instead, correspondents file the early version of their stories for the specialty program "Inside Politics," which airs at 4:30 P.M. eastern time. Political pieces are channeled first to "Inside Politics" then made available to "PrimeNews" and other broad-based programs, which have their pick of the political stories later in the evening. This procedure gives general news shows like "PrimeNews" a smorgasbord of political news from which to choose, although it puts CNN political reporters on a very early deadline.

The structure in place at ABC facilitates coordination between newsgathering and production around the purpose of designing a specific news program. The comparable mechanism at CNN enables the production of many news programs on an ongoing basis. "World News Tonight" is tailormade; "PrimeNews" is off the rack. Yet, despite these differences, "World News" and "PrimeNews" told the campaign story in a similar way. This convergence indicates a common denominator to the thinking underlying the decisions made at each network. The ABC political unit, working in tandem with program producers and correspondents, approached the election in essentially the same way as the CNN political unit, the producers of "Inside Politics," and the producers of "PrimeNews," regardless of their different organizational imperatives.

Staffing: Lean and Mean

Both networks assigned personnel to cover the election story on a candidate-by-candidate basis. From an organizational perspective, this approach had the advantage of being predictable, enabling the use of candidate schedules to anticipate staffing needs and obviously contributing to the political emphasis of election coverage. However, the decision to cover the election this way, although unquestioned by newsworkers, was by no means easy to carry out from an organizational standpoint. At times, the procedure strained limited resources. This was particularly so during the early primary stages when the field was large. When Ross Perot became a sustained presence in the mediated version of the election, the decision to cover him required an unexpected and expensive commitment of additional correspondents, producers, and crew.

The strain was probably greatest at CNN. Even though CNN's reporters file more stories than ABC's, CNN operates, as one executive put it, as "a lean, mean fighting machine," with a smaller and less differentiated staff. Both networks typically sent producers, correspondents, and camera crews to cover the candidates. ABC also employed reportorial producers, or "off-airs," who were assigned along with other production personnel. Off-airs functioned as fact finders for producers. They traveled with the candidates, taking notes on items they believed would be potentially useful in constructing stories. These would be passed up the chain to program producers, who would make decisions about news content.

During the early primaries, ABC dispatched off-airs to cover each declared contender in order to have someone on watch all the time. In some instances, off-airs were the only constant link between the network and the candidate, as correspondents and producers shuttled in and out. As the field narrowed, off-airs became part of a larger, more permanent media presence.

In contrast, CNN could not maintain a production presence on all the candidates all the time during the early months of the campaign. Rather than abandon the candidate-oriented approach to the story, the network utilized what one executive referred to as "zone coverage"—engaging in the practice of pooled reporting, whereby networks share resources—in order to cover every candidate appearance prior to the New Hampshire primary. Once the field diminished, it became easier to cover the candidates regularly with correspondents and field producers, although correspondents did not always have their own producers.

The result was a somewhat more fluid organizational pattern at CNN, which on occasion could become disorganized. A number of employees acknowledged that things were at times chaotic. Gathering the news required long hours and hard work, and newsworkers for both CNN and ABC noted the difficulties of trying to keep up with rapidly moving campaigns. "Disorganization is endemic," said CNN correspondent Charles Bierbauer. "You show me an organization that doesn't have any, and I'll show you one that's inert."

Pitching Stories

Story ideas, as we will see in chapter 10, may originate either in the field or at a bureau. When they emanate from correspondents or producers, they are typically "pitched" or "sold" to executive-level decision-makers. Employees of both networks discussed the marketing of story proposals in these terms. Either through conversation or written memo, they would offer up what they perceived to be of news value to those at the top.

Because the two networks have different organizational needs, the amount of competition involved in selling story ideas varies greatly between them. In keeping with ABC's more differentiated organizational structure, and owing to its focus on specific broadcasts, selling a story at ABC is a more competitive venture than at CNN. At ABC, a larger number of people are pitching stories for a far more limited amount of air time. One producer estimates that, taking into account all the subjects covered by "World News," there were hundreds of people pitching stories for little more than twenty minutes of air time every day.

For campaign news, off-airs would join producers and correspondents in pitching stories or "story elements" to program executives, thus increasing both the volume of material available to the network and the number of people competing to get their ideas on the air. Obviously, most ideas were turned away. One producer likened the situation to having a newspaper with only a front page, leaving nowhere to put non-headline stories.

The reverse is true at CNN, the never-ending electronic information station. Given its need for news around the clock, pitching stories takes on a different form. According to a CNN executive producer, "It's basically not pitching, it's more like, what do you have?" In contrast to ABC, where employees face a competitive environment, CNN employees face the pressure of being able to come up with enough ideas to fill their massive news needs.

Air Time and Filing Stories: Feeding the Beast

The same is true with getting on the air. CNN was described by several employees as the "beast" or "big monster" that says "feed me, feed me" all the time. Between the specialty needs of "Inside Politics" and the ongoing general news rotation, political reports did not sit on the shelf. In contrast to ABC personnel, who cited often fierce competition for air time as a given at their organization and at any other broadcast network, CNN employees discussed the constant struggle to keep up with network needs. One said that, rather than competing to get on the air, "It's more like, please take us off for two minutes so we can go get some coffee."

More stories aired means more stories filed. At CNN, correspondents file completed pieces far more often than at ABC. The difference, again, reflects how the networks are organized. Carin Dessauer, who worked at ABC during the 1988 presidential campaign, is associate political director at CNN. She explained the difference as a matter of "constantly looking forward." She said, "It's a challenge, when you're on twenty-four hours a day, to try to stay on top of the news in that twenty-four-hour period and work on stories down the road, to be ahead of the curve in reporting. You don't have people who file a story once a week or twice a week like you do at ABC. Most people file stories almost every day in some bureaus."

Deadlines: Early and Often

More stories for more news programs translates into more deadlines at CNN. Deadlines are a problem for all television newsworkers, but for CNN producers, correspondents, and executives alike they were by far the most frequently mentioned constraint to performing their jobs. Deadlines at both networks impinge on last-minute story editing, the ability to cover events scheduled late in the day, and the potential to polish stories for broadcast.

As one of the last steps before completing a story, editing work takes place as late in the day as possible. At ABC, the 6:30 P.M. "World News" air time necessitates that story scripts be approved, videotape edited, and the final story fed to the network in the hour or so leading up to the broadcast. The later the events being covered, the later this process will start, and campaigns, which hold nonstop events and commonly run late, typically added to the pressure to delay. Consequently, some producers said that in 1992 they were left without sufficient time to shape or structure the story the way they would have liked. Quite frequently, final editing decisions or script changes competed feverishly with the program deadline, and it was not unusual for completed pieces to be on their way to the network after "World News" had begun or even as the story was being introduced by Peter Jennings.

Because "Inside Politics" ran at 4:30 P.M. eastern time, CNN correspondents had even less time than their network counterparts to file their stories. National correspondent Gene Randall echoed the sentiments of his colleagues, calling the early deadline "the biggest problem I faced," especially when the campaign went on the road: "We had 'Inside Politics' at 4:30 in the afternoon, and that meant that the deadline for collecting news would be three in the afternoon eastern time. And you know you get out of the eastern time zone and you're really in trouble. On the West Coast it's ridiculous. You'd have to have the story wrapped up by noon." In the frequent instances when candidates started late or ran late, the early deadline was particularly difficult. A candidate's staff does not necessarily schedule events around the early CNN deadline. Correspondents were left to work around the limitations and to develop their stories with whatever material they could get.

If deadlines were early at CNN, so were they often. "The other networks have to worry about one report at the end of the day," said one CNN producer. "We have a revolving deadline." Commonly, stories prepared for 4:30 were updated for use later in the evening, particularly if the specialized needs of "Inside Politics" differed from the more general interests of the regular evening news shows. Correspondent Charles Bierbauer said that after filing a story for the early deadline, "you updated it for 6:00 P.M. and you updated it for 8:00 P.M., as opposed to having the relative luxury of being able to sit through most of the day and then sit down and write something presumably cohesive and coherent."

Sometimes CNN correspondents didn't have enough time to file. That left producers with the task of reconciling the different institutional needs of the campaign and the network. Producer Chuck Conder called this a major challenge: "We struggled with that on some days. It would entail one or more of our news team dropping off of the campaign and trying to catch up with it later on commercial flights. That was the case with Clinton, and sometimes with Jerry Brown. It was the constant craving that CNN as a network has for absolutely the most recent thing the candidate said." The end result was a demanding daily schedule even more relentless than the severe agenda imposed by the broadcast networks. This situation not only manifested itself in the product, in the form of relatively less analytical coverage on the cable network, but also took its toll on those who had to keep it up. "I wanted to have pulled my last all-nighter in college," joked a CNN correspondent. "I'm too old for this!"

Something in Common: Logistics, Technology, and Economics

Concurrent with these differences in how CNN and ABC are structured, staffed, and run, three distinct organizational similarities affect the two news operations. Everyone covering the presidential election sensed the press of logistics, particularly at CNN. These included largely mundane but highly critical problems of moving people, machinery, and information over vast distances against deadline pressure, often under conditions of great uncertainty. Interwoven with issues of how to get there from here were matters of technology, which made rapid reporting possible but greatly complicated the mechanics of coverage. Finally, there was the guarded economic climate of both networks, which, although a presence, was hardly a debilitating force to covering the 1992 campaign.

"Horrific" Logistics

Like deadline pressure, logistical concerns ranked among the most frequently mentioned obstacles faced by newsworkers at the two networks. In one respect the two problems were intertwined, with deadline requirements mandating that logistical problems be successfully navigated within a specified time frame. Deadlines aside, problems of communication and transportation are common to life on the road as a reporter and to how television in general covers a campaign. In this regard, deadlines and logistics affected both networks in the same way, even if CNN personnel faced the deadlines earlier in the day and more frequently.

Solving logistical problems is typically the work of those operating behind the scenes. Accordingly, at both networks, producers and executives were more likely than correspondents to raise the issue of logistical problems, often in graphic detail. Accounts of logistical predicaments real and imagined included satellite problems, remote places without telephones, figuring out as you land in Altoona how you're going to get your report back to Atlanta, changing tape at a crucial moment of a campaign event, and planning feverishly to find the nearest satellite uplink while in the proverbial middle of nowhere. "TV," said Charles Bierbauer, "is 90 percent logistics, 5 percent reporting, and 5 percent whimsy." ABC correspondent Chris Bury was more blunt: "The logistics," he said, "were just horrific."

The responsibilities of each role dictated what people worried about. Correspondents were concerned with getting the elements they wanted for their story and feeding it back to the network in time. Producers agonized over an array of things, primarily involving the complex movement of a host of people, videotape, and hardware. One listed as his primary logistical concerns "getting from place to place. Making sure that the correspondents have enough time to follow their stories. Making sure all the equipment is in the right place. Making sure that everyone gets to where they need to go at the right time." Another producer saw her logistical tasks in terms of endless details: "Let's make sure the camera works. Let's make sure the tape isn't bad. Let's make sure that there's a transmission point in order to take that tape and feed it. What if it goes down? What if our cell phone goes dead?"

At the higher levels of each organization, logistical issues involved putting together all the pieces of a complicated operation. Carin Dessauer itemized her main concerns as CNN associate political director in terms of the big picture: "What are your resources, how many people are out in the field, how many people can you get out into the field, how much money can you spend to do this story, how much air time do you have to play with, how many stories can you do, how many bodies do you have to work with on pieces down the road?"

Technology Great and Small

If broadcast and cable television share a common logistical plight, then workers at both operations will draw sharp contrasts between what they do and what newspaper reporters do. Several television personnel noted, some with envy, that newspaper coverage is far less complex. ABC correspondent Charles Murphy said that television reporters are "locked into [using] an uplink truck or a microwave," which requires getting to a place where one is available. Otherwise, there is no story. Newspapers, in contrast, are simple; "They pick up a pay phone almost anywhere and dictate."

It is true that television's logistical nightmares are attributable as much to the technology of broadcasting as to self-imposed deadlines and the requirements of the road. As with logistical considerations, technology affects CNN and ABC in much the same fashion, although it is clearly more critical to the twenty-four-hour news format. ABC existed well before satellites were used in television news, but it is impossible to imagine CNN doing what it does without them.

The rapidity and versatility of news coverage owes its existence to big-ticket technological items. Everything revolves around satellite technology. Satellite uplinks make possible the instant transfer of information. In 1992 they were more plentiful than even during the 1988 campaign, and they were regularly booked by networks, as one producer put it, the way you would book an airline reservation. Satellite trucks traveled with the campaign during big events like the Clinton/Gore bus trips, providing a roving uplink for immediate media use. Satellite pagers made it possible to contact colleagues from virtually anywhere.

Some technological devices far less sophisticated than satellites were nonetheless critically important. These were commonly available items adapted to the specific needs of television news. One producer said, "We couldn't have survived without a cell phone," which was used constantly for communication in the field, or without a fax machine, because, "It's hard to find a *New York Times* when you're out in East Bumba, Louisiana." Whereas ten years ago much information was sent by telephone, today correspondents can type their scripts on a laptop computer while traveling on an airplane and send it along to the bureau via modem. Likewise, they can receive wire reports or background information the same way.[2]

Technology is perceived as an asset by some, a hindrance by others. "It's great," said one producer, "but it can also be a major pain." Certainly, it speeds things up, but then, things were fast enough already. Technology is both credited with and blamed for creating CNN's early deadline. And there are the inevitable inconveniences. Appliances may be heavy, and they have to be transported. Sometimes that trip to an out-of-the-way uplink is unavoidable. And, like so many of us, some correspondents live in fear that the computer is going to eat their script.

If technology is a mixed blessing for those who use it, without question television news as an institution exists in its present rapid-fire, go-anywhere form because of it. It understates the case to say that television news operates at an entirely different technological level from when Epstein wrote about network organizations in the early 1970s.[3] Then, cameras used film, which had to be shipped by airplane to a facility for development before it could be used on television. At the time, Epstein accurately noted that servicing video technology made story selection its servant. Contemporary technology is far less constraining, allowing television to broadcast instantly, as one producer put it, "while literally standing out in the middle of a field in the middle of Wyoming."[4] The complex logistics developed by both networks for reporting election news assume the availability of a reliable advanced communications system, and most of the time, this is the case. A fundamental premise of both operations is that the camera can go to the event; it need not be the other way around. Gone is the problem of dropping a story from a newscast because the film will be a day late or because an event is taking place in an inconvenient location.

Of course, technology has its limits. As Chris Bury tells it, "Cell phones work where there are cells. And a lot of places, there weren't cells. And computers work when you can plug into a phone system and get into the modem, and when they don't, they don't." In these cases, television coverage does "go back to the sort of 1960s technology of reading the script into New York." But these are minor obstacles compared to the technological constraints of a generation or even a decade ago. If they were more than that, network news organizations built around flexible advanced technology would cease to function. Consequently, broadcast and cable television news have unprecedented freedom to determine the content of coverage without being curbed by technological barriers.

Economics: "We're Still Out There"

Given dwindling profits and decreasing audiences at the three broadcast networks, it's easy to imagine how economic conditions could constrain election coverage, particularly at ABC. However, this does not appear to be the case. Few respondents included the admittedly sensitive issue of economics among the obstacles they face in their work, and when prodded, convincingly argued that economic circumstances have only a marginal impact on what they do. Staff at both networks admitted to being more cost conscious than in past years, as well as to engaging in the usual grumbling that often accompanies belt tightening.

But they submitted that financial restraints are more likely to be applied to investigative matters, where the investment could be steep and the outcome unknown, and feature stories, which are often expensive to produce. Breaking news is at the core of what both networks offer, and big stories will always be protected. The 1992 election was classified this way by both networks, and each in its own fashion made the commitment to cover it. CNN had the aid of a $3.5-million Markle Foundation grant specifically earmarked for campaign coverage. At ABC, according to correspondent Mike Von Fremd,

> Our Vice President Bob Murphy made a conscious effort, even in the face of [parent company] Capital Cities' tightening its belt, to say this is important, we have to spend it, and we're going to make this known. Particularly on the Clinton bus trip, we just went out and spent whatever it took. Eight years ago did we spend even more? Heck, yes—we were making so much money we didn't know what to do with it. We're more prudent now, but we're still out there.

Senior Political Correspondent Jim Wooten of ABC acknowledged that financial constraints must be there but said, "I don't see them," adding, "I'm not doing anything different this year than I did in 1980 or '84 or '88 or '68." However, others claimed that they were more conscious of money than they had been in the past. Whereas ABC did manage, unlike the other broadcast networks, to maintain an editorial presence on each candidate early in the race, in some instances it amounted to an off-air without a camera crew. If pictures were needed, creative methods had to be arranged to get them, such as borrowing a camera from an affiliate station. At CNN, even with the outside funding, trade-offs involving how to spend money were a regular part of doing business.

But these considerations did not stop either network from covering the campaign as it wished. In at least two instances, news judgments preceded economic criteria in the decision to spend money. One situation involved Ross Perot, whose presence as an unanticipated third candidate in the race cost each network additional crew, correspondents, and producers. Both CNN and ABC made a significant investment to cover the Perot campaign, as did their less financially healthy broadcast counterparts. Their common news judgment that Perot was a worthy component of the election story superseded fiscal concerns in a decision that one CNN executive said sent all budgetary estimates out the window.

A second instance of news judgments trumping pocketbook calculations involved ABC's coverage of the Gennifer Flowers fiasco. When the *Star* first reported Flowers's allegation that she had had an affair with Governor Clinton, ABC dispatched several people to Little Rock to investigate the charges. It was, according to one producer, a significant investment of time, travel, and personnel. One of those sent to investigate was Von Fremd, who said, "I'd report every single day to our executive producer, and to [Political Director] Hal Bruno, and to Peter Jennings. And they said, keep finding out, keep learning about her, but we have no intention of reporting one word of it because in our estimation it still hasn't become a credible story. But, we do want to get all the facts for ourselves and not rely on others." In the end, Von Fremd said, ABC "put a lot of effort into the investigation and reported none of what we were finding out."

On large-scale matters, decisions outweighed rather than succumbed to economics. Television election coverage maintained its familiar form despite leaner times, at least at the two networks chosen for this study. It is true that ABC is generally considered to be in better financial health than its two broadcast counterparts and that CNN had private funding. There were rumblings from ABC and CNN personnel that the other broadcast networks may have suffered a bit more deeply from their financial woes. But the difference was colored in shades, not bold strokes. In the end, all covered the campaign in effectively the same way and made the extra commitment of resources needed to cover Ross Perot.

Some have also argued, with Epstein, that this well-known shape of television election news followed from the economic logic of the medium. In other words, what the audience saw was the product of how the operation decided to invest its resources. Thus, such things as maintaining high ratings and happy affiliates were central to choices about coverage. Without rejecting the obvious importance of market factors to any business, the findings presented here suggest a greater economic impact on form than on content. CNN and ABC had different economic needs, yet they conceptualized the election in the same way. Consider that ABC News was charged with using the evening report to attract and hold an audience for the network's nightly entertainment programming, whereas CNN provided a service akin to newsradio, from which viewers might bob in and out. Accordingly, such things as the placement and length of stories varied between the two networks to accommodate their respective audiences, as we saw in chapter 2. But the content of coverage was remarkably similar.

Furthermore, given the way employees of the two networks described the economic environment, it appears that decisions about content follow more directly from how newsworkers perceive their respective roles than from resource allocation. Material on Gennifer Flowers was withheld because it was deemed unnewsworthy, even though money was spent to collect it. Ross Perot was given coverage because of judgments about the (personal and political) nature of campaigns and assessments about how the independent candidate fit into this schema, even though budgets were tight and covering Perot was expensive. Organization established the framework within which the election was covered, but what newsworkers did within this context and why they did it mattered far more in the evolution of election news content. These items, matters of procedure and personal orientation, will be considered in the next two chapters.

10

Newsmaking Routines: "This Is Not Brain Surgery"

The person in the field is always going to have a slightly different view of what they believe the story that day is in their own little bailiwick. Now, the people back at the desk do have more of an overview. They know what the other candidate is saying, they know what his surrogates are saying, they know what happened in Iraq, which may color what it is they want from your candidate that day. And basically, you make your case as best you can. The story can be driven by some person you don't even know someplace in your bureau, or it can be driven by the day's events either inside the campaign or outside the campaign. It depends how forcefully you want to make your argument.

—Candy Crowley, CNN correspondent

Routines follow from and are intertwined with the organizations they serve, but they are also a response to external constraints. Some routines of campaign coverage—for instance, the ongoing activities of moving correspondents and crews over long distances on short notice—are born of logistical necessity. Correspondents who write stories while airborne and send them by modem to their home bases perform a routine made possible by the available technology. Similarly, routines of election news coverage navigate a path between the goals of the news organization and the goals of the campaigns themselves.

The substance of routines is determined in part by the purposes they seek to accomplish. As correspondents, producers, camerapersons, and executives engage in the process of creating something called election coverage, their methods are collectively oriented toward this end. Through routines, all parties work together to create the televised image of the election that viewers see at home. At both networks, these routines are a function of a regularized, ongoing give-and-take. When we examine routines, we look at the process by which election news is negotiated.

The routines employed by CNN share a common denominator with those used by ABC. This is partly because, despite their organizational differences, the two networks share a familiar understanding of television election coverage. To the extent that both are involved in producing news about the election for a television audience, they share a similar purpose. They pursue that purpose in much the same way. To a great degree, they perceive election news to be composed of the same elements, which they cover in a similar fashion. Consequently, the procedures described by newsworkers at both organizations for getting election news on the air transcend most structural differences discussed in the last chapter.

The shared nature of routines is also partly attributable to the actions of the political campaign, which impact all broadcast outlets similarly. As Candy Crowley notes in the above passage, the story may be shaped at any time by events internal or external to the news organization. The strongest external influence, save for the possibility of breaking nonelection news, is the campaign itself. Both networks, having committed to a campaign-centered understanding of election coverage and having allocated resources accordingly, are at the mercy of the campaign for the information and pictures they need for their reports. Correspondents and producers in the field are particularly susceptible to the machinations of the campaign, just as they are subject to the demands of their home base. The routines they use to negotiate both sets of influences reflect this situation.

This chapter will examine the routines that mediate both the internal demands of the network and the external constraints of the campaign. The focus will be on how newsworkers make sense of their environment to produce election coverage. Then, in chapter 11, we will examine the assumptions about election news that inform the establishment and practice of these routines and, in the process, give election news on both networks its common content.

Internal Operations: Routines Within the Organization

Collaboration: A "Committee Process"

CNN and ABC share the fundamental belief that election coverage should be campaign-based; additionally, they agree to a great extent on the procedures to be used for covering candidates. At both networks, campaign news results from collaboration. Whereas upper management makes the final decisions on large questions, both networks operate on the basis of an open flow of ideas from executives at headquarters to correspondents and reporters on the road and back again from the field to Washington, Atlanta, or New York. Employees at all levels of both organizations called the choice of story subjects and the development of reports a joint effort; one correspondent called it "a consultation with management, where management has 51 percent of the vote."

CNN Associate Political Director Carin Dessauer said the process involves "a lot of give and take." For planning purposes, in 1992 correspondents kept management informed of upcoming campaign plans, and management suggested ways to cover them. Stories took shape out of the negotiation and discussion involved in reconciling inevitable differences of opinion on how to proceed. Dessauer described how this process looked from the Washington, D.C., desk of CNN:

> Usually you have a correspondent calling in to talk to Jack Smith [a senior producer], and they would say, OK Jack, this is what is happening tomorrow, we suggest the following story. Clinton is going to be in New York before the New York primary, and there is a lot of attention between Clinton and Brown. We'd like to take a look at what types of voters they are attracting. What do you think? Jack thinks about it, they kind of fine-tune what they're thinking, and we have a sense of what the highlights of the next day's stories are going to be the day before. We usually talk about it sometime that night, with Jack and Tom Hannon, and Chris Guarino, the senior producer of "Inside Politics." Everyone is talking because there are other developments taking place out there that could warrant another angle to the story. Then first thing in the morning there's the daily 7:30 conference call with the key players [management and personnel in the field], where we would run through what was in the papers that morning and see if there was a new story that developed overnight, or that somebody on the campaign trail learned, or that we learned about very late in the night. It could mean we had to change a decision about a story we wanted to do.

As the day progressed, collaboration would continue through regular telephone contact between the field and the desk. At ABC, the focus was on individual news programs. According to Political Director Hal Bruno, the process was straightforward.

> The off-air reporters and the correspondents who are covering the candidates report in to the show every day, several times a day, to say here's what's happening today. And the executive producer makes a decision, should they do something on it that day, is it something newsworthy or interesting? You get stuff in from all over the country. And you're trying each day to report what's happening. This is not brain surgery.

CNN's Gene Randall called the daily routine a "committee process," which for the correspondent on the road began with a daily, early morning call to Jack Smith.

> I would give him a breakdown of what was going on that day, and he would have an overview of the entire political day. He would let you know what was happening at other campaigns, and then you'd have some general idea of where the day

was going. And then, you would simply stay in touch as the day went along. And by the time you got to three o'clock in the afternoon eastern time, we'd all be working toward the same end, which would be getting a spot on "Inside Politics."

By mid-afternoon, the shape of the day's "Inside Politics" program generally would have been set, with all the contributors having a fairly clear idea of what they were doing. Around the same time, ABC personnel would be working toward the later deadline for "World News," staying in regular telephone contact with senior program producers in New York.

The process was held together by constant communication. One producer said the production staff was "the link" between correspondents, crew, and home base. A CNN field producer assigned to the Bush campaign said, "You were constantly checking in with your headquarters in Atlanta and Washington, telling them if Bush was on schedule and telling them what he was supposed to say, and they would tell you if there was any other news that you needed to get."

Story Editing and Approval: Top-Down

As deadlines approached, final editing and script approval took place at headquarters. An ABC correspondent explained that at his network, a script designated for broadcast would be sent to "the rim," the term derived from the shape of the desk in New York and used to describe "World News" senior producers.

> They would edit the script, tell us what they liked and didn't like, and what we had in there that they didn't want or what we didn't have in there that they did want. And through this revision process you might go through two or three scripts before you get the one which is satisfactory to the rim. Once you have that you edit it. It could be for matters of style, it could be for matters of substance, but they weigh in on each script.

The process was comparable at CNN, where the emphasis was on speed and accuracy. According to producer Marty Kramer,

> We have the producers on site go through the reports, and then we have producers back in the newsroom, either in D.C. or Atlanta, depending on where we are, also go through them. They have been studying wires, they have been listening to other sources, so that way you have someone who is not totally wrapped up in that day's coverage going through the reports to make sure that they're accurate and factual and correct. We try to get as much information into our reports as accurately and as quickly as possible.

At ABC, when the script was approved, it was designated for broadcast on "World News Tonight." At CNN, there was yet another step before a filed piece was included on the evening news program. Producers on programs like "PrimeNews" would cull through the day's political stories, including the entire "Inside Politics" program, which was made available as a package for later use.

Political stories were selected for "PrimeNews" in accordance with the general news needs of the program, which airs at 8:00 P.M. eastern time and is picked up for worldwide distribution on CNN's international service. With an eye toward the general news audience, Executive Producer Scott Woelful favored election news with broad appeal. Interview segments from "Inside Politics" were generally not used. Reports that were selected were embellished when necessary with details on the basics of the campaign because, as Woelful put it, "You can't assume people know who won the New Hampshire primary." As to how selections were made, "You come in and you take a look at what's out there, and it's a mix between what appeals to you and what's an interesting story, what's an important story, what stories you've done too much on or you think you need to do more on. You look at what works into the whole scheme of coverage on this show, which was a snapshot of what happened that day."

Political stories competed for air time with national and international news the way they would on "World News." Consequently, the breadth of coverage encompassed the same set of items as the ABC broadcast, which senior "World News" producers agreed was comparable in terms of overall content.

Originating Stories: Bottom-Up

In general, ideas may originate from the field and work their way up the chain of command, or they may emanate from the political desk, upper-level management, or, at ABC, from program producers. According to Hal Bruno at ABC, "The most common origin of a story is a reporter in the field selling it to a show producer or executive producer." Correspondents at both networks were quick to agree that their determination and initiative does and should inform story content because of their ability to capture what one called the "dynamic" of the campaign trail. "You've got to be a synthesizer," said another, "and it's almost impossible to do that anywhere except where the story is being reported."

Correspondents said that in 1992, their story ideas typically came from what they saw following the campaign on a daily basis. Many ideas emanated from what all parties to the process called "news of the day" items arising from candidate events, actions, or statements. Often, this focus entailed horse-race-oriented "here they come, there they go" stories chronicling the campaign itinerary. Sometimes, correspondents claimed ideas would occur to them over time as they experienced life in the field. Such was the derivation of the ABC piece about local press coverage on the Clinton bus tours, discussed in chapter 3. Chris Bury, who reported the story, explained that its origins were in observations of "what a smooth operation Clinton had for getting positive local news coverage and how they really milked the local news mar-

kets for all they were worth. That was just something we noticed out on the
trail and decided to pitch."

Less frequently, specific story ideas originated at executive levels removed
from the campaign trail. This process sometimes entailed ironing out different perspectives between those covering the campaign and those suggesting
the story idea from afar. Kim Schiller was an ABC producer on the Clinton
campaign late in the fall when "World News Tonight" executive producer
Paul Friedman assigned a story about the size of the candidate's crowds,
which he perceived to be unusually large. Schiller agreed that the crowds were
interesting but hesitated to do the story because, "What was interesting about
the Clinton phenomenon was that it started in August with the bus tours, and
the size of his crowds increased from August on. We sort of balked at doing
the story because it was not new to us. You could expect these crowds in October. It was a phenomenon in August." Nonetheless, ABC had not yet run a
story about the size of Clinton's crowds, a fact easily overlooked on the road
where large crowds were a fact of life but quite noticeable at home base. The
story was subsequently produced, and it was broadcast during the waning
days of the campaign.

Whenever differences of perspective such as this occurred, they were generally ironed out through negotiation or discussion. Numerous newsworkers
said that, for the most part, the fact that everyone was operating with the same
basic set of assumptions about what was newsworthy and important mini-
mized large-scale disagreements. More frequently, differences arose when, as
one correspondent put it, a "breaking story" in the campaign conflicted with
the desk's "preconceived notion of what they'd like." How smoothly such
differences were resolved depended on the nature of the discrepancy and on
the individuals involved. Some downplayed the matter while others tended to
agree with the correspondent who said, "There is natural competition between inside people and outside people in our business. People inside often-
times don't have a feel for what we go through on the outside; they, on the
other hand, feel we are a bunch of whining prima donnas who never want to
follow their directions." Of course, when a final decision was required, it
came from the inside.

External Constraints:
Routines Imposed by Campaigns

Campaign coverage was built around the candidates and their organizations
at both networks in 1992. Correspondents and producers talked about how
they were "with Clinton for a while" or "assigned to Tsongas during New
Hampshire." The nature of the assignment naturally caused television personnel to rely heavily on the campaigns for much of their information. At
some point, this tendency inevitably necessitated bending the newsgathering

routine to the will of the candidate or fighting the campaign organization to gather what television considers political news.

Campaigns generally provide reliable structures for coverage in the sense that they endure as long as the candidate is viable, but they are far from always accessible to reporters.[1] Correspondents and campaign operatives engage in a dance over access. When campaigns are well organized, media oriented, and doing well, correspondents find them forthcoming and easy to deal with. But few campaigns are all these things all of the time, if ever. Consequently, in 1992 newsworkers tended to struggle with the people they half playfully referred to as their captors; in fact, correspondents were at times caught between the agenda-setting efforts of the candidate and his staff and the logistical, time, or creative pressures of the network.

The Clinton campaign received universally high marks for being well organized and media oriented. These qualities made life smoother for those assigned to it and made it easier, according to some, for the Clinton people to get their version of news on the air. The Clinton campaign regularly arranged information packets for correspondents to use as background to their daily reports and planned for television's logistical and technological necessities. Jerry Brown's campaign operated at the other end of the organizational spectrum, paying little attention to fundamental aspects of planning, like arranging a place for reporters to sleep at the end of the day.[2] Most other campaigns operated within these two extremes.

Regardless of tactical sophistication, campaigns always attempted to regulate the message they sent to correspondents. Operatives naturally wished to portray their candidate in the best possible light, which was always easiest when there genuinely was something good to say. Good news facilitated access with the press and made the information-gathering process easier. Said one producer, "When you ask the press secretary how much money they raised last month and donations are coming in, the answer comes, well, we raised $2.4 million, with $1.6 million in matching funds. When the money starts drying up, it's, oh, you have to call someone in the home office."

Of course, in the fall, newsgathering was frustrated by the sheer complexity of the campaigns that had been successful. Inevitably, layers of aides were deposited around the candidates and the size of the press entourage swelled, making it more difficult for individual correspondents to have access. Compounding the situation was the tendency for campaigns to become conservative in their dealings with the press as the days tick by, aware that the risks of a misstep are greatest as future opportunities to correct them decrease.

Both networks anticipated this problem and tried to compensate for it in part by having an early presence on each campaign. This way, their representatives would be familiar, and perhaps favored, faces in the fall. Nonetheless, there was no question that the opportunities for easy one-on-one dialogue with a candidate or his assistants diminished sharply after the primaries.

This forced correspondents to alter their routines. Gene Randall, who covered Bill Clinton for CNN, said there wasn't a lot of access to the candidate in the days leading up to the election, and that posed a problem. Other campaign sources were available, but "you had less involvement of the candidate in a less formal setting than a speech, so you'd have to scramble a little bit more. I think it kept us from doing as effective a job as we might have done as the campaign went along." Candy Crowley also covered the Clinton campaign. Reflecting on the situation in late October made her nostalgic for the previous winter.

> In New Hampshire when the draft story broke, I got a call, I think it was about nine o'clock, to cover it that day. Clinton's over at such and such hotel, and I went over there, and I knew he was upstairs. I waited for him to come down, and we were the only crew there. He stopped, and I met one of his guys. Toward the end, you couldn't get near the guy. The larger they become, the more of a story they are, the less you're able to cover them. So, I long for that little day in New Hampshire, when it's just me standing there in a hotel lobby.

Tactics employed by a campaign to control their message can be strong. News personnel accept this as part of the job but are always seeking ways to deal with it. CNN's Bob Franken itemized the forms of "coercion" routinely used by operatives against the press in order to limit access to information. These include "physically blocking your camera, refusing you access, verbal intimidation of a variety of sorts, trying to prevent you from asking the questions you might want to ask of the candidate by walking away politely or silently, or sometimes less than politely." To compensate, Franken fought back. He said, "In the case of the Clinton campaign, they sometimes got pretty close to the line in terms of being physical. In my case, I'm large enough that I would be physical right back. They would put their hand in front of the camera, or would push you a little bit, and I'm not shy to push back. This is not unprecedented. Other campaigns do it, too."

In less intimidating ways, as well, newsworkers felt that the candidates were often able to control the agenda. But the campaigns, in turn, were likely responding to the way television conceptualized the campaign as a string of daily events. Campaigns had their "event of the day" planned to tie in to their "theme of the day"; inasmuch as reporters felt constrained to cover the campaign from an event-oriented, daily perspective, they relinquished some control over coverage to the campaigns. Several newsworkers protested their inability to get the candidate to go to a particular location or comment on a certain subject.

Of course, the campaigns did not always control the news; at times, they confronted a story or a story angle beyond their best efforts to control. Some nonissues, such as the pot-smoking allegations against Jerry Brown, arose out of the news organization's initiative and so dominated the media's interest that for periods of time little else was reported. During these times, which Larry Sabato described as "feeding frenzies," the best a campaign could hope for was to control the damage caused by a critical mass of reporters pursuing one line of questioning.[3] In this regard, the ongoing push for access pitted the campaign's need for positive exposure against television's demand for daily, event-driven, interesting, campaign-oriented political stories. There was, as one television executive put it, a "constant tension" between the two that was so commonplace as to be routine. Reporters expected it and worked around it.

Ultimately, the campaign cannot survive without television, just as it cannot survive long stretches without good press. Consequently, candidates need television reporters for exposure as much as, if not more than, television reporters need candidates for news. ABC's Mike Von Fremd feels this gave him an advantage over the long run.

> In this day of television, if you're a television correspondent, it ain't that hard anymore. Because they want to be seen, they want to be heard, and if you work for any of the big four networks, you're probably going to be able to get the access you need. You're probably going to be able to do anything. When they're running for office, when they're out there trying to get elected, I don't think they pose too many obstacles anymore.

For the political reporter and producer working on the 1992 presidential election story, obstacles were the name of the game. Newsworkers at both networks used their routines as ammunition. Whether created by the structure of television news or imposed by the campaigns, impediments to covering the story ranged from finding ideas and negotiating their development, to writing and editing under pressure, to struggling physically and psychologically with campaign representatives for control of the agenda.

Such obstacles were addressed through a variety of commonly employed methods: constant observation in the field; regular conference calls between the newsroom and the road; ongoing negotiation of story content; making one's presence known to campaign aides; even shoving a little when necessary. Still, if routines typically follow from the constraints of the campaign trail and how newswork is structured, they are equally consistent, as we will see, with assumptions common to the television news community about what makes a political story.

11

Newsworker Orientations: "Inside the Bubble"

A campaign becomes sort of a hermetically sealed community.

—Bob Franken, CNN correspondent

CNN's intention to narrowcast the news around the clock was unprecedented on television, and the network was organized around a unique set of objectives. The organizational structures of CNN and ABC support different command chains, staff sizes, deadlines, story volume, and levels of competition for air time. Nonetheless, it would not be easy to pair workers in the field with their respective networks simply on the basis of how they approached campaign coverage in 1992. Routines defied organizational differences as personnel at both networks went about the business of gathering election news in much the same way and ended up with strikingly similar products. Newsworker perspectives on what constitutes political television—whether at CNN or at ABC—are cut from the same cloth.

The two networks, indeed the television community, conceptualize campaign coverage in very much the same way. The choice to send correspondents and producers to interact with the campaign was informed by a commonly shared sense that election coverage is about (selected major party) campaigns. The shape and form of that interaction likewise followed from a collectively held understanding of what constitutes political news and how to gather it in the face of the constraints posed by political operatives and organizational imperatives. In short, what we have come to know as television election news owes its existence to how those who create it are oriented toward television and elections. Differences over coverage particulars and disputes over story specifics aside, the people who brought the election campaign to the American public were operating in a community of shared orientations.

These orientations were not divinely inspired or automatic, nor were they correct or incorrect in a normative sense. But they were communal and commonplace, and they shaped the news Americans saw on television.

"Orientations" refer to an individual's awareness of the world in relation to the self. I prefer this term over "values" or "norms" because the items I will address in this chapter relate to personal perspectives reinforced by the community. Sometimes newsworkers are aware of these orientations, or aspects of how they are inclined to see the news world; sometimes they are not conscious of them but would likely admit to them if they were brought to their attention. In any case, these points of view are important in shaping election news. The terms "value" and "norm," which conjure up real or idealized standards for behavior, properly could be applied to some but not all of the items addressed here; indeed, some of the things we will consider have been discussed elsewhere as "values."

Richard Hofstetter, in arguing for "structural" rather than "political" bias in television's coverage of the 1972 election, states that news is the product of choices informed by values—in this case, values inherent in the medium itself. The commercial imperative to hold an audience through interesting, appealing, dramatic news accounts leads newsworkers to favor those aspects of the political campaign that fit the bill, notably competitive and character-oriented items.[1] News selection follows implicitly from what matters most to those doing the choosing, or as other observers put it, "A powerful system of logic underlies the news and provides implicit boundaries on the parts of the world that are newsworthy and the parts that are not."[2] Likewise, Herbert Gans speaks of "values in the news," which stem from judgments made by newsworkers whose assumptions about reality translate often unknowingly into the stories that are reported.[3] The selective nature of political communication implies the existence of a set of ideas about what is or should be considered news.

I believe the term "orientation" best suits the items discussed here, given the tendency for news personnel to address their world and their work in strictly personal terms. This notion incorporates value judgments about what constitutes the news but does not restrict the discussion to this narrow area. It emphasizes the fact that news is the product of individuals working within a bureaucratic framework, not simply the product of an organization. The news show is the end result of a string of choices made by people playing roles from executive producer to off-air producer. Their options are facilitated by how they understand political news as much as by the institutional imprint of the television environment. The professional imperative mandates that newsworkers apply individual judgment to the difficult choices they face regularly, even as a common community circumscribes those decisions by reinforcing a set of specific approaches to the news.

The fourteen orientations addressed in this chapter are aggregated from the responses given by the newsworkers interviewed for this project. Not every respondent mentioned—directly or indirectly—each of these items, although all of them were widely addressed. Neither were the respondents prompted to mention any particular orientation; they were asked simply how they do their jobs and what obstacles they face in their work. Recurrent themes in their answers formed the basis of the material discussed here. I do not mean to suggest that the following list of orientations is absolute or complete, only that it is sufficient to understanding how election coverage is derived. Additional orientations are both possible and likely.

A list of newsworker orientations is presented in Table 11.1, together with the impact each is assumed to have on election coverage. Distinct orientations are linked with particular components of the complex election story discussed in Part I. Thus, different aspects of election coverage, such as the tendency toward horserace, process, and nonissue items, are traceable to particular perspectives on coverage.

The Idealized Self

The first item on the list in Table 11.1 refers to the commonly held sense of what election coverage should be. This is a normative standard that many newsworkers impose upon themselves, a yardstick for self-evaluation. On a regular basis, the television product falls short of the ideal. Normative self-judgments take several specific forms, but all revolve around the wish for television election coverage to be more substantive and less superficial than it usually is; thus, newsworkers would like to be able to cover the issues more and the horserace less, diminish the prominence of polls, deemphasize pictures, or at CNN, cover the campaign in greater depth.

Newsworkers at both networks were aware of and sensitive to the widely articulated criticism that television pays too much attention to the horserace at the expense of the issues. Some were defensive about this critique, whereas others offered it willingly. Invariably, the subject of issue coverage was discussed in terms of an ideal standard of accomplishment, with respondents saying things like, "There is room for improvement" because "we ignore the issues" or "favor" the horserace.

For many, the quantity of issue coverage was inseparable from the idea of good coverage. Covering the issues was equated by an ABC correspondent with "more substantive coverage" and by a CNN producer with "covering the campaign better." Added ABC's Morton Dean, "Every four years after an election, there are meetings about how better to cover the campaign next time. And every four years somebody will say next time we have to cover the issues."

TABLE 11.1   Orientations and Their Impact on Campaign Coverage

Paramount Orientations	Impact on Campaign Coverage
Idealized self	Unrealized
Self-interest	Structures content; process emphasis
News is obvious	Structures content
Play it safe	Reinforces the obvious
News is events	
News is dramatic	Horserace over issues;
News is conflictive	political orientation
News is predictable	
News is best if easy to cover	
News is unusual	Horserace strategy; nonissues
News is personalized	Candidate-centered coverage
News should be objective	Nonideological coverage
News needs context	Analytical coverage
Perception of audience	Reinforces coverage pattern or idealized self; promoted issue coverage in 1992

Numerous respondents, without provocation, defended the quantity of coverage devoted to the issues, arguing with invisible critics that there was more substantive—meaning issue—coverage than some people think. Anticipating the discussion in chapter 4, they accurately perceived that, in 1992 at least, significant attention was paid to domestic economic issues. But the high level of sensitivity with which the subject was treated indicated great awareness of and concern for the criticism that television is shallow. Likewise, the widespread twinning of issues and substance was evidence of an internalized measure of what should constitute responsible election coverage.

At CNN, a twist in this reasoning involves the concern that coverage on the all-news network is broad but not deep. Largely in response to criticism that CNN is essentially an airborne clipping service, and consistent with tendencies for self-examination about matters of substance, CNN employees can be particularly sensitive to this suggestion. One employee said that concerns about "bad breadth" had motivated the network to self-consciously attempt "more meaningful" stories as opposed to "sexy pieces" like "car crashes and suicides." In the electoral arena, issues of depth had the same impact as generic worries about substance. These concerns led to (often successful) attempts to emphasize issues on vehicles like "Inside Politics." For election coverage in general, however, issues about issue coverage continue to stir concerns.

A comparable degree of defensiveness was also evident when the subject turned to television's use of public opinion polls in its coverage. Again without provocation, newsworkers who themselves raised the subject felt compelled to downplay the influence of polls on how the election was portrayed.

A CNN producer, discussing how story topics were chosen, mentioned the daily polls conducted by the Gallup organization for the cable network. In keeping with concerns about shallowness, the polls were promoted as being "very in depth, and that really helped drive us." Moments later, in response to my request for more details, she corrected herself: "We weren't poll driven. I don't want you to go away with that impression. It was really just to see what the candidates were making for news. The candidates made news, we covered them, and we just put it on the air."

A similar exchange occurred with a senior ABC News official while we were discussing how Ross Perot became noteworthy when his public support blossomed in the spring of 1992. This surge of popularity was evident, the respondent said, because "you start seeing trends, polls start reflecting things." He then immediately qualified his statement, adding, "not that we're driven by polls alone. That's not it at all. It's so many things. Polls are simply a part of it."

But others were quite direct about the prominent place of polls in political reporting, admitting that "we're driven by the polls to some extent because that's national opinion," that polls are "overused," or that "we've all been polled to death." As with issue coverage, some newsworkers openly criticized how data-oriented they felt coverage had become. An ABC producer expressed the sentiment that "too many reporters have fallen prey to the notion that the polls show thus, and so that's the way it's going to be." And a CNN correspondent compared television's use of polls in 1992 to a "Harold Pinter theatre-of-the-absurd play," given the manner in which networks ultimately yielded to covering each other's poll results. Great sensitivity to the addictive potential of polls, coupled with the wish to downgrade their influence, contributes to the self-conscious contours of an idealized portrayal of the election in which the "right" thing to do is clearly not to let polls overwhelm coverage.

The same may be said of newsworker sensitivity to the role of visual imagery in shaping coverage. Even though the data addressed in Part I indicate that pictures only marginally influenced election coverage, the potential for this to happen coupled with past criticism on this matter contributed to the same sort of reaction that respondents had to polls and "trashy" coverage. A certain discomfort permeated discussions of the use of visuals; some respondents would speak about it only "off the record."

While acknowledging that items will be covered even without pictures, a CNN producer admitted to a difference of opinion with colleagues over how imagery should be used, saying, "There are some people who believe that if you don't have it on camera, it didn't happen. I don't personally believe that. I think if you got it on camera, that's great, if you don't have it on camera, well, it's still news." But another respondent self-critically explained, "We're particularly guilty, in television, of going for a great picture." For instance,

"There was a Buchanan campaign event in San Antonio where he put on a raccoon hat and took out a little rifle and aimed it. Well, that's a great picture. You have a presidential candidate with this coonskin hat on and he has this gun and he's aiming. It's going to show up on television."

The uneasiness with which newsworkers acknowledged that television is by definition visually oriented underscored the perceived connection between reliance on catchy imagery and a tendency toward superficiality. Attitudes toward all these items—substantive content, polls, and pictures—spoke to concerns shared by many in the broadcast community about the substance of their product. Their comments about process coverage further indicated their depth of concern about deviations from the ideal. Process coverage, as we have seen, at times self-consciously deals with such topics as "why television doesn't cover the issues" and "whether television is overly dependent on pictures." As one newsworker put it, "We report on how naughty we are! We often report on how we'd like to stick to the issues and stay away from the dirt." When I asked why television didn't simply report the issues rather than devote air time to the fact that they would like to report the issues, this respondent was unsure but said,

> Let me tell you this. I think all news organizations are striving to stay away from the sleaze stories. But after it's reported somewhere and people start hearing about it, it's our job to do a story about it. You can't ignore something that people have started hearing about on their radio stations, that they've seen on maybe some talk show, that showed up in the New York *Post*. At that point, we can't ignore it.

In other words, other orientations override the archetypal wish to be more substantive. Herein one finds the primary reason why television searches for but cannot obtain its ideal. In the above case, "sleaze" coverage was perceived to be the result of what other news outlets were doing, which we will shortly observe invokes an orientation about "playing it safe" and not straying too far from the journalistic hoard. Others explained why they fall short of their ideal in terms of the need to fill the demand for interesting gossip (an orientation I call, "News is dramatic"), the need to "steer coverage," as an ABC producer put it, within the confines of the event-driven mentality of the horserace ("News is events"), or the need to avoid too many difficulties in getting material ("News is best if easy to cover").

Other orientations, ones rooted in the everyday reality of newswork, take precedence over the imagined ideal. If television election coverage is not dominated by issues, or absent poll data and pictorial constraints, it is not because the medium is staffed by shallow or superficial people. On the contrary, the newsworkers interviewed for this book were universally self-aware, subtle thinkers who generally felt the dissonance between what they produce and what they would like to produce.[4] The ideal is held at bay by a series of orientations that fit sensibly with the manner in which election coverage is performed but that generate results at odds with newsworker wishes. Paramount among these orientations, and consistent with tendencies toward self-awareness, is a keen feeling of self-interest by those involved in political coverage toward the unique environment in which they live. More than any other orientation, this feeling structures the product they bring forth.

Self-Interest

Something akin to a chemical reaction takes place between newsworkers and political officials on the campaign trail. Professional boundaries are altered by common experiences and concerns: the frenetic pace of travel; the relentless, unyielding deadlines; the pressure of performance; life in the public eye. They share different objectives and market different products, but campaigners and correspondents over time become united by a perspective only the participants can understand. To be sure, professional training and a strong orientation toward balanced reporting help mitigate against the loss of ideological detachment. Serving time with the political campaign, however, has the effect of drawing newsworkers inside themselves, leaving them unable to differentiate between what one insider called "your life" and "the rest of the world." For those covering it and living it, the campaign becomes the main point of reference and a source of fascination. This orientation is reflected in coverage.

David Maraniss wrote from experience about the phenomenon for the *Washington Post*.

> "The bubble" is what surrounds the traveling road show of any presidential campaign. It includes the candidate, the staff, the press, the plane, the bus and all the electronic gear of the 20th-century hustle. Yet it is not so much a tangible phenomenon as a metaphysical one, a way of looking at things, at once cynical and cozy, but mostly just weird. It is where you find both the real story and an utterly false one, a speed-blurred picture of a very large country.[5]

Correspondents and producers at both networks described this phenomenon, often in bold language, talking of "the community" in which "you eat, sleep, and breathe" with the same people every day without end. Perhaps the most descriptive account was offered by ABC producer Kim Schiller.

> We all live in this cocoon, in a completely different world from anyone else, those of us who are covering the campaign. You're there all the time, morning to night you live together in this strange world. You see crowds and outside people, but you live in your own community. It swells and it decreases, but basically there's a core of people who are always in this community. I was lucky, I mean, every weekend I got a day off, which was very unusual. Some people were never outside the bubble, especially at CNN. A CNN producer had two large suitcases that he would pack, and he would be out maybe a month and a half, two months at a time without ever having a day off or going home, without ever leaving the bubble.

In this environment, the campaign appeared to take on what one correspondent called "a life of its own," divorced from everyday reality, and became a "source of fascination" in its own right. The effect was exaggerated by the fact that many of life's ordinary, mundane aggravations were accommodated, but at the cost of restricted personal freedom. For instance, as Schiller noted,

> Most people never have to go through an airport experience. You get chartered to wherever you're going and the bus is waiting for you when you get there. You get off the bus and the hotel people have your keys ready for you. On the other hand, your life is not your own and you're completely out of control of your own comings and goings. You're literally herded into pens—the press pens as they call them. And you're told where to go and where to sit and what time to get up.

Common membership in the cult of celebrity also perpetuated the campaign's unique seclusion. Correspondents in particular were likely to comment on the Hollywood status of presidential candidates, symbolized by but not limited to the rock star treatment granted Clinton, Gore, and their spouses during their national double-date tour of America. One journalist perceptively noted that the candidates were not alone in this respect inasmuch as "the newsmakers and the news coverers have gotten mixed up in that whole broad category we regard as public figures." There are, after all, celebrity reporters: highly visible marquee figures who are grist for the same *People Weekly* articles and tabloid put-ons as movie stars and presidents. On this score, no distinction is made between Bill Clinton and Sam Donaldson;[6] the candidate and the traveling reporter, the candidate's aide and the field producer, have more in common with each other than either has with the general public. It is a privilege derived from life in the bubble.

To hear the participants explain it, the bubble analogy applies to more than simply the campaign environment. Inhabitants of the East Coast newsrooms occupied a place in the extended family of fast-forward motion that describes equally well the presidential campaign and television news production. Piecing together news elements so as to generate stories is a process akin to the proverb of the blind men attempting to describe an elephant based on their encounters with different limbs. As correspondents and producers "fly all over creation with one guy in this little cocoon," executives sit in a "room without windows," removed from developments in the field, asking for news elements that one high-level respondent admitted often didn't make sense to the people on the road. Collaboration takes on a sense of urgency when viewed from this perspective, for no one is ever situated such that she sees the whole picture. Those in the "room without windows" are bound by mutual self-interest to those in the "cocoon"; the protective metaphysical layers of the hermetically sealed campaign extend to the entire world of election news production.

All involved have a tremendous emotional investment in maintaining this environment and making it work. Television newsworkers, who tend to take an active role in seeking out and developing stories,[7] are quite naturally going to be attracted to this strange world as a source of news. It doesn't take a large leap of faith to expect that they would inevitably videotape it, write about it, and televise it. Nor should it be surprising that so much of what is produced about the campaign that doesn't directly invoke the bubble is fueled by what newsworkers perceive to be interesting from within their cloistered setting.

The manifestation of self-interest is apparent in the attention given to several of the election news topics addressed in Part I. It is most evident with process coverage, or coverage of how the campaign is covered, which by definition derives from self-involvement. "We're interested in how the campaign is covered," Kim Schiller offered, "because there is a certain fascination with the bubble." Others agreed, sometimes in stronger language. Said one correspondent, "It's journalistic incest. Our turnaround discussing ourselves is egotistical and weird. The lines get blurred and we end up covering ourselves."

Newsworkers expressed the sentiment that self-interest penetrated every level of newswork at both networks. Several admitted to feeling conflicted about airing process stories or to trying to find ways to justify them as items of interest to the general public. But everyone speaking on the matter acknowledged the enormous pull of life within the campaign as an irresistible source of material. CNN producer Marty Kramer believes it's a prerequisite perspective for participation in high-level political coverage.

> The people who are in the news business are fascinated with it to begin with, otherwise they wouldn't be there. They wouldn't be working the crazy hours that we work, and the seven, eight, twelve days in a row that they sometimes have to put in to get the story covered, if they weren't fascinated with the process to begin with. So, they think that because they're fascinated with it, other people are also, and I don't know. I think that there's a place for that, I just don't know if it's in the nightly newscast.

CNN's Bob Franken agreed, calling process coverage "parochial" and attributing it to a baby boomer attitude. He said, "I think that we often cover things that are near and dear to our hearts and exclude things that are equally significant but which aren't near and dear, now that the yuppies, the baby boomers, basically control the press. We cover stuff about cellular phones rather than problems of drought, or farm problems, or anything like that."

Some suggested that process items are grist for the hyperactive television mill on occasions when there is nothing else to cover. In essence, when there is no "news," so to speak, newsworkers on a deadline may look inward toward the bubble. A respondent assigned to the Clinton/Gore bus tours lamented that the tours were excellent publicity for the candidate but "almost never contained any news," as defined by some of the orientations to be discussed below. To compensate, and in order to generate a story, life on the bus became an acceptable topic to report and an obvious source of material.

Self-interest also plays a role in promoting horserace coverage. The community in which campaign news is found and reported is built around winning. Correspondents and producers may be there looking for a good story, but the bubble would not exist for them to enter if not for the paramount political purpose of electing a president. On the road, newsworkers said, it was hard not to get wrapped up in who was ahead and by how much because these matters were the overriding concerns of the political people on the journey. Inevitably, a horserace orientation permeated everything.

Of course, political reporters needed little coaxing. Several newsworkers openly admitted that they looked for horserace news because it was of personal interest to them. Some acknowledged that it could be fun, that a good race could get the juices flowing. Getting into the game could alleviate the monotony of long days on the road. One correspondent said, "When you've got two strong, tough guys going for the biggest prize, it can be ferocious. And that can be very entertaining." It might or might not have captivated the audience, but the horserace certainly engaged the media contingent in 1992, as in other election years.

The method by which experiences were translated into horserace coverage further indicated the importance of self-interest in structuring election news content. Obviously, judgment is involved in making coverage decisions, and practitioners will claim the professional prerogative of knowing the standards to apply. But there is some evidence to suggest that, in tandem with other orientations that reinforce what is newsworthy, the details correspondents found personally interesting had a better chance of making it to air. This notion qualifies newsworkers' claims that the campaign controls the message (discussed in chapter 10). Within the framework provided by the campaign, the correspondent's feelings about the campaign may determine the details of the news agenda.

Perhaps the best example of this factor came from ABC's Chris Bury, who contrasted the ease with which he covered the first Clinton/Gore bus trip with the difficulties he faced after several excursions on the road:

> The first one was quite fascinating and quite rich *from my vantage point.* Because it was Clinton right out of the convention, and there was genuine excitement. I mean, it was a lot of good advance work, but there was genuine enthusiasm and excitement for the Democratic ticket. To see the whole act of Hillary and Bill and Al and Tipper, the whole sort of generational road show. The first one produced a wealth of interesting stories. But by the fifth or sixth or seventh, they got to be just silly little public relations gimmicks and the thrill was gone, *at least for me.* I was very happy to do my last bus trip.[8]

Arguably, the bus trip was no less gimmicky in Ohio than it was in Wisconsin, Florida, or Illinois. Likewise, the novelty and excitement of the experience was shared by many who turned out in remote communities all over the country, whether it was during the first tour or the last. But from the perspective of the correspondents, the thrill of the tour waned because they were experiencing it continuously. This point of view was captured in the television coverage. Thus, the national audience experienced the bus tour the same way the correspondents did—and the correspondents quite naturally saw the excitement at the beginning and the hokeyness at the end. To cover the bus trip from the point of view of those experiencing it for the first time would have required the reporter to suspend the first-person perspective in the face of great boredom wrought of redundancy. It would, however, have generated a different account of the story.

In 1992, self-interest may have also enabled coverage of the economic recession. Bob Franken made an interesting and provocative observation about why television paid so much attention to the matter in 1992.

> This economic recession got covered much more thoroughly than previous ones because this one for the first time affected white-collar workers, which is our class. If it affected blue-collar workers, so what, big deal. We'd do some stories on it and that would be it. This one affected us, therefore it got more coverage, and the argument could be made that because of the coverage, it became self-feeding. Now, that latter one I'm not sure I'm ready to believe, but it's certainly possible.

Although it is difficult to say if this is a widely held impression, Franken's analysis is consistent with the overall role of self-interest in structuring coverage for television. Whether or not economic stories fed on one another, the possibility that self-interest fueled economic coverage on a medium not typically inclined to cover issues is noteworthy in its own right. Certainly, the economy-as-politics story can be traced to other sources, such as poor economic indicators, pictures of the unemployed, and the effort made by both networks to focus on issues. But that effort, while effective, was effectively single-minded in scope, focusing in large part on coverage of "the issue" instead of issues per se. And that makes the possibility that personal experience played a role a curious one. Self-interest may not have been the only factor fueling coverage of the recession, but it certainly provided one reasonable explanation for its durability in 1992.

From within the bubble, newsworkers turned their own interests and their interest in themselves into news. This approach made process coverage possible, promoted horserace coverage, and might even have contributed to issue coverage. From the cocoon to the room without windows, the bubble structured the lives of newsworkers and informed their product; fascination with their own lot was evident in choices about what to report and how to report it. This observation is consistent with the self-assessment evident when news personnel invoked their ideals, with the self-consciousness that led newsworkers at all levels to constantly review their performance and at times plead with critics to understand how disappointed they often were with their own work. Self-interest is the overarching orientation of the television community; all others either follow from it or bend to it.

News Is Obvious

One orientation that follows naturally from self-interest is the sense, widely held among newsworkers, that campaign news is simply obvious to anyone who looks for it. "Not that I can't explain it," said one respondent, "it's just that when you've been in the business, there are certain things that you know are going to be news." Others likened this news sense to "instinct," to knowing what "feels right." Said one newsworker, "I think there's a gut reaction. It's some sort of thing in you, some sort of gene or something that helps you know the story. It becomes obvious to you."

CNN correspondent Candy Crowley believes reporters simply think alike.

> Reagan spokesman Larry Speakes used to have this phrase which at the time I never agreed with. He'd look at all of us in the press and say, "Y'all like blackbirds on a pole, you know, one of you takes off and so do the rest of you." I think there's a certain amount of that, and part of it is, we do tend to think alike. I mean, reporters do know a good story when they see it. Not that we think alike politically, but think alike like, boy, this'll be a great story and that'll be a great story, so we know one when we see one and we pursue it. I think the blackbirds on a pole metaphor could be true.

Repeatedly, newsworkers expressed the sentiment that the campaign existed apart from their conscious awareness of it. They regard election news as something that happens in their environment, not something they create or even actively effect. This impression persisted despite the awareness they had of living in the closed, distorted campaign environment. Various interviewees said, for instance,

> We cover the campaign that is there. People think we invent this thing, that we determine it, and that's not true.

> I think it's basic journalism, covering the story that's out there.

> It's quite possible that out there in Oprah-land, there's something lying in the weeds, some issue, some moment. There's no way we can anticipate it. There may be a moment out there that helps to define the campaign.

In other words, they feel coverage is the result of reporters "discovering" rather than "anticipating" the news and not a function of choice.[9] This perspective reinforces the professional standard of the dispassionate observer, provides a rationale for news content, and guards against charges of intentional bias. It also shifts the focus away from the role of personal orientations in story selection. But one need not argue malicious intent to claim that a host of perspectives and judgments establish how newsworkers will see the campaign or its defining moments and consequently affect what they will report about it.

The perspective that news is obvious works in tandem with the orientation toward self-interest in structuring election coverage. Self-interest allows the television news community to define campaign coverage in its own terms, and the belief that news is obvious provides the rationale for denying that self-interest makes a difference. In truth, whatever is worthy of coverage "out there" is determined by what appears obvious and important from inside the bubble, a point of collective self-reference distorted by the media-campaign environment. Whatever reality check is applied in the process of selecting what to report, it is made against a common, skewed standard that includes the assumption that coverage is determined by "the story" rather than the story being a product of coverage.

Play It Safe

Television newsworkers will make sure not to stray too far from the competition, be it electronic or print. This behavior serves to reinforce bubble-induced coverage standards. Despite competitive pressures to be first with the story, media personnel at all levels are oriented to playing it safe. They talk of checking with other outlets to make sure their brand of the story is not too far afield of what others are reporting. This collaborative process has the effect of reinforcing "the obvious." If a story is being carried by the competition, where the same ideas apply about what constitutes election news, newsworkers assume it is reasonable for them to use it as well. "If there was a story out in the *L.A. Times,* for instance, that something happened with Clinton back a couple of years ago," offered a CNN producer, "of course we'd try to pursue that and maybe make that the news of the day."

It is a curious procedure, considering the professed lack of choice involved in determining election news. Reinforcement from other news outlets seems redundant if the story is obvious and inconsistent with looking to the campaign, rather than to other reporters, for the news. At the very least, if the story is similarly apparent to all journalists at all networks, newspapers, and magazines, verification should invariably yield duplicate results. But this does not always happen.

Essentially, television newsworkers turn to other news sources more as a guide for behavior than as a source of validation, although both are desired objectives. The universally acclaimed prestige press are the beacons, most notably the *New York Times,* the *Washington Post,* the *Wall Street Journal,* sometimes the *Los Angeles Times,* and of course the other networks. Charles Murphy, who covered Ross Perot for ABC, explained that the decision to devote air time to the independent challenger crystallized following much in-house discussion once the independent began to receive attention in the *New York*

Times. He said, "We talked about it, and I said to the executive producer, you know, this guy's catching on down here, you better pay attention to him. Well, well, yeah, we know that, they say. But then the dawning hits. It seems to hit the three networks and CNN—it seems to dawn across all these editorial desks the same day. The *New York Times* has a lot to do with it, of course. That's sort of a guide they use."

Other respondents said they routinely looked toward the elite press "to see what information they have, to see if they have something we don't." Recall the CNN producer who relied on fax machines to transmit the *New York Times* to remote places. I asked him whether having the paper would influence his story. "Well, sure it would," he said, "I mean, if another newspaper is reporting something about the candidate we're covering, yeah, that would influence our story. I've got a perfect example for you. The *Wall Street Journal* had a list of four names that Clinton was looking at for vice-president the week before the convention. That very much influenced our coverage that day."

The perceived purpose of checking what others are reporting may be to play it safe from a professional standpoint, to keep up with the story as it is defined by the competition. But in fact, the process involves searching out the prescribed boundaries of coverage set by elite media and continually monitoring and protecting the parameters collectively employed for reporting the election. These routines may appear to simply provide a reality check for newsworkers. But they have the effect of compounding the impact of the bubble by creating an insular environment where reporters are constantly incorporating the judgments of the larger community of journalists into their own stories.

Promoting Horserace and Politics

The three orientations discussed thus far—self-interest, the obvious quality of the news, and playing it safe—provide a basis for understanding election coverage. Collectively, they work to structure election news content by determining and reinforcing the predominant understanding of coverage as viewed by those immersed in the campaign. All subsequent orientations may be interpreted against this background. Perspectives that lead news personnel, for instance, to see coverage in terms of action or drama are manifested in election coverage as horserace stories, in part because that's what seems exciting or dramatic from within the campaign-media bubble.

Five orientations in particular combine to make horserace coverage a more likely topic of television election stories than issue items while reinforcing the political nature of election news. Newsworkers generally share a sense that events constitute news; that news is dramatic; that news is conflictive; that news is predictable; and that news is best if it is easy to report. The first three of these are recognizable as well-understood tenets of newsworthiness; the dual wish for predictability and ease of coverage is only reluctantly acknowledged. In the campaign setting, they combine to orient newsworkers away from their professed ideal of issue-based reporting.

Most newsworkers see the news as coverage of events. "Your story line," according to a CNN correspondent, "was dictated by the events of the day." In election campaigns, this type of coverage usually involves horserace items. As Michael J. Robinson and Margaret A. Sheehan put it, "'horse races' happen. ... Policy issues, on the other hand, do not happen; they merely exist."[10] Candidates rise and fall in public opinion polls, win and lose primaries. But issues are stated in position papers, which perhaps garner coverage when initially announced but, once public, simply sit there unless revised by the candidate.

One newsworker noticed that Jerry Brown's proposal for a flat income tax was introduced before the New Hampshire primary. It remained a centerpiece of the governor's campaign through the primary season. But not until Bill Clinton attacked it prior to the New York primary did it become a television agenda item, fundamentally because it had become a pawn in the electoral war of words. Before New York, Brown posed no viable electoral threat, and the other candidates (and the media) virtually ignored him. As he surfaced as the final obstacle to Clinton's nomination, his ideas drew fire from the Arkansan and notice from television producers.

Another respondent saw this emphasis on events as contrived, as a manifestation of the artificial standards that define what is and is not news within the bubble. The television-campaign environment was invested in activity, constantly in motion. As a consequence, issues that the general public might deem important stood their best chance of getting regular air time when grafted to events. This happened, for instance, when the release of new unemployment statistics supported a story on the candidates' job proposals. But even when issues were covered in this manner, it was the event, not the issue, that drove the coverage. One newsworker felt that health care deserved far more media attention than it received during the campaign but lamented that it wasn't worth waiting for Blue Cross and Blue Shield to go out of business for it to happen.

The orientation of newsworkers toward events is evident in routines that emphasize capturing trends. Several respondents drew clear distinctions between isolated happenings, which are not newsworthy, and sequences of incidents, which are. Correspondents attempt to anticipate which single events might become trends worth reporting. Mary Tillotson, who covered President Bush for CNN, described the process she went through in deciding how to cover the people dressed in chicken suits who began appearing at Bush rallies in October to taunt him about his reluctance to debate Governor Clinton.

The first couple of times the Chicken Man appeared, we didn't use it, but we shot footage of it. By the time Bush got to Texas for a weekend series of campaign appearances, they had started bringing up cops to cordon Chicken Man out of the events. At that point, we went back and collected various Chicken Man intrusions that we had taped and put them into our piece. At almost any political event you go to, you would run into protesters. But this had developed into more than an isolated event.

Kim Schiller, an ABC producer assigned to the Clinton campaign, referred to this routine of collecting elements for subsequent use as "saving string." Toward the end of the campaign, for instance, Schiller noted what she felt was a pattern of growing enthusiasm among campaign operatives and started "saving string" for a possible story. "Over the course of a week or so," she said, "we had noticed that there was this sort of exuberance going on, and I began making notes about where I saw it and keeping tape so that when we put it all together, we had several examples of it." As is typical of the hunt for trends, the enthusiasm of Clinton's aides and the Chicken Man story both involved horserace trends rooted in the campaign.

Such reliance on campaign events is consistent with television's need for a daily fix of election news. When a correspondent is attached to a campaign, the most typical way to cover it is by a "calendar-driven" approach that emphasizes what the candidate is doing day to day. In the media-campaign bubble, stories have to be produced every day, the campaign is in motion every day, and the candidates—craving regular exposure and knowing that television is event-driven—perform for the cameras every day. Campaign events provide a natural forum for stories—and the only forum that is readily apparent on the evening news.

An alternate approach to calendar-based coverage is what one respondent called "issue-driven" coverage, which would require the reporter to develop background on the campaign's main issues and ideas. But this approach would compel the reporter to leave the bubble and gain the perspective necessary to view the campaign more broadly than is possible from the field. Theoretically, a steady flow of stories could be produced this way, but they would involve an entirely different type of effort and would not likely be event oriented. Instead, election coverage plunges ahead from within the bubble with daily, incident-driven accounts.

Sometimes, though, at least in 1992, the hunt for newsworthy events failed as correspondents strained to find items to report. Under these circumstances, rather than reevaluate fundamental orientations toward coverage and look elsewhere for stories, newsworkers became imaginative and sought ways to piece together events to fit preestablished coverage ideas. When there was nothing obvious to report, one CNN official said, "you became a little creative" and tried to cultivate horserace items. An ABC employee acknowledged, "If there is no story that is apparent, you sort of generate one."

Perhaps the best example of this is the way the medium can use the president—the most newsworthy of public figures by television's standards—to, as one respondent put it, "make it sound like there's news, and you don't even have to make it up."

> Especially in the dead of summer, when Congress is not in session and there's not a lot going on, there's nothing really big and important. But you can always go to politics and do "the president is out doing whatever he's doing." And then you do a story behind that, which is "his challenger is out doing whatever he's doing." And it seems big and important, even though it is not necessarily warranted by the activities of the day.

But, if it really is a slow day, this takes imagination.

> Sometimes the White House team has to really scrape together disparate elements and pile them together and make it seem as if there's an important story coming out of the White House. They're not hyping it, but they are nonetheless making something where other days they might choose not to do anything at all with it.

In instances such as these, television maintains its commitment to daily event coverage at the cost of presenting stories lacking "obvious" campaign news value. It is easier to endure an occasional in-house white lie about the perceived importance of a story and go on with the show than to reassess and refashion how campaign news is gathered. So the reporters make an effort to find events that at least appear to satisfy both orientations.

In truth, newsworkers would prefer to report not just events but dramatic, conflictive events. This objective further encourages reporting about the horserace at the expense of issues. Echoing the newsworker who said a contested horserace can be very entertaining, respondents offered a preference for "exciting" or "spectacular" coverage and for "political drama." Witness coverage of Jerry Brown, which peaked when he was the lone challenger to Bill Clinton; during the early primaries, those covering him had difficulty getting on the air. Similarly, coverage of Bob Kerrey declined when news executives perceived that he was not going to be a factor in the horserace. And, as we saw in Part I, the quantity of horserace coverage varied with the amount of drama present in the race. When the field was either muddled or resolved, with excitement either pending or past, media attention diminished.

Indeed, respondents at both networks said the decision to invest in election coverage came only after executives were convinced that the election would be contested. In midsummer 1991, with George Bush basking in the warmth of a military victory in the Persian Gulf, the consensus opinion was that the 1992 election would be a mandate for the incumbent. Without political conflict, it literally would not be worth the investment necessary to cover it. Why spend the money, one respondent asked, when you already know who's going to win? ABC's Mike Von Fremd said the turning point came at his network when they realized Bush might be vulnerable.

> Everybody was thinking for a while, we're going to be able to save a fortune because there won't be a presidential election. But then I went out and covered Clinton throwing his hat in the ring in Little Rock, and I came back and told my bureau chief that I couldn't believe the amount of hostility toward Bush out there, and he laughed at me. Then, when Pat Buchanan showed just how much displeasure there was even within Bush's own party in New Hampshire, that's when it really changed.

As the horserace intensified, network executives no longer thought about saving a fortune. Doubts about the cost-effectiveness of sending a full complement of anchors and correspondents to the national conventions gave way to questions of how, not whether, to do it. And of course, when Ross Perot became a player, expenses only went upwards. Television had found its story in the dramatic, conflictive events of a contest no one anticipated.

Commensurate with these orientations toward exciting experiences are two others with their origins in how people—newsworkers or otherwise—often approach work. One involves a quest for predictability, the other a yearning for the path of least resistance. They are not orientations that respondents spoke of proudly, but they did emerge from multiple interviews as fundamental approaches to the work world.

At face value, the fact that television news likes predictability seems to contradict the idea that the unusual, man-bites-dog story is inherently newsworthy and a journalist's dream. Some observers, such as S. Robert Lichter, have noted that horserace stories dominate the news because they are "less predictable, hence potentially more newsworthy"[11] than repetitious stump speeches or issue position papers. In the overall scheme of things, this is quite true; as the three-way autumn horserace became increasingly volatile, the television community perceived it as a far better story and gave it more coverage. But in the everyday process of producing political television, unpredictability can be a nightmare. The organization has a vested interest in knowing that deadlines will be met and the product will be completed on time, which requires knowing as much as possible in advance. "Regardless of how everybody likes to tell you that the news business really can turn on a dime," said a CNN correspondent, "they would much prefer to know the night ahead what you're going to report the next day."

Management is not alone in this sentiment. Facing logistical confusion, early deadlines, and the fast-forward throbbing of the presidential campaign, newsworkers in the bubble also seek to find their way through safely. They share with those at home base a need to see as far into the future as possible. Often, this is no more than a matter of hours, or even minutes. But the demands of the job lead reporters to look for news in familiar, known places.

No theme is more familiar than the horserace, and no other type of story is as easy to predict. Campaign stops, always announced in advance,[12] can easily be mined for a horserace angle. This is why the morning conference calls always considered what the candidates were going to *do* that day and why producers and correspondents tended to feel that the candidates controlled the agenda. The newsgathering process was structured in such a way as to turn scheduled events into horserace copy in time for "Inside Politics" or "World News." Even at times when the contest appeared uncertain, details of the horserace clung to the same familiar formula. Knowing exactly what candidates would do and say when facing political uncertainty enabled newsworkers to diminish instability in their lives and meet their deadlines with reliable copy.

The horserace was also an easy story to cover. Respondents particularly disliked talking about this aspect for fear it would make them appear lazy. After all, if they worked harder, would they not achieve their substantive ideal? Some blamed television's format, saying how difficult it is to fit an intelligent treatment of a substantive matter into a two-minute framework. But most said some of their decisions were just matters of what was easy and what was hard to do. In the words of a producer, "Complicated issues are hard pieces to do. And they take time. And you have to talk to a lot of different people. You have to go to the economists and the experts and the authorities at the universities who spend time studying these things."

Others confirmed that it is virtually impossible to construct an issue story without leaving the bubble because academics or "experts" must be included to give the work legitimacy. Moreover, the orientation toward events usually requires some connection, through videotape, text, or both, between the issue content and "what the candidate is doing today." If this link can be accomplished using videotape of the candidate's day or copy about the issue in light of some new event, it still doesn't change the fact that issue positions are hard to explain. CNN correspondent Brooks Jackson drew the comparison to horserace coverage.

> There's been too much horserace coverage to the exclusion of stuff that's harder to do, like why health care costs are driving the economy to the point of collapse. Because it's easy to call up your chums at the campaign, but it's hard to get your arms around a complex subject. In other words, it's just easier to cover personnel problems at a presidential campaign than it is to explain detailed issues.

Jackson's CNN colleague Candy Crowley echoed the sentiment, saying the horserace is a television favorite "because it's easy." She said, "Because all you have to do is commission a poll. I mean, it's *easy*. It's easy to write: 'As Bill Clinton pounded his way through the northeast, polls show that he's de-da-de-da-de-da; George Bush, meanwhile, is besieged by de-da-de-da-de-da.' And you've got a story."

In much the same way that the horserace and poll-driven stories are easy to write, process stories are simple to report. This factor reinforces television's natural interest in its role in the campaign and facilitates coverage of coverage. Every correspondent is acutely aware of the place of the press in the election, so knowing what to write in a process story takes little effort. Plus, the mechanics of reporting the story are simple: Just "turn the camera around," as a producer put it. Indeed, from the standpoint of ease of coverage, process stories are simply horserace items with the camera pointed in the other direction.

Respondents cautioned that the difficulties of covering a particular story do not necessarily determine coverage. Nevertheless, these difficulties do influence coverage by working together with other orientations that favor horserace stories over issue pieces. Television newsworkers have a vested interest in finding dramatic, conflictive events that are both predictable and easy to cover, and this leads naturally to the mixture of horserace and issue items detailed in Part I. Whereas issue stories may be invested with great value and appeal, these ideals are not strong enough to overcome the draw of practical concerns that dictate that campaign news be easy to report and interesting to hear. Horserace items satisfy these requirements and can be reported without leaving the bubble.

News Is Unusual

Repeatedly, newsworkers underscored that news means new and that they are interested in and responsible for discovering the different and the unusual in the campaign. Otherwise, as one respondent intimated, why should anyone care about what is reported? However, the quest for the fresh and uncommon story is complicated by several factors. First, it conflicts with orientations about news that entreat predictability and ease of coverage; it is hard to find unusual material in commonplace events. Second, it is curtailed by the tendency for newsworkers to satisfy their hunt for regularized coverage in the daily occurrences of a campaign designed for repetition and consistency. Third, the meaning of unusual is readily confounded in the campaign-media environment, where small changes in a candidate's inflection may be interpreted as bold alterations in the campaign's strategy, prospects, or effectiveness.

Respondents frequently spoke of looking for the tiniest of nuances, of hunting down even minor changes in the candidate's stump speech, of assessing modifications in emphasis that the candidate would use as he addressed different groups. Such deviations were freely interpreted to mean that the campaign was attempting to reach out to a new block of voters, panicking in the wake of the latest polls, trying to alter its approach, or gaining confidence and feeling able to take risks. Television's thirst for the atypical led its personnel to mine the bubble for anything even remotely different and guaranteed that once found, such items would be regarded seriously—without consideration of the possibility that a change in the candidate's inflection at a rally in Denver was motivated by, say, a shift in atmospheric pressure.

Without fail, newsworkers offered that the main benefit of remaining on the campaign trail without leave was the ability to pick up subtleties and shades of meaning that might escape the correspondent or producer who was rotated in and out. With the mandate for "obvious" news requiring a campaign focus, personnel had little choice but to twist their predilection for the unusual toward the relatively minor matters regularly available to them. Like the individual looking for lost change under a faraway streetlamp because the light is better there, items both unusual and germane but astride the campaign bubble were not likely subjects for coverage because they happened beyond the purview of those following and living with the campaign.

Once the decision was made to cover the campaign as a series of daily political events, producers and correspondents had little choice but to look for shades of change in order to satisfy their inclination for the unusual. "We don't as a rule cover what the candidate says," offered a network producer, "because it's standard stuff." But that's what reporters are exposed to most of the time because, as this producer and many others acknowledged, "at stop after stop after stop, the candidate goes out and does his standard speech." There is little choice but to look toward even the most seemingly insignificant changes in the candidate's routine for something "different or new, and see if there's a story to be done about it."

Something is deemed unusual when a newsworker finds it interesting. From the correspondent's viewpoint, for example, the first Clinton/Gore bus trip was unusual, new, and interesting, and thus newsworthy; the second one was not. Likewise, on an everyday basis, against a backdrop of great redundancy, journalists tend to be drawn to particular types of nuances. Accompanying the shifts in a candidate's words or tone, which get reported as horserace strategy, Robert Benenson suggests a list topped by "errors of fact, dramatic pronouncements, overstatements, verbal gaffes and hints of scandal."[13] These, he offers, make for the most memorable stories.

They also generate the sort of copy I have been calling "nonissue" coverage. The orientation toward unusual news is consistent with television's fascination with the prurient: candidate sexual exploits, draft dodging, pot smoking, and the like. This factor helps to explain the consistent pattern of nonissue coverage we addressed in Part I whereby particular nonissues would come and go, usually with great haste, but both networks had something on the burner almost all the time. The tendency to include nonissues as a regular component of coverage is essentially a manifestation of the need for the unusual. In a campaign format noted (and valued) more for its predictability than its novelty, nonissue stories provide a certain level of intrigue. Moreover, nonissues are covered in predictable ways, often characterized by packs of reporters yelling questions at candidates and aides.[14] When interesting non-issues arise, they provide novelty without challenging any of the other orientations newsworkers hold about campaign reporting.

The only problem with nonissues is that they almost always have a short shelf life. This type of coverage requires an ongoing search for the unusual, which must be accomplished through investigative work if novel items are not forthcoming from the campaign itself. Indeed, the term of a nonissue on the evening news is bounded largely by how long newsworkers believe it to be unusual. Once it loses its novelty, a nonissue may fade into another topic. By this token, during the long hiatus between February and September when specific allegations were being made about Bill Clinton's draft history, reporters blended the item into more generic, image-oriented coverage of character. More likely, used nonissues will disappear entirely from television's agenda, like so many tempests about a candidate's health or Murphy Brown's baby.

Such was the case with the first and perhaps most memorable nonissue of the 1992 campaign, Gennifer Flowers's allegation of extramarital activity on the part of the Democratic frontrunner. Contrary to widely held popular impressions, the Flowers nonissue received intensive coverage for only a short period of time and then vanished from the evening news. Assuming it was the sort of unusual campaign event television would find attractive, I asked newsworkers why they decided to stop covering the story so quickly.

Several respondents echoed the sentiment that the Flowers story was swiftly dropped precisely because it was no longer deemed unusual. Gennifer Flowers was determined to have little credibility as an accuser, and given television's orientation toward events, without additional allegations to fuel further coverage there was nothing new to report. Then, when Clinton addressed the issue on "Sixty Minutes," "that kind of ended coverage because the allegation was out there," said a producer, "and we had to go on to other things." A correspondent agreed: "You can't just every day mention, 'Bill Clinton—comma—alleged of having an affair with Gennifer Flowers—comma—alleged to have dodged the draft—comma—and also who claims he never inhaled his marijuana—comma—today went to Wichita.'"

The decision to drop the story followed a lot of thought at the highest levels. Executives at both networks said they spent a lot of time discussing how to cover the matter, ever aware of the widespread criticism aimed at the media following previous forays into candidate bedrooms. ABC anticipated the issue with an editorial meeting in September 1991 after Clinton declared his presidential bid. Cognizant that allegations of extramarital activity were possible, the network decided as a matter of policy only to lend credibility to the story if there was proof. Hence, the search for leads in Little Rock. When the allegations went unsubstantiated, they were not broadcast.

Ultimately, however, the choice not to cover the Flowers nonissue was as clear as the distinction between the unusual and the commonplace. A CNN correspondent put it this way:

You can't ignore Gennifer Flowers on the day that she comes out and says this stuff. You can't ignore the second day when he's telling reporters it's not the truth. You can't ignore the third day when he and Hillary are on "Sixty Minutes" trying to put this thing to rest. You can't ignore the fourth day when you're talking about strategy to get the Gennifer Flowers thing behind you. But after that, after you do the "he says, she says," where do you go with it? You necessarily have to drop it.

Moreover, there was a widespread sense among the press corps that, whatever the validity of the charges, a candidate having an extramarital affair was simply not that unusual and dissecting one on television was not as novel as it would have been at one time. Sometimes aware of their own troubled marriages, correspondents felt uneasy, as one put it, "blasting somebody for his humanness." A producer who covered Clinton put it this way, "We spent a lot of time thinking and talking about what was appropriate. I know that I did not enjoy asking questions about Flowers. I prefer to ask questions of a more substantial nature than, 'Did you sleep with her?' I don't think anybody likes that. I think everyone was uncomfortable with it." Lacking originality, the Flowers saga vanished from the evening news programs as quickly as it began, relegated to interminable coverage by tabloid television but deemed uneventful by the regular press. It had run its course as a nonissue, leaving the networks to hunt for a new one. They did not have to wait long; allegations that Clinton evaded the draft, with all their novel implications, surfaced one week later.

News Is Personalized

In Part I, we saw how cable and broadcast coverage emphasizes persons far more than institutions. On television, presidential campaigns are about people, most notably the people running for the office, and not about parties, organizations, interest groups, or a host of other institutional players who could readily be considered premier contributors to the work of getting elected. This orientation follows from a reporting perspective that favors readily interviewed, easily photographed individuals over abstract, often physically distant institutions. So strong is the orientation toward personalized reporting that newsworkers—who regularly confront the most trying institutional restrictions imposed by the campaign—nonetheless emphasize individuals over campaigns in their coverage.

Correspondents are assigned to *campaigns,* but they cover the *candidates.* Newsworkers are wedded to the institutional prerogatives of contemporary presidential organizations, to the agendas and logistics of the traveling show, but when they speak, they address the words and behavior of the individual running for office. Even strategy, albeit sometimes cast in terms of what the campaign hopes to achieve, is largely personalized to the candidate's ends. The orientation toward individuals and personalized coverage is so deeply rooted among television newsworkers that covering the person is synonymous with covering the obvious.

Reporters are told to "cover the body," literally to follow everything the candidate does. News originates with the individual, and anything the individual does is potentially news. CNN producer Marty Kramer, who covered George Bush, said, "You have to go everywhere the president goes as a body watch. Everything the president does has potential news value. When the president has a public event, we go. Even if we think there's not going to be any news, we go anyway." The same was true on the Clinton campaign, which Chris Bury covered for ABC News. Bury noted, "We were on full body watch on Clinton. In other words, we traveled with him full time from just after the New Hampshire primary until the general election. Either I or another correspondent was with Clinton all the time."

What happened on full body watch reflected how easily the tendency toward personalized coverage fits with other newsworker orientations, specifically the emphasis on events and awareness of "the obvious." Bury said, for instance, "We covered every single event. We would try to either report whatever the obvious news story was, or we would try to splice together a particular theme, either from one day or over a period of several days, which we could weave into a package that would be suitable for "World News Tonight." Consequently, stories about candidates dominated the news. Television's orientation toward personalizing events generated the candidate-centered coverage evident in every topic from issues to process.

News Should Be Objective

Unbiased, unslanted reporting has been a tenet of journalism since the decline of the party press. As a pure form of coverage, objectivity is difficult to define and impossible to attain. But this difficulty does not diminish the value placed on objectivity or the extent to which newsworkers will tenaciously assert that their work is unprejudiced.

So great, in fact, is the orientation toward objective reporting that respondents adamantly defended their ability, derived of professional training and experience, to avoid being swept away by the current of campaign events. Even those who acknowledged the distorting effect of life in the bubble argued that they managed to maintain a healthy perspective about the world around them when it came to writing the story.

Newsworkers are familiar with the risk of developing "tunnel vision." As a CNN producer put it, covering people you're living with so closely can be "like a snake biting its tail." The problem was widely mentioned in the interviews I conducted, although respondents differed on how they imagined it might affect them. Some worried about "going native" and covering the campaign in a manner favorable to the political occupants of the bubble. Two respondents likened the fear to the "Stockholm syndrome" of falling in love with your captors. Another feared the opposite response, saying, "You come to know the candidate so well that you end up inevitably regarding him as a son-of-a-bitch."

Whatever the imagined effect, the same remedies were offered to guard against tunnel vision: understanding the problem, keeping professional distance, and relying on the people back in the "room without windows" to put things in perspective. As with any difficulty, tunnel vision is especially dangerous if newsworkers are oblivious to it. A CNN correspondent admitted, "You have to be aware of it. If you're not aware of it, you've got a big problem. It manifests itself when you're out in St. Louis or Wichita or Omaha or someplace, and you say, 'I've heard this speech six times this week already.' You just have the sense that you're only hearing one side of the story." A colleague offered a more direct method for being on guard—perpetual skepticism: "I am an equal opportunity iconoclast! Whoever it is, I don't believe them!"

Unspecified but staunchly asserted professional qualities are commonly mentioned as an antidote to lost perspective. The first comment below comes from an ABC producer, the second from a veteran ABC correspondent, and the third from a seasoned CNN reporter:

> People who do this are pretty experienced journalists. They're a certain breed, because they're willing to ruin their lives for nine months of one year out of every four. So I think there is some trained objective. People learn how to be objective in this situation, they learn how not to groupthink.

> It doesn't take an ounce of intelligence—it might take a little experience—but it doesn't take an ounce of intelligence to separate your ideas from your work. I mean, if you're professional about it, it's not hard. If you want to keep it out, you just do. You don't even think about it.

> You could go through the Phil Donahue–type discussion about what you do psychologically, but it's all old hat. You just do your best to withdraw.

Another respondent added, "You're not working in a vacuum," and one said that having "outside eyes and outside minds within your organization" could help mitigate against tunnel vision. To the extent that home base operates outside the campaign bubble, which is to say physically rather than metaphysically, there is some truth to this statement. Ongoing negotiations about story content between the newsroom and the field do give coverage a certain balance, at least within the parameters of commonly shared orientations toward what constitutes election news.

Blatantly partisan reporting is easily recognizable and out of the question; one correspondent said he faced castration at the hands of his executive producer if his work began to reflect a particular political perspective. On more subtle matters of news value, routinized give and take produces compromise.

Candy Crowley related how a clash of generational outlooks with a CNN supervisor guided her coverage of Bill Clinton's draft record.

> When the draft story broke, I thought, "So what? Everybody I know did this. I know people who went to Canada." But I went ahead and did the story because they insisted, because I had a news manager that's sixty-five years old, who said, "This guy's dodging the draft." That's an instance when a desk had a totally different view than me. He was outraged, so we provided a really good balance to one another in our personal reactions to the story. The committee process worked well. It was a generational blind spot on both our parts, but together we had a whole vision.

In order to maintain a claim to objectivity, correspondents and producers invoke procedures for producing copy that may be defended as objective.[15] They share an approach to coverage that deemphasizes blatantly ideological material and substitutes equity for objectivity by presenting balanced, opposing views. This practice gives election coverage its nonideological character and balanced story form.

As they fly all over the country with the presidential candidates and watch them calculate how to garner electoral advantage from each day's events, correspondents readily see the candidates as nonideological figures. The nature of candidate coverage reflects this vantage point, and the volume of it leaves little room for attention to other actors whose approach to the presidential election might be viewed as more ideological. These individuals—activists, candidates of sectarian parties, and their supporters, to name a few—share the disadvantage of not being a part of the campaign gaggle and are easily delegitimized as insignificant by a medium that is quite attentive to the twin desires of maintaining objectivity through minimizing ideological references and, whenever possible, simplifying coverage.

By applying the political criterion of covering only those candidates who "can win" (a standard unevenly applicable to Ross Perot in 1992), both objectives are accomplished. Coverage focuses on the political over the ideological and remains confined to the familiar bubble. Add the practice of balancing the comments of the few remaining subjects of coverage, and the claim to objective reporting is almost complete. It leaves only the logistical question of how to "fairly" cover everyone in a large primary field, but that is a far more limited concern.

Newsworkers complained about how difficult it was to balance the words of five primary candidates in the context of a two-minute television story. Issue pieces, which require far more explanation than stories about a candidate's strategy or standing in the polls, were certainly out of the question. This led newsworkers back to political items and to the political standards that guide coverage and inform objectivity. Relatively manageable horserace stories were more feasible than issue pieces in television's truncated format, even with a large field. Balance then became a function of performance, with attention "fairly" given to candidates who, by television's "objective" standards, were running ahead. Hence, those covering less competitive Democrats complained that they could not get their material on the air. In the two-candidate Republican race, the decision was easy: Include an element from Pat Buchanan's day along with White House coverage or run a Buchanan piece back-to-back with a Bush piece. The same procedure was subsequently extended to the major party nominees and at times to Ross Perot.

Even with careful attention to how a story is balanced, "objective" reporting is bounded by other choices. Newsworkers decide what is germane to the election to begin with, and what is germane is usually the competition between major party frontrunners. Balancing an allegation Bush makes against Clinton with a response by Clinton is equitable if the campaign is seen as a two-party seesaw but not if it is viewed more widely. This type of story excludes airing a rejoinder by any of the multiple minor presidential candidates who exist outside the bubble and therefore off-camera. Similarly, a "story" may potentially have three, four, or a dozen "sides"; assuming away other perspectives is a form of prejudice that is masked when the duality of "balance" is equated with impartiality.

The choices that correspondents make are consistent with the view of the campaign from within the bubble. Given the parameters of that world, they are defensible as objective. Correspondents dutifully keep the campaign free of ideological bias by aiming the bulk of their coverage at politicians and covering them as they see them, as motivated by self-interest and political acquisition rather than ideology. By further limiting coverage to the politicians in the bubble—to the major candidates of the major parties and the occasional popular billionaire—they can maintain balance in their stories, which within the prescribed order certainly looks like objective reporting.

News Needs Context

Chapter 7 explored why both networks, and especially ABC, use analytical coverage. The orientation requiring that news be put into context for the viewer is related to this practice. The networks place a *value* on analytical coverage—apparent in the manner with which some CNN personnel were offended by the observation that "PrimeNews" was less analytical than "World News." To suggest that coverage is not analytical is to (unintentionally, in this instance) assert that the news operation is not doing its job. Analysis is equated with putting the news into context, which in turn means doing more than simply relating the headlines. In a medium rarely cited for its depth, newsworkers have an investment in being able to do more than simply report the "who" or "where" of a story. Being able to provide a reason for "why" something happens was emphasized time and again as an integral part of being a good journalist.

Perceptions of the Audience

I end this litany of orientations with an account of what newsworkers imagine their audience to be like. I do so because respondents frequently raised the topic, indicating that it is of concern to them, and because, unlike all the items that have come before, there is no consensus about who watches political news and what items interest them. Rather than enforcing action, perceptions of the audience serve as a reinforcing mechanism, either for acting on orientations that structure election coverage in a manner the audience is perceived to like or for holding on to the idealized wish for a type of election coverage the audience is believed to want.

Ratings indicate that the television news audience is a bit older, whiter, and less well educated than the nation as a whole. CNN, which comes with a monthly cable fee attached, attracts marginally higher income viewers. Traditionally, television viewers are not highly informed about or interested in news events. But talking to television newsworkers yields no sense of a disinterested audience. Executives at both networks had a firm and accurate grasp of audience demographics. Ideas about the "typical viewer," however, are many and varied.

Take the situation at CNN. The "Inside Politics" producer did not have a sense of what the "PrimeNews" audience looks like, and the "PrimeNews" line producer could only guess that "Inside Politics" attracts "people that were interested in getting more involved in politics and political junkies." But producers at each program had definitive ideas about who was watching their shows. Executive Producer Scott Woelful said his political selections for "PrimeNews" assumed his viewers were less politically informed than those who would "seek out" "Inside Politics." Chris Guarino described the "Inside Politics" viewer as one "more in tune with what's going on in politics," but added, "That's very much characteristic of what you've got at CNN." But what does the CNN viewer look like? Woelful believes it is "somebody who wants to sit down and watch an hour of news, or a half hour, or however much time they give it." Another CNN producer put it this way:

> I think that our audience tends to be the person who probably reads his newspaper every day, and maybe reads more than one newspaper every day. It's more than just the average viewer, because otherwise they wouldn't be tuning into an all-news network. They put us on in the morning and we stay on all day. Or they put us on in the evening, they watch "Crossfire," they watch "PrimeNews," they watch Larry King, they get the news again, and then they go to bed.

As many views as there are of who is in the audience, so are there opinions about where viewer interest lies. A number of respondents offered that viewers are not concerned with candidate strategy, motivation, or "inside baseball" items. Yet one respondent offered, "I think the public's interested in spin doctors. Sure, they're interested in it." There were equally mixed opinions on whether the audience is as interested in the horserace as television personnel are. Some respondents expressed the sentiment that electoral competition captivates the audience; others said the audience is indifferent or even that they "hate" it. Several newsworkers felt the audience has a penchant for the horrible and the mundane: "earthquakes, disasters," and gossip. "Almost everyone you meet loves gossip," one respondent offered. And several respondents stated perhaps more than the obvious by offering the impression that different people are interested in different things.

Given such disparity, it is impossible for newsworker perspectives about the audience to collectively motivate how the election is reported in the same manner that shared orientations influence choices about what to cover and how to do it. Instead, audience impressions serve either as a reality check for those who believe the audience wants or approves of what they are doing or as justification for the idealized perspective of what television election news should be. Those who believe the viewers want to hear about candidate strategy and motivation and believe that's what they're getting may find comfort in the assurance that their job is being well performed. "If it's interesting to us," one respondent said, "I guess I perceive that it's interesting to the audience." Those who believe that viewers do not care about all the attention television pays to itself may find reinforcement in this impression for an imagined, loftier news product.

If it is to be the rule that vague notions about the audience have little impact on coverage, then let there be an exception. In 1992, the widely held belief that the audience was concerned with the economy advanced issue coverage beyond what recent history suggests would otherwise have been a secondary role in campaign coverage. In this instance, views about the audience did more than simply reinforce preexisting coverage patterns. Atypically, a consensus among newsworkers about audience interests and concerns fueled television's curiosity with political issue coverage. As we saw in Part I, television's investment in economic reporting had multiple roots that appeared to be particular to the 1992 election. To these, it may be added that an unusual orientation (consensus about the audience) helped to fuel an aberrant phenomenon (large quantities of issue coverage). It seems unlikely that issues will receive a privileged spot in future elections held under different circumstances.

One final observation: The shared belief among newsworkers that the economy was a major audience concern came not from contact with the audience but from proxies believed to reflect audience concerns. As correspondents listened to what the candidates were saying, talked to campaign operatives, and in some instances discussed the issues with friends and peers at dinner parties and functions, the images of unemployed workers that they glimpsed as they zoomed across the country with the campaign were reinforced. News personnel were able to conclude that the economy was of overriding concern to the audience without ever having to leave the bubble.

12

Breaking the Rules

Orientations shared by the community of television newsworkers motivate how and where they look for election news. Common perspectives support similar routines and procedures for getting the story and form the underpinning of television's portrayal of the campaign. The evening news takes its shape directly from the perspectives of its creators. Consequently, the election picture focuses on the personal, political, nonideological, and analytical; features horserace stories and a steady complement of nonissues; and emphasizes material of great interest to those who produce it. Even though the result is often at odds with the stated wishes of those responsible for creating it, the way election coverage is conceptualized is too entrenched to be readily changed. At present, the routines simply are not geared to producing the sort of issue-oriented, "responsible" coverage many newsworkers claim to crave.

So deeply embedded are newsworker orientations that when confronted with obstacles to their normal approaches to coverage, correspondents and producers prove to be immovable objects. This chapter will examine two such situations. One, posed by ABC executives, involved an attempt to pull content closer to the issue-based ideal by implementing an experimental policy directive during the general campaign. The second, posed by the unconventional organization of the Perot campaign, forced newsworkers to confront how to cover a candidacy that disregarded their expectations. In both cases, adherence to established ways proved stronger than either obstacle.

Authorizing the Ideal:
ABC's Policy Agenda

Ever wishful for substantive news programming and keenly aware that critics find television lacking, ABC attempted an experiment during the general election stage of the 1992 campaign designed to remaster the horserace-heavy, issue-thin mix of election coverage traditionally found on the major networks.

Through a series of high-level decisions, the network endeavored to reorient its election coverage on "World News Tonight" toward greater and more detailed attention to campaign issues and away from concentration on horserace matters.

It was a two-pronged attack. To bolster issue coverage, ABC decided to devote the recurring "American Agenda" segment of "World News" to investigations of the major candidates' issue positions. This plan simply required conscripting for election use a staff and format already dedicated to issue coverage. The "Agenda" segments are longer than the typical evening news piece—generally three and a half to four minutes in length instead of ninety seconds to two minutes. They are designed to enable correspondents to present the background necessary to establish a rudimentary understanding of the issues, which newsworkers repeatedly noted are far more complex to set up than event-driven horserace items.

With a half-dozen correspondents and twice as many producers, the "Agenda" staff was already equipped to handle a full complement of issue-oriented reports. "Agenda" correspondents regularly addressed such issues as education, the environment, drugs, crime, and money matters. They were to remain on these beats during the fall campaign, tailoring their coverage to include the records and proposals of the major candidates. The adjustment was a simple one that required essentially no change in how "Agenda" pieces were produced or how "World News" was structured. Said Political Director Hal Bruno of the choice to use "Agenda" staff and time slots for campaign issue coverage, "It was a decision that made itself. You've got a formula like 'American Agenda,' so you're naturally going to use it in your campaign coverage."

It was also a decision that worked. As noted in Part I, the amount of attention that ABC paid to policy issues increased dramatically during the general election stage of the presidential campaign, largely because of the "American Agenda" effort. Because the structure for reporting issue pieces was already in place and did not need to be altered, the network was quite successful in its bid to add issue coverage to the evening broadcast. That is exactly what they did—*add* issue coverage, as opposed to *replacing* horserace, nonissue, or process coverage with issue material.

In significant ways, "Agenda" pieces stood apart from regular political coverage. They were generated by a pool of correspondents and producers who were not following the campaign's daily activities or caught inside the campaign-media environment. No orientations needed to be challenged, no routines changed. The production of "Agenda" pieces did not have to compete with the daily frenzy of life with the candidate. Those responsible for their creation were free to engage in the more complicated construction of longer, less easily researched stories. Even the space allocated for "Agenda" items in the broadcast was typically distinct from other campaign coverage. Coming as they did late in the program, the "Agenda" segments offered protracted, more feature-oriented, back-of-the-book items.

This is as it was intended to be. The network had a unit capable of doing the work that it was able to call upon without causing any real dislocation. For two months, a regular component of "World News" was "borrowed" to serve as an election feature. The ease with which this aspect of the policy was implemented, and the facility with which it was maintained through election day, stood in contrast to the more problematic nature of the other part of ABC's quest for substance in election reporting.

The second line of attack was more complicated, involving structural changes in how campaign news was gathered and reported. In a deliberate effort to downplay the attention given horserace matters and make coverage "more nutritious," as Jeff Greenfield put it, a policy was enacted to instruct producers and correspondents to develop more comprehensive, less candidate-oriented pieces. These were to air in a recurring segment called "Campaign Focus." Topical rather than event-oriented, "Focus" items were conceived to explore such questions as how the Republican's "family values" message was playing with the electorate or how the candidates were doing in the South. Meanwhile, more traditional horserace coverage, the "here-they-come, there-they-go" stories about the candidate's day, would be given less air time. They were to be relegated to segments called "Campaign Watch," which briefly summarized daily political events, and "Campaign Notes," one- or two-line items of a more marginal political nature, related by Peter Jennings. "Campaign Watch" segments would be expanded to full stories only on days when candidates were deemed to have done more than simply come and go.

The entire package was brought together with custom red, white, blue, and gray graphics announcing whether a story was a "Focus" piece, part of a "Watch," or a "Note." Jennings would introduce each section accordingly with phrases like, "In our Campaign Focus tonight," or "We have two Campaign Notes," which supposedly cued the audience to the format. In fact, the entire arrangement was introduced with great fanfare on September 9, 1992, when Peter Jennings, speaking directly to the viewer with the utmost of process-oriented self-concern, announced in detail the motivation for the change. Working on the assumption that the audience cares, Jennings opened the third segment of "World News" as follows:

> Now for the political news. First, an explanation. We're aware that a lot of you are turned off by the political process and that many of you put at least some of the blame on us for the way we cover political campaigns—or do not cover them. And so for the next couple of months we're going to try to make better sense of it all in several different ways. We'll keep a "Campaign Watch" every day where we'll give you the day's headlines, and we'll only devote more time to a candidate's daily routine if it is more than routine.

He continued with an indication that although horserace coverage might be taboo, process items were a different matter, saying, "There'll be less attention to staged appearances and sound bites designed exclusively for television. We will focus our coverage more on how the battle for your vote is being fought—the television campaign, for example, or how a message is being refined, say, for the suburbs." Finally, Jennings concluded, "We will examine very closely how the candidates are responding to your concerns on what you told us are the most important issues. Beginning next week, our 'American Agenda' reporters will lay out just where Mr. Bush and Mr. Clinton actually stand on everything from job creation and health care to the environment and education. So, let's get on with it."

So began ABC's experiment in a different, more substantive version of election coverage. Still, self-interest preceded substance. Just as the entire format announcement was rooted in television's concern for itself, the first "Campaign Note" of the September 9 broadcast was about television, specifically Dan Quayle's ironic appearance in a local station's promotional announcement for "Murphy Brown." The next day's "Campaign Note" was equally self-interested, relating footage from CNN's "Larry King Live" on which Tipper Gore called her husband, who didn't recognize her voice, and asked him for a date.[1]

After these process items, there was, alas, the horserace. For the two days following Jennings's pronouncement, despite the intended format change, "Campaign Watch" segments contained full-length reports from the campaign trail that bore a stunning resemblance to the many horserace stories that had come before them. On September 10, there was a piece on a major Bush campaign address. On September 11, there were two pieces, the first on the political motivation behind a Bush decision to send arms to Saudi Arabia, the second on Bill Clinton discussing family values. Not until September 12 did the "Campaign Watch" segment feature a headline version of horserace material.

The format unfolded haltingly for the next two months. At times, horserace material was effectively deemphasized, but on other occasions full coverage was devoted to the candidate's day when it was arguably not "more than routine," as Jennings had put it. As election day approached, "World News" paid growing attention to the rush of daily campaign events, and a policy designed to recast coverage away from the horserace became increasingly confining.

It was never an easy policy to follow from the field. From the start, the experimental format violated the predictable, daily, "obvious" orientations that newsworkers brought to their jobs, causing confusion and some consternation among those called upon to implement it. Kim Schiller was a producer on the Clinton campaign. She said that even when the philosophy of the new format was set down in a memo to correspondents, it was a bit hard to grasp.

> It was always a little confusing to us. When we were on the campaign we were always trying to figure out whether we were a "Campaign Watch" or a "Campaign

Note." They had these little titles for these things, and we could never quite figure out who we were trying to serve. It was kind of funny, you know, we made fun of it in a sense. From our point of view we never quite understood what it was that we were or which category we were trying to fill.

Schiller navigated her way through the confusion by trying to assign familiar ideas to unfamiliar labels. "'Campaign Watch,' it seemed to me, was 'the news', whatever that happened to be," she said, by which she meant the event-oriented news of the day, what the candidate was doing. But "Campaign Focus" was a bit more difficult to conceptualize. Given these curious labels, Schiller said she developed coverage ideas by relying on a familiar procedure: tailoring story proposals to mirror items the network was picking up. "We would offer a story and they would say, 'no thank you.' And then we'd offer another story and they'd say, 'no thank you.' And, then we'd offer another story and they'd say, 'yes.' Then afterwards they'd say they liked that story. So the next time we're offering stories, of course we would go with something like the third story that got sold the last time."

But one effect of the policy was that fewer stories were sold. Reports of the "Campaign Watch" variety—the type typically produced on the campaign trail—were discouraged, at least for a period of time. In their place, newsworkers were urged to file stories involving trends that developed over a sequence of days that could be run as "Campaign Focus" items. These stories were more complicated to construct than the daily items. Chris Bury agreed that the format made covering the Clinton campaign more difficult than it had been before the policy was implemented. He said, "It made it a bit complicated. Because from the time during the primaries until the week after Labor Day, we out in the field pretty much covered the campaign as it had always been covered, you know, on a daily basis. And, we tried to get whatever story we could on the nightly news. After that format was instituted, it became slightly more difficult for us to get on with the daily events."

Ultimately, the difficulties spread back east. As election day neared and the horserace intensified, ABC moved away from its directive, at least in part, backsliding to the more traditional daily coverage. The reason Chris Bury gave for this shift was instructive.

> By the end when it got down to the crunch in late October, *there was so much news* that we reverted to the daily coverage. *There was just so much news coming out* that it became impossible to stick with the strict format. There was just a tremendous appetite by the time it got down to the last couple of weeks of October, that people just wanted to know what Clinton and Gore and Bush were saying day by day.[2]

Deeply enmeshed orientations had won out. The perception of so much obvious news emanating from the campaign and so many people clearly wanting to know about it overtook the network's alternate approach. The campaign, in essence, *was* the daily events and horserace developments, and as the drama and conflict inevitably built to a final and, in this instance, contested outcome, it was difficult for anyone, including those with the final say on program content, to imagine covering the campaign any other way. To those who reported it, this material was obviously news and it needed to be covered more urgently than the problematic stories that the experiment required.

The lesson of the ABC experience is that orientations precede structure. The network's attempt to impose a superstructure, as it were, on the way election news was reported ran into difficulty because newsworkers were asked to reconceptualize long-standing approaches to what constitutes election news and how it should be gathered. In contrast to the ease with which the existing "American Agenda" segment was folded into the political story, the "Campaign Watch" directives raised problematic questions about how newsworkers saw the election world. By placing restrictions on coverage, the format change confounded "the obvious." By seeking trends rather than events, it complicated the easy, daily, personalized fashion of gathering election news. As viewed from the bubble, it would appear a confusing experiment because it was superimposed on newsworkers, asking them to change their product without first redefining their orientations toward campaign coverage.

Ultimately, the shared orientations of the entire news community came into play, and as election day drew near, coverage reverted back to the familiar. As Chris Bury said, there was simply too much news, meaning too much of the obvious and familiar, to let the format get in the way. In the end, the common orientations that bound correspondents in the field to executives at "the rim" overtook the experiment, encouraging the production and broadcast of prosaic, daily, candidate-oriented, horserace-driven material. The inclusivity of the bubble was confirmed.

Playing His Own Game: Perot's Elusive Campaign

ABC's efforts to alter the content of election coverage presented newsworkers with a challenge to their orientations from within the organization. The make-up of the Perot campaign presented a similar type of trial but from an external source.

From the start, Ross Perot was an uncommon political figure. Without a party or past political ambitions, singular in his ability to command vast quantities of television time through his personal fortune, the maverick from Texas defied classification as a typical would-be president. Having backed into the presidential action following an announcement on "Larry King Live" that he would run if people would put his name on all fifty state ballots, the multibillionaire proceeded to wage a campaign that confounded all media expectations about how a presidential candidate behaves. In truth, this was part of his appeal; if news is unusual, then Perot is most certainly news.

His could only loosely be called a campaign organization. The effort was centered exclusively on Perot himself, who made both large and small decisions on behalf of the "campaign" without first sharing them with the media. At the start, his bid was staffed by volunteers and personal aides from the Perot empire. There was a brief effort to conscript political professionals to run things, but Perot resisted attempts at decentralization. Then he abruptly dropped out of the race during the Democratic convention in July only to re-emerge in the fall as a one-man show.

If not for his money and his mass appeal (which, of course, would not have been established without his money),[3] it is questionable whether Perot would have been covered much at all. As it was, the criterion that television will only attend candidates with a chance of winning is dubiously defensible in Perot's case and perhaps only applicable during Perot I, when polls indicated he could be a serious contender. In the fall, Perot maintained a following, was included in the presidential debates,[4] and remained a colorful individual, but he had little chance of victory. Nevertheless, for a medium fascinated with colorful individuals and not very interested in institutions, he was a natural for coverage.

Newsworkers' attempts to find a way to report on the Perot campaign proved difficult because of how Perot conducted himself. "I wouldn't even classify that as a campaign," said Charles Murphy, who covered Perot from ABC's Dallas bureau. Tony Clark had the same assignment for CNN—and the same reaction. He said it took a while before he could convince his superiors in Washington, D.C., that Perot did not feel obliged to follow the familiar set of rules.

> For a long time it was difficult to make our counterparts at the network understand that you simply could not ask a question of the campaign and get a response. It was difficult for us to explain to our counterparts on the political assignment that they were not responsive. We kept saying, "We can't get an answer." Then they finally understood. If we could not get an answer, they understood why.

Chuck Conder was assigned to Jerry Brown and Bill Clinton before CNN sent him to produce Perot coverage. He drew a sharp distinction between how other campaigns operated and how Perot did business.

> Other candidates, if a question came up related to a news story during the course of the day, where if welfare was a big story in Washington and you wanted to get a response on that issue from one of the other candidates, you could either go to them directly and ask them a question related to that story or you could go to a spokesperson. With Perot, you could never do that because Perot was the only person who could speak for Perot. And if he wasn't available—and he never was—then you couldn't ask him any questions about what was in the news on a given day.

Because Perot ran for president his way, he disregarded several assumptions about campaigns that newsworkers use to build their stories. In addition to limiting his contact with reporters and personally controlling all campaign information, Perot did not hold regular events or even provide "news of the day." He often refused to go on camera. He was unpredictable. To newsworkers oriented to covering campaigns on a daily, event-oriented, predictable basis, the result was frustration.

It was difficult for newsworkers even to report fundamental "here-they-come, there-they-go" stories, for Perot so rarely either came or went. "We would go for days," said Chuck Conder, "when Perot was just sort of camped out in Dallas." Added CNN Associate Political Director Carin Dessauer, "He was always doing his own thing." For television's purposes, this did not amount to much.

Several newsworkers insisted that Perot didn't understand television's needs, or that if he was aware of them, he simply did not care if they were met. Tony Clark believed it was the former, recounting how the campaign would distribute copies of their commercials on the wrong size videotape, and how once during a rare Perot event, the press plane "landed forty-five minutes after Perot started speaking." Chuck Conder, conversely, was left with "the impression that the campaign was set up the way Perot wanted it. He wanted to set the agenda, not let the news media [do it]."

All this led to media frustration, but as we saw in Part I, it did not diminish the amount of attention television paid to Ross Perot. In early summer when Perot I was at its height, the candidate would plunge from sight for long periods of time and still receive more press than the nominees of the two major parties. A producer working on another campaign at the time said the other candidates were out every day practically begging for coverage, while the press was simply waiting for Perot to appear.

Hence the question: If all the correspondent saw of the Perot campaign was a candidate limiting his exposure, ducking the media, and refusing to answer questions, what could he say in his report? The answer: Just that. Much of the time, Perot coverage offered essentially that the candidate wasn't *doing* anything; rather than turn away from covering the campaign as a series of events, newsworkers reported on their absence. The passage quoted below, reported for ABC by Morton Dean, was typical of the sort of coverage Perot received, and it attests to another assertion the correspondent made about the Perot campaign: "There was no there there."

> Perot made it clear he would limit the kinds of questions he would answer during his campaign. [Perot: "I will not spend one minute answering questions that are not directly relevant to the issues of concern to the American people."] As usual, Perot was annoyed by reporters' questions, especially about his reported use of private investigators. [Perot: "Look, I don't care what you do—just have fun, play 'gotcha,' I don't care."] It's expected that Perot will continue to operate in a

highly unorthodox, unpredictable manner, limiting public appearances, ignoring political reporters, while spending a lot of time and money on TV.[5]

Stylistically, Perot stories bore the familiar tone of election news. But so often they were content-free, even by television's standards. The above passage addresses familiar process concerns about covering the story, like how the reporter's questions are being received and the status of the candidate's relationship with the press. Only, in this case, the candidate is not answering the questions and has no relationship. In essence, it explores a process that is not. It was the best television could muster given its tendency to try to pour new wine into old bottles.

Accordingly, Perot was covered mostly as a horserace phenomenon. Minus daily events, and apart from coverage of the fact that there were none, newsworkers could rely on the drama and conflict of a third candidate with national support to address how Perot was influencing the broader contest. By relying on material under their control, they could cast their approach in terms of how Perot was affecting the presidential race. One method for doing this was to report how he was doing in the polls. Another, available during Perot II, was to cover his television commercials as though they were campaign events.

Perot's standing in the polls added an element of uncertainty and excitement to the campaign. "For an independent candidate to come in there and even have a crack at being considered was a big story," said CNN producer Kip Grosenick, "and that's why we were constantly monitoring how he was polling. In the early going, back around the California primary, he was running first in the polls, and that's a big story." Even later in the year, when Perot was no longer positioned to win the presidency, the effect he was having as the odd man out in a three-way race was the justification given for continuing to report his numbers.

However rationalized, reporting poll data was also easy to do. It posed none of the hardships faced by newsworkers trying to fathom the Perot campaign on an everyday basis; the networks commissioned the polls and had all the statistics and graphics they needed to construct horserace items. As with poll coverage elsewhere in the campaign, these items satisfied television's uncomfortable fascination with the daily numbers.

Covering Perot's commercial blitz is a bit harder to justify on the merits than saturating the screen with percentages, although it did provide newsworkers with the same advantages. Campaign ads are not controlled by the candidate. If correspondents need access or producers want footage, both are available, albeit in processed, videotape form. Commercials are easily accessible, and even the longer ones are quick and easy to view.

Accordingly, when Perot decided in the final weeks of the campaign to convert a tiny percentage of his personal fortune into the largest television political advertising campaign in history, it was big news. It could be argued that there was news value in the novelty of the event that justified some attention. But television went further, covering the details of the campaign ads in an on-going fashion and essentially treating Perot "infomercials" as substitutes for the campaign activities newsworkers depended upon but the independent rarely staged. Television commercials were covered as though they were *events* in the familiar manner to which newsworkers are accustomed to covering a campaign. The finale to the Perot campaign, which played out almost entirely on paid television, was supplemented by free coverage on the evening news that intimated that something was really happening.

Covering the Perot ad campaign dubiously legitimated a product that the candidate created under conditions of utmost control. By equating Perot's commercials with the rallies, speeches, and press conferences of his oppo-nents, television news suggested they were equivalent functions. But com-mercials—even very long ones—are not events as they are usually defined and presented by television news. There are no public appearances, no crowds, no interplay with the press, no opportunity for reporters to get a "sense" of the candidate. Newsworkers in need of material to fit their orientations toward campaign reporting latched on to the ads as a vehicle for "covering" Perot. As a consequence, in the effort to circumvent the obstacles he posed, they lent credibility to a process purposefully designed to exclude them.

Newsworkers argued that there were few choices available to them. This was certainly true given how political campaigns are universally conceptual-ized by the television community; there were, under the circumstances, few perceived ways to proceed. One strategy that newsworkers could—and did—apply with little conflict was investigating Perot's background. Offering that it was something he'd "like to think we would have done anyway," Morton Dean said looking into Perot's past was a way of getting a sense of who he was and where he came from, which, in this instance, was not available to the press through the familiar channels of direct contact.

This avenue resulted in a number of nonissue items about Perot's past be-cause there was much about his background that was unusual. Between the two networks, questions were raised regarding possible past discrimination in his hiring practices, the veracity of his claims about seeking POWs and MIAs in Vietnam, whether he bent the rules to build his fortune, and so forth. Given the lack of material under the control of correspondents and producers, nonissue stories were a natural way to fill the void in Perot coverage.

In this manner, Ross Perot became a horserace phenomenon, and to a lesser extent the subject of process and nonissue topics. But noticeably missing from the Perot story was coverage of the issues. For the man who claimed he wanted to run for president because the other candidates were not addressing the hard questions, his absence from this aspect of campaign coverage was glaring. Reporters said they had no choice; Perot wouldn't speak in specifics and didn't have much in the way of concrete proposals. Bush and Clinton did not call him on this because both felt it was in their strategic best interest not to engage Perot in a dispute that could alienate his supporters or push them toward the other opponent. The press did not have at its disposal a familiar method for probing the candidate, and Perot was free to say, when asked, that the answers were all in his book. Chuck Conder said Perot rarely held press conferences, but "in those rare instances when he was asked specific questions, he'd simply hold up the book and say 'it's in the book.' There's not much you can do with that as a reporter."

What was in the book? According to Tony Clark, not very much. Clark said, "It never gets down to solutions. In his book, he talks about health care, and his solution for health care was let's get people together and discuss the best ways to come up with the best health care policy. Drugs, let's enforce the laws. He was going to deal with the deficit when he started his TV blitz, but he spent as much or more time talking about himself and his family." As for foreign policy, Clark said, "He never talked about international issues. What would you do in Yugoslavia, Somalia? Those things he never really talked about."

Ultimately, the evening news portrayal of Ross Perot was the product of newsworker orientations forced to adapt—in some instances, unable to adapt—to an unfamiliar environment. There was no media-campaign bubble from within which newsworkers could maintain a disorienting but familiar perspective. Ross Perot broke the rules by campaigning in a vacuum rather than a bubble; no one was allowed in, and public contact was minimal and controlled. This unconventional approach caused confusion and posed difficulties to newsworkers. The problems of covering the Perot campaign were eventually solved by applying predisposed ideas about campaign coverage to the Perot enigma in whatever ways seemed best.

Lacking regular events, correspondents talked about the lack of regular events or made events out of campaign ads. They found drama, conflict, and predictability in poll figures. They found unusual occurrences in the nonissues of Perot's past. If nothing was obvious in the usual way, then the unusual fact that nothing was obvious became news. Ironically, this most personal of presidential campaigns confounded a medium that places a premium on individuals because this individual was so well protected from press exposure.

An alternative to saying "nothing is happening here" is simply to say nothing. But this option was beyond the purview of newsworker orientations, which assumed that campaigns *happen*, therefore something must be available to report. If a third party was adding drama and conflict to the horserace, then this had to be reported. If presidential campaigns are personalized, then *he* had to be reported. This logic reinforced the decision to commit resources to cover Perot, which once done imposed an organizational demand for news that had to be met. This demand was fulfilled only when newsworkers found a way to satisfy what they set out to find.

As for Ross Perot, playing a different game worked in his favor. He demonstrated that those who can afford to violate newsworkers' expectations about a campaign can maintain control over how they are covered. Notwithstanding critical nonissue coverage, which he could do nothing about, Perot was well served by television. He managed to say little and do little yet remain a constant presence on the evening news and a force in the presidential race. No one can say what his personal fortune would have bought had daily helpings of free television not reinforced his role as a serious player, but save for allegations of massive wrongdoing, having your name in the news is always better than not having your name in the news. Every good salesperson knows this, Ross Perot included.

Following the campaign, Perot indicated he was not eager to relinquish the spotlight, and television demonstrated it was willing to oblige. When I spoke with Carin Dessauer two months after the election, she explained why she would cover a Perot press conference if he decided to hold one: "Perot got 19 percent of the vote in the general election. He had the resources to put together the campaign that he did and run the high-tech commercials that he did. Had he gotten 3 percent of the vote and he had a press conference today, I doubt we would cover it." Even after the election, Perot's terms are television's terms.

PART III

Conclusions

13

The Public as Political News Consumers

Just as television news personnel rely on analysis to place news reports in context, in the concluding chapters of this book I shall frame my findings in terms of their implications for the public and American politics. The public and its institutional arenas are places where the content of television election news, and the guiding forces that shape that content, are of considerable concern. I will first consider what the substance of television news coverage means to the news viewer, then, in chapter 14, I will look at the role television news plays in the broad context of the American political system.

Think of the average person as a news consumer who has a choice about whether to seek information about politics. Should he or she decide to do so, the different media offer a virtual shopping mall of options, ranging from traditional print and broadcast, to all-news radio, to the cable capabilities of CNN, C-SPAN, and even MTV. More recently, afternoon and evening talk shows have become vehicles for political discourse where candidates and elected officials take questions from studio and home audiences. And as long as Ross Perot maintains his interest in politics and his personal fortune, the "infomercial" will be a forum for political "news." Clearly, there are far more sources of political information than there were just a few years ago, and the television viewer who depends on one evening broadcast for all her news is fast becoming an anomaly. This book has looked at only two of these choices, and I must draw my conclusions about what they offer with the knowledge that news consumers may shop elsewhere if they do not like what is being sold.

Nonetheless, cable and broadcast networks are two of the most important outlets. Their news programs are pitched to the general news consumer looking for a more digested version of politics than found on C-SPAN and a more detached account than may be found on a Perot "infomercial." CNN and

ABC are among the most heavily consumed sources of political news—the big department stores anchoring the media shopping center. ABC is fond of reminding its audience that more people turn to this network for news than to any other source; indeed, evening broadcasts are critical to an understanding of political communication because they still attract large audiences. And networks still regard the evening program as the centerpiece of their news operations. The broadcast networks still make large investments into high-salaried anchors who shepherd the evening news audience through the gates of prime time programming. On cable news, where comparable audience judgments do not apply, the "PrimeNews" telecast nonetheless lives up to its name as first among equals, commanding an early pass through the network's daily news stockpile and offering as hosts CNN's most visible anchors.

The similarities in the way CNN and ABC covered the 1992 election are significant, given the importance of these networks among media options. Switching back and forth between CNN and ABC would cause little disruption to the viewer, who would see on both outlets the same political figures engaged in the same campaign actions for the same partisan reasons. On CNN, there is less diversity in coverage than the proliferation of television channels might suggest. The Cable News Network offers variety and convenience but not different offerings about politics. Whatever potential cable may hold for new perspectives on the news, it has yet to materialize. So, when I draw conclusions about electoral politics on television, I am discussing the cumulative impact of CNN *and* ABC. In their similarities, they reinforce each other.

Among the manifold ramifications of how these two forums portray the election, several stand out from the analyses presented in Parts I and II. I will look first at the similar thematic emphasis of "World News Tonight" and "PrimeNews" and consider, to paraphrase Jeff Greenfield, the overall nutritional value of the product that news consumers buy. I will then consider the sensitive and important issue of bias—both ideological and structural—as it appears or does not appear in television news. I will conclude this chapter by examining the relationship between the cynical nature of coverage, especially television's ongoing, in-depth analysis of its own political role, and public attitudes.

Issues or Trivia?

Newsworkers at all levels, together with critics and academics, place a premium on making television news substantive and informative rather than entertaining and trivial. In truth, the people who bring you the evening news would like it to be informative *and* entertaining, but when these two values collide, the shared orientations of the television news world push the product inexorably toward the latter. The secret, then, is finding fresh, enjoyable ways to fashion substantive material, but this goal is often difficult to attain. Substance is invariably equated with issues on the campaign trail, and these are difficult to mold into story elements of any fashion, no less appealing ones.

If television election news is historically short on issue coverage, it is not for lack of awareness, concern, or effort. Ever self-critical, newsworkers are constantly looking for ways to improve the amount of attention they give to the issues, and for them, issue coverage stands as a mark of quality in a medium noted for its superficiality. Executive-level meetings are devoted to the subject; as we have seen, ABC News even attempted to redesign its political coverage of the 1992 fall campaign to make it more issue-oriented.

But issue coverage is always an uphill battle because it takes more than concern, good intentions, and even policy directives to enhance the depth of television reporting. If the home audience in 1992 saw a more issue-laden account of the election than they did in past campaigns, it was because of the fortunate convergence of two factors out of the direct control of the networks: a poorly contested horserace and a conflictive, overriding policy issue. These elements are unlikely to coincide very often because a matter of great national importance would be expected to produce a strong, competitive field of candidates. In political terms, economic conditions of the sort that emerged in 1992 typically point to a political opening for challengers of all stripes. That this did not happen in 1992 is simply a fluke.

Timing, of course, was everything. Had economic doldrums caused George Bush's popularity to sag several months earlier than it did, he may have drawn a stronger field of Democratic and even Republican opponents. This scenario would have opened up a competitive horserace that would have naturally hauled attention away from economic matters. Issue coverage, which primarily constituted concentration on domestic economic matters, outdueled horserace coverage for attention on both networks only when the contest was muddled, resolved, or in hiatus. In a competitive election more conducive to the frontrunner–main challenger–longshot mold of years gone by, we would expect few of the fallow periods that pockmarked the 1992 campaign. In this more likely scenario, horserace matters would be expected to overwhelm issue material—as they did during the more competitive periods of the 1992 election. Good intentions aside, the temperature of the horserace still determines the amount of attention television will give to the election.

So likely is it that a hot policy issue will produce a good horserace that I would not expect to see the conditions afforded the networks in 1992 to reappear anytime soon. Future elections may well hold competition without a dominant issue (as in 1988), or both competition and dominant issue, but neither of these combinations would promote issue coverage. Furthermore, it is well worth remembering that so much issue coverage revolved around economic questions in 1992 that even with conditions conducive to what the networks call substantive coverage, the resulting product was limited in its range. Many domestic policy questions got little more than a turn or two in the public eye; most foreign policy issues were not covered at all.

Given these likelihoods, is it reasonable to conclude that the product the news consumer views is badly lacking in fiber? Is television's tendency to equate issue coverage with substance a valid assumption? My answer to these questions is equivocal. Television's perception that issues provide substance is consistent with a romantic view of democracy that regards voting as a function of informed choice on the weighty matters of the day. Long before there were sound bites and spin doctors, there was evidence that most people employed far more parochial concerns when making up their minds, like party identification and their immediate personal circumstances.[1] More recently, there are indications that viewers pay intermittent attention to rapidly broadcast information and often do not commit it to long-term memory.[2] In saying this, I do not mean to justify widespread ignorance of issue particulars or to argue that issue coverage is of limited utility if people do not integrate it into their voting decisions. Rather, issue coverage may not be the panacea for frivolity the networks make it out to be, and television's difficulty covering the issues may be commensurate with giving the customer what he wants.

It may be more useful to evaluate substance by looking at the overall message television sends to its audience about elections, campaigns, and political figures. Horserace, image, and even nonissue items have substantive components. Taken as a whole rather than in the sentence-by-sentence fashion of the research project, cable and broadcast news reports tell the viewer that the election is about a quest for power among a small number of flawed individuals who engage in interpersonal competition at great expense for personal political gain. The American public is given the results of a year-long background check conducted by the media as reporters sort through the candidates' character, potential for performance, and other largely personal concerns. The numerous subtexts that follow from this investigation offer surrogate measures of how well suited the candidates are to being president—how well they plan strategy; whether they were ever unfaithful or dishonest; and, of course, how well they relate to the media.

There are grains of substance, sometimes large ones, to all these matters. Selecting a president entails making choices about individuals and policies, and issues of trust, character, experience, and performance envelop concerns that are as substantive as whether a candidate would impose a flat tax on income or enact a middle-class tax reduction. Television is not wrong to address these matters, and it is too hard on itself when it fails to recognize that meaningful material is encrusted in some of its favorite themes.

But this approach to election coverage is not without significant drawbacks. The sense of the election that the audience gets from consuming this version of television news is governed by political criteria that are obvious and interesting to television newsworkers but that represent only one perspective.

Television assumes, for example, that the election is about individuals rather than institutions; political parties and interest groups are tangential to the main event, and the only institution that seems to matter much at all is television itself. The media play a pivotal role in the competition for office; consequently, television is more interested in this competition than it is in the competition over ideas. Political gladiators are featured doing battle in the electoral arena, while the campaign is portrayed as a nonideological pursuit.

The point is not that other conceptualizations of the campaign are better suited in a normative sense to how democracy conducts itself, for they may well not be. Rather, the message is that other conceptualizations of the election *exist*, albeit beyond the purview of network television news coverage. Viewers will not be privileged to them if their main source of news is electronic, for whether they turn to the broadcast networks or to the all-news cable format, the picture they get of the campaign will reflect what political reporters find interesting and important. Cable offers the choice of more news, but it is essentially more of the same news presented in a more convenient format.

In this regard, questions about the content of election coverage should focus not on its supposed lack of substance but on the overriding perspective that informs what often is useful, meaningful coverage. A person can survive on either fast food or whole grains, but a diet of the former precludes awareness of the taste and value of the latter. Television news simply resembles a large order of burgers and fries. A current morning network news program is fond of advertising itself as "breakfast for your head." But viewers should ask, as with the evening reports, What's on the menu? Often, the answer is: Sustenance, but laden with fat and cholesterol.

Hence, the other drawback of looking for substance astride issue coverage: the great potential for news to be fraught with irrelevant distractions. Television is particularly susceptible to this kind of presentation,[3] and without a doubt, coverage of the 1992 election was filled with unnecessary moments. Obviously, these included some of the nonissues, but there were other indulgences as well. Such things as public opinion polls, arguably useful in gauging the horserace, at some point became a focus of coverage, making measurement into a main event. Potentially meaningful character concerns were regularly reduced to candidate slogans offering little more than the distracting rhetorical pleasantries of "trust versus change" or the promise of "a place called hope." And of course, there were the arcane maneuvers of campaign and press useful only to those whose self-interest introduced it to the campaign story.

Newsworkers routinely equate issue coverage with substantive coverage because there is very little fat in something as obviously important as trade policy or health care. As newsworkers move away from the issues, they run the risk of being drawn to items that are appealing but trivial sideshows to the electoral event, thereby condemning themselves for, as one newsworker put it, their "naughty" ways. In truth, election items can and do offer both substance and trivia to the viewing audience, which seems to muddle through the offerings in indiscriminate fashion.[4] Framing questions about substance strictly around issues overlooks this point.

Partisan Bias

The charge that mass media reporting is slanted toward a particular perspective is a hot-button issue that inflames observers from across the ideological spectrum. From the left, critics argue that an ideological bias reinforced by the corporate structure of news production restricts the ability of the media to question the motives or actions of the ruling class. They claim that newsworkers, blinded by a common investment in the status quo, are unwilling and unable to challenge the legitimacy of society's dominant political, social, and economic institutions.[5] From the right, critics claim that a left-liberal tilt among newsworkers generates antipathy toward conservative politicians and their ideas. In 1992, Vice President Quayle brought this controversy to the fore by calling the press part of a "cultural elite." Bolstered by studies showing newsworkers tend to have progressive attitudes,[6] conservatives argue that liberal perspectives naturally find their way into reporting.

This critique is particularly germane to election coverage because it emphasizes the partisan actions of political figures. So intent are critics on arguing for the existence of liberal bias in election coverage that the debate has continued despite the victories of Republican presidential candidates in five of the last seven elections. Perhaps coverage has been slanted but ineffectual. Regardless, the allegations are frequently heard, and not just by professional media watchers. "Millions of Americans," reported *Time* in a piece appearing two weeks before the 1992 election, "remain passionately resentful of what they consider a marked liberal bias" in the press.[7]

How did CNN and ABC News election coverage fare on this count in 1992? Two things are necessary in order to demonstrate liberal bias: First, evidence that the more conservative candidate, President Bush, received worse coverage than his opponents, and second, if there is evidence that he did, the values and attitudes of those responsible for election news must be proven as the cause.

"Bad press" may be defined several ways. Candidates may be associated with unfavorable topics. They may be excluded from discussions of favorable items. Or they may be portrayed in an unflattering light by the use of adjectives that convey a negative impression of their ideas, their records, or their personae.

The first type of bad press is quite common to election coverage. Nonissue stories, which rarely fail to consume air time, are invariably unfavorable. All major candidates, and a few minor ones, have been the subject of nonissues at one time or another. In the list gauging the amount of attention given the ten most heavily reported nonissues, Bill Clinton received the most fanfare, followed by Ross Perot and George Bush (see Table 4.1). Between CNN and ABC, 552 statements about these nonissues implicated Clinton, 167 were about Perot, and only 36 featured Bush.[8]

But nonissues constitute only one topic where candidates may be portrayed badly. Horserace items can be unfavorable if they show a candidate losing or falling behind, as every unsuccessful primary challenger found out. Among the survivors, Bush was portrayed more poorly than his rivals on two key, recurring items. Opinion polls, a staple of television election reporting, consistently showed him lagging behind Clinton. And television's near-obsessive need to find debate winners and losers tagged the incumbent with worse spin than his two rivals.

Then there are policy issues. On this count, Bush received perhaps the worst coverage of all. With television addressing economic conditions often and in disparaging terms, being associated with the economy rarely meant getting good press, and no candidate was more frequently paired with poor economic conditions than George Bush. As I noted in chapter 4, because he was the incumbent, he was portrayed in terms of national economic circumstances three times as often as his Democratic rival. Most of this coverage was negative; the overall assessment of an economy in decline permeated television coverage and was liberally associated with the president's performance. In fact, the total number of negative references to Bush outdistanced all mentions of Clinton and the economy, be they negative, positive, or mixed. Taken collectively, these references clearly implicated Bush as being responsible for the nation's economic woes.

This assessment seeped into coverage of the president's image. Matters of capability inevitably centered on Bush's handling of the economy instead of, say, the Persian Gulf War. This focus generated negative evaluations of an attribute that had previously been widely considered as one of his strengths. On this score, the president lost twice—from the attention paid to his handling of domestic matters and from the lack of concern about his foreign policy pursuits. He was also at a disadvantage because posturing between the candidates about how to handle the economy crowded out coverage of the questions he was trying to raise about his opponent's character.

In sum, George Bush was the subject of less than favorable reporting. He wasn't the only candidate to receive bad press, of course. Nor did he always come out worse than his opponents: On nonissue matters, he probably received the best treatment. But on items central to the Bush campaign's theme of "trust" versus "change," television coverage played to Bill Clinton's strengths.

Nonetheless, it is difficult to discern whether this was caused by ideological bias. In order to claim that liberal tendencies among newsworkers motivated this pattern of coverage, there must be evidence that newsworkers had partisan reasons to present one candidate (for parties are rarely addressed) in a more favorable light than the others. The argument would be that newsworkers, commonly united in the belief that America would be best served by a liberal alternative to George Bush, consciously or unknowingly advanced a view of the campaign that emphasized matters favorable to Bill Clinton.

There is little evidence that this happened. Instead, coverage of the 1992 campaign reinforces Michael Robinson's observations about the 1980 election, that "in campaign news reporting—the one form of journalism which ties directly to voting—partisan bias counts for next to nothing."[9] Given how newsworker orientations structure reporting, the kind of coverage Bush received followed naturally from what newsworkers perceived to be obvious news rather than from partisan concerns. Once correspondents and producers, relying on audience perceptions, came to see the recession as a central component of the election campaign, it became difficult for Bush to recast coverage in more favorable terms. Any incumbent presiding over a sour economy, regardless of partisan affiliation, would "obviously" be perceived by newsworkers as responsible for those circumstances and could expect to receive the kind of coverage Bush did. This is how the press perceived Jimmy Carter in 1980. Absent the sense that the economy was in trouble in 1984 and 1988, incumbents in those years were not saddled with this particular kind of bad press, large deficits notwithstanding.

Quite possibly, this negative emphasis fueled Bush's chronically poor ratings in public opinion polls, which television dutifully reported. This cycle nevertheless cannot be traced to partisan motivation. Opinion polls are predictable and they illustrate conflict; these qualities argue for their repeated use in election coverage regardless of what they say. Among horserace items on which Bush fared poorly, only his debating performance was strongly susceptible to subjective interpretation. But again, no evidence exists for partisan evaluations of the outcome. Established "standards" for performance, consistent with the news community's benchmark orientation, generated the ubiquitous, ever-stilted conclusions about who "won" and who "lost." There is always room for play in applying these guidelines, but criteria like staying with one's game plan, looking "presidential," and not making gaffes remained the qualities against which all candidates were evaluated.

Ultimately, the bad press that other candidates received had its origins in the same bundle of orientations that informed how Bush was covered. Bill Clinton's draft record, his alleged extramarital affair, and other like sagas of the long election year received attention because they were, for a while at least, regarded by newsworkers as "unusual" events punctuating the monotonous daily routine of the campaign trail. The event, not the candidate or his partisan inclinations, makes the story newsworthy. Had the roles been reversed, had Bill Clinton been the incumbent presiding over a long recession and George Bush the challenger with a string of character-oriented questions in his past, coverage would have been reversed as well. Right-wing critics wishing to allege partisan bias would simply have had to look to other aspects of coverage to try to make their case.

To the degree that the evidence supports a claim of bias in the news, it is bias of a structural type of the sort discussed by Richard Hofstetter, who writes, "Television has many attributes that facilitate reporting specific kinds of information in specific ways."[10] We have seen how the perception that "news is obvious" structures a series of orientations about what is unusual, event-driven, dramatic, predictable, and the like to determine the shape of election news on cable and broadcast television. Items beyond the purview of these orientations will not be reported. Matters that do not play out where the light is good will be excluded from the agenda. This subjectivity is clearly a form of bias and perhaps more worthy of examination than unsubstantiated claims of partisanship. Material kept from the media agenda will surely be omitted from the public agenda.

To return to a question raised at the beginning of this chapter, What does the substance of television news coverage mean to the news viewer? If television portrays the election as a contest for power, it is hard to imagine the audience regarding it any other way. If it emphasizes a small group of political actors and a limited number of behaviors framed by political motives, this is likely how the audience will think about politics. The "obvious" is reinforced not just for the newsworkers but for news consumers as well.

The same dynamic applies to process coverage, which finds its origins in the structural bias of the medium. In the distorted world of the campaign-media bubble, it is hardly curious that the cameras turn irresistibly backward toward television itself, and newsworkers at all levels acknowledged that interest in their own lot tugged at them like strong undertow, pulling them against their stated wishes farther out to sea. Self-interest masquerades as news as reporters relate their own experiences to an audience that does not share the same concerns.

Many newsworkers were at a loss to see how the choices they made about covering the coverage could add to audience knowledge of the election. Some admitted that it contributed nothing useful to the public's ability to decide how to vote. Others acknowledged it was far more interesting to those on the scene than to people watching at home. But, because it satisfied a strong, selfish need, it was hard not to do process coverage, even if it contributed little of value.

But process coverage potentially poses a greater concern than simply cluttering the screen with material of more interest to producers than consumers. So much of what correspondents say about candidate-media relations describes life in their world—which they admit to be false and distorted. Covering the coverage results in a picture of the media in the campaign that could leave the viewer doubting everyone—candidates and their aides who try to manipulate reporters as much as the press that tries to stop them. Depending on television's ability to influence viewers, the self-serving bias that makes election coverage into a contest between candidates and those covering them could facilitate viewer cynicism about the political process and those who are part of it.

A Cynical Audience

Cynicism is central to the picture of the process presented to the television audience. Consider the various images of the election campaign communicated to the viewer in 1992. Candidates were shown to behave in self-serving ways, engaging the media in a struggle to win favorable coverage. They were shown to be motivated by the wish to be portrayed in a positive light, no matter how phoney, in a game where image is everything. To obtain this, they engaged in behind-the-scenes maneuvering with the press, which portrayed itself as an adversary in an ongoing struggle for control of the message that would reach the voters. No one was noble or particularly principled. Even the reporters, through the relentless attention they paid to their own needs, appeared as party to a dysfunctional process rather than as guardian of the public interest.

The audience was left to sift among the images of this power play for conclusions about the political system. It was not difficult to decide that politics is simply about power, that power is about personal gain, and that the candidate who figures this out and exploits it best is the most likely to prevail. Finding reasons to participate in the election, enthusiastically support a candidate, or feel good about the electoral process was far more problematic.

If the public is not quick to become this cynical, correspondents willingly point them in this direction through the analysis they bring to their coverage. In the interest of putting events into context, reporters on CNN and particularly on ABC provided an analytical framework for coverage. Necessarily, the perspective they supplied offered a view of the campaign from the media's perch. Viewers were told about the *real* reasons behind candidate actions, which invariably involved manipulation of others, particularly reporters, for personal political gain. Nothing was benign or to be taken at face value. When the media did not let the candidates "get away with it," viewers were told of how the candidates' efforts were futile; when candidates did succeed in "getting their message out," viewers learned of how adept they were at controlling others—their opponents, the press, and of course the audience. The most successful of these were the candidates who inevitably led in opinion polls, the people for whom the American public was asked to vote.

The press did not fair any better. By placing television in the center of the campaign universe, correspondents aligned themselves with the political figures whose motives they constantly questioned. They became partners in a relationship, locked in a dance in which candidates and reporters flaunted their mutual mistrust. The candidates attempted to manipulate the reporters, who revealed their plight to the audience only to have the candidates respond with further attempts at control. These subsequent efforts were predictably passed on to the viewer as well. Candidates led, reporters followed, the audience watched—and the message was clear. Sometimes the roles reversed, and the reporters hounded the candidate with questions about issues they could not avoid, leaving the reporters to tell the audience that the candidates were trying hard to leave those issues behind them and would do so if only the press would let them. Reporters led, candidates followed, the audience watched. But the message about the process didn't change.

For the viewer inclined to see this dance as cynical, television presented little evidence to the contrary. But to argue that television's approach to election coverage reinforced or enhanced public cynicism requires making a strong claim about the influence of the media on the audience. On this matter, our knowledge is inconclusive. For a long time, the prevailing wisdom among students of the media was that the impact of the message on audience attitudes and behavior was quite limited.[11] Recent evidence suggests otherwise. Especially for viewers with limited education or political interest, television messages may in fact inspire which items we consider important. Shanto Iyengar and Donald Kinder argue this point, claiming television has the ability to emphasize or deemphasize political information, establishing the terms by which the public will make political judgments. They find the effect to be particularly strong when an item leads the broadcast, which election news invariably does as the horserace approaches the finish line.[12]

Iyengar and Kinder write primarily of performance-based items. Their evidence supports the claim that linking George Bush with poor economic conditions affected the way the public thought about the president when considering how to vote. With character-based judgments, the effect is less clear.[13] So on matters of public attitudes, it is difficult to decipher how people will react to exposure to reporter judgments.

This argument has not stopped others from claiming that the message on the screen instills in viewers doubts about politics and American political institutions. The argument that televised messages erode public trust in government and politicians,[14] or generate "videomalaise" among heavy users,[15] is bolstered by the decline in levels of public trust and efficacy witnessed during the years when television sets became standard household furnishings. Unfortunately, the evidence is not as strong as the claim; Vietnam, Watergate, and widespread social unrest also mark this period, leaving me to wonder whether cynical television news messages foster, reinforce, or simply coincide with increases in public cynicism.

One thing can be said with confidence: Viewers who wish to find support for the feeling that politicians care little about people like them need look no further than the evening news. On any given night, on cable and broadcast, that message is hammered home in less than subtle fashion. On all the miniseries that collectively composed television election coverage of the 1992 campaign, correspondents talking about their experiences presented politics and government as an ordeal. Through the analytical turns applied to the story in the name of "context," and especially from material detailing coverage of the coverage, viewers were exposed to a single perspective—the media/ campaign perspective—which raised questions about the actions and motivations of all involved in the quadrennial campaign rite of electing a president.

To offset television's ability to structure how people think about politics, Iyengar and Kinder wistfully call for the medium to present "multiple portrayals of campaigns," each reflecting a different perspective on the nature of politics.[16] This is unlikely to happen. Television naturally and "obviously" presents one perspective, singular in its self-serving, self-referential nature. So long as the collection of newsworker orientations responsible for coverage remain in place—and no forces exist to controvert them—the American public can stay tuned for more of the same every four years.

14

Television as a Political Institution

Network television provides its consumers with a perspective on the political world. In its news reporting capacity, it affords the viewer the opportunity to partake in political and cultural experiences of national and international concern. It is where the American public can turn to share news about national emergencies, learn of new places, hear the latest advances in medical research, or watch and listen to the people running for president.

But television does far more than this, of course. It is also home to countless advertisements for hair loss remedies and denture adhesives. Broadcast networks offer the familiar array of drama and comedy programs for the mass audience, while cable provides a bundle of shows geared toward specific segments of viewers. Cable is where people can indulge their desires for perpetual weather, music, sports, and stock reports, for new or old movies, for children's shows, religious inspiration, comedy, home shopping, and a wealth of other services. It is even a living museum of television's past; for those who feel nostalgic about the medium, cable is the place old network programs find immortality.

Television provides these choices because it is designed to entertain more than to educate or instruct. CNN does not advertise itself as an educational network; cable television offers a "learning channel" for that. Rather, it relies on the entertaining quality of information to attract an audience that finds fulfillment in tuning in to accounts of the latest events. The broadcast networks count on the same factor, plus the star quality of their anchorpersons, to reach a broader, more generic audience than cable. For the broadcast network, the evening news is a success if people stay around to watch "Roseanne."

Television's role in political discourse is tangential to its mission. But because the flickering tube has the unique ability to hold the attention of countless millions, its utility as an instrument of politics is obvious and was evident even when the medium was in its infancy. Initially, television was a vehicle by which candidates could engage in wholesale politics on an unprecedented scale. Today, it is far more than that. In its news reporting capacity, television negotiates the terms of politics with candidates and elected representatives. Newsworkers are part of the political action, as witnessed by their activities in the media-campaign bubble that defines the rules by which campaigns are conducted and election news is produced.

It is not by design, but television has come to function as a political institution. By this I mean that television is structured in such a way and newsgathering is conducted in such a fashion as to have an enduring role in American political decision making. If politics involves the allocation of resources, analysts need look no further than television's version of the presidential campaign to see how the medium helps negotiate who gets what, when, and how. Ask the candidate who lacks the organizational base necessary to warrant coverage in New Hampshire if television plays a role in political decision making. For that matter, ask the candidate whose personal fortune provides him with a televised platform.

By saying this function is institutionalized, I mean the political role of the media is facilitated by the manner in which newsgathering is structured. Being an institution entails more than just the simple existence of organizations for newsgathering; it involves the common set of operating principles that unite those structures in a communal approach to news. Timothy Cook submits that television may be seen as an institution inasmuch as newswork follows routinely from a collection of roles, rules, and procedures that have developed over time for the purpose of serving society's need for communication.[1] Election coverage certainly demonstrates these criteria. Presumptions about what constitutes election news and how to gather it transcend whatever organizational differences follow from the distinct missions of broadcast and cable television. Correspondents and producers at both organizations approach the political world in the same manner, guided by widely held orientations about how to do newswork. Television is in this sense an institution; in fact, it is the only institution television is interested in reporting about.

In this regard, television holds a place among the network of national institutions in which political decisions are made. As a regular matter of governance, television's news function is intertwined with the work of the three branches of government, just as media access to the White House, Congress, and the judiciary is critical to the production of television news.[2] From an electoral standpoint, television maintains a critical place in the political process relative to another institution, the political parties. The relationship is noteworthy because the two institutions perform overlapping functions. As linkages to the public, both parties and media serve as conduits between the electorate and officials or their would-be rivals. Each engages in the process of channeling information between those who inhabit or wish to inhabit other institutions of government and the general public.

Two trends over the past few decades have made this relationship particularly tenuous: the decline in the ability of political parties to perform the intermediary function and the concurrent development of television as a potent political force. The impact of these twin trends is most notable in primary elections, where parties perform the critical task of candidate selection. In the name of democratized decision making, the parties moved toward a decentralized method of delegate selection starting in the late 1960s. This change entailed replacing closed, consolidated caucuses with open primaries. As the number of primaries proliferated, the business of winning party nominations shifted to the public arena, where the key relationship is between politician and voter. This new approach was supposed to have the effect of empowering a wider range of constituents in the nominating process, but in fact it transferred power from the elite domain of the party convention, where matters were decided in the old system, to individual candidates and the media. Candidates benefited from the ability to circumvent the party in strategic planning and, with the help of changes in campaign finance laws, to raise funds for primary challenges. The media gained importance as the natural vehicle for the ensuing public relations effort.

Some theorists argue that the unbridled ability of candidates to reach the public through television accelerated the decline of political parties[3] and that television's emphasis on persons rather than institutions facilitated recent trends in ticket-splitting and weakened partisan identification.[4] Whatever the cause may be, the effect is clear: Television intervened as the main institutional link between candidate and public and became central to any candidate's effort to win a party nomination. The medium filled the void left by the political parties. And presidential campaigns assumed their now familiar protracted, frenetic form.

These changes set the stage for the creation of the media-campaign bubble as the accepted, predictable environment in which the candidates reach voters and television finds election news. The manner of running for office assumed the form of a prolonged horserace as candidates began to hopscotch the country for months at a time in what amounted to a long string of individual statewide media campaigns. Naturally, newsworkers riding with the horses experienced the campaign this way as well. ABC Political Director Hal Bruno said that television only covers what the candidates—and the parties—give them: "We did not create this process. The McGovern-Frazier reforms of 1970 created this system of primaries and caucuses. They created a horserace from New Hampshire onward through the February, March, and April primaries. They created this process in 1970, and all you have to do now is count delegates. People don't understand this."

Of course, television covers it according to its own criteria. So the process that television did not create becomes a story about numbers: organizational size, money, delegates, and victories. Bruno said,

> It becomes a weekly test of who wins or loses. If you win you get the money to keep going. If you lose you run out of money. That has happened every single presidential election since 1972: If they don't win they don't get the money, if they don't get the money they're out of the game. If you do not cover that aspect of it while it's happening, what should you be covering? Should we ignore the fact that Dukakis [*sic*] didn't have the money to keep going because he couldn't keep winning? It was that simple. The other thing is the delegate count. Every single election since 1972, since this process came into being, at a certain point the delegate count takes over. It doesn't matter what the delegates say or what they do, if the delegate count builds up for one candidate, that candidate is going to be nominated. It happens every single time. It happened this time with Bill Clinton.

By the same token, Bruno defended television's inclination to predict a race as an inevitable outgrowth of how the race is run.

> It's clear to everyone at some point what the outcome's going to be. In 1972, it became clear that George McGovern was going to have the delegates. Hubert Humphrey knew it and Ed Muskie, and everybody, and there was no point in having a stop McGovern movement. Same thing was true in '76 with Jimmy Carter, and with Ford and Reagan. Ronald Reagan tried to spook everybody into thinking he had hidden strength, but he didn't have it and we knew he didn't have it— everybody knew Ford was going to be the nominee. The same thing happened in 1980 with Teddy Kennedy. There came a point where no matter what Teddy Kennedy did, Jimmy Carter had the delegates. Now, you would be misleading people if you didn't report that this is the fact of life. And we go through this every single time, where everybody says, well, the news media's declaring it over. It isn't that at all. It's there, and nobody's ever been able to beat that.

Missing here is television's active role in setting and evaluating the expectations that determine whether resources are won or lost. In this regard, television has a hand in determining when the race is over and how it is resolved, shaping as much as reporting the final declaration of victory.

But, in one important respect, Bruno was exactly right. When television sees the horserace and calls it news, it behaves according to how it understands the political world. By supplying television with a long string of meaningful tournaments and supplying candidates with the opportunity to contest them on television, the parties have given the medium the occasion to act as master of ceremonies for the presidential campaign. The medium is free to report what it sees. If from behind the camera the world looks like one long sporting event, and this "obvious" observation finds its way into coverage, television has not failed in its role as purveyor of campaign news. To the contrary, it is doing exactly what it is designed to do.

The problem is that television is not structured to perform the functions of a political party. As an entertainment medium, its primary purpose is to distract. It may also inform, especially if the information has an entertaining quality. On this count, the parties obliged when they served up the nomination-by-marathon format. But this fact does not alter how television functions. Daily recounting of life on the trail is no substitute for the traditional two-way link between public and party that predated the media campaign.

Television simply is not a suitable substitute for political parties. It cannot aggregate public interests, lend stability or legitimacy to the political system, or require accountability from presidential candidates. Worse yet, because of the orientations of political journalists, the televised picture of the election actually mitigates against these outcomes. As television becomes the default replacement for political parties in election campaigns, it serves to weaken the link between the public and its institutions of governance.

Consider for a moment the functions that political parties can perform but television cannot. Political parties serve to bring together groups and individuals with diverse interests and concerns under one large organizational umbrella. This function is most prominently emphasized at the national level through the process of negotiating the ideas that constitute the platforms both parties generate at their quadrennial national conventions. The mechanism facilitates governing a complex, multicultural nation with a decentralized political system by providing a focal point for expression and a forum for compromise.

Consequently, political parties work to provide stability and legitimacy to a complex political system. Larry Sabato writes, "They represent continuity in the wake of changing issues and personalities, anchoring the electorate as the storms that are churned by new political people and policies swirl around."[5] Parties temper political change through tendencies toward moderation born out of the need to build the broad-based political support necessary to electoral victory. In much the same way, they manage some of the conflict inherent in our fragmented political structure, underscoring the ability of the system to process demands.

Moreover, parties demand accountability from their candidates. Running under a common label in America does not require uniformity of ideas, but it can provide the ligament that holds a candidate to his promises and connects both to the voter. Prior to reform, parties would seek candidates who broadly speaking subscribed to a set of values and ideals readily identified with their institutional label. Voters could use this information to guide their vote choice and, if so inclined, their partisan identification. The nominee was the party's representative, not his own.

Television is ill-equipped to do these things. Communication between reporter and audience flows one way. Viewers are not engaged in the political process as much as they are observers of it. Even if television covered the campaign as a give-and-take over policy objectives among individuals and groups, the experience of watching television still could not replace participating in an actual exchange. But television does not even do this much; it focuses instead on the personal agendas of candidates who speak through the medium to the voter. Even for the attentive viewer, television tenders little more than couch potato politics, offering the vicarious ordeal of political conquest rather than the interactive experience of interest aggregation.

Instead of lending stability and legitimacy to the political system, television coverage of the election raises doubts about politics and everything it touches. As noted in chapter 13, although political television may or may not enhance public cynicism, it certainly relates a cynical message through the relentless attention it pays to how candidates manipulate the rules of the television era. By personalizing politics and focusing on what it takes to win an election in an age where strings are pulled in view of the camera, television raises and reinforces doubts about the veracity of political actors and the desirability of a process sullied by their actions. In addition, by publicly scrutinizing its own behavior and motivation, the press raises questions about the lone institution portrayed in the televised account of election news.

In contrast to the manner in which political parties once demanded accountability from their nominees, television requires only that candidates speak in terse sound bites about matters that need not be substantive. When candidates sidestep reporters or fudge answers to their questions, television responds by talking about what the candidate *did* rather than by examining the substance of what he *said*. Reporting on a candidate's personal, political motives serves simply to reinforce the medium's primary message about the cynical manner in which the game is played. With repetition, this message cannot come as a surprise to viewers; they have heard it many times before. Candidates know this, but this knowledge does not undermine their political objectives. Left unchallenged, they are free—indeed, encouraged—to issue more sound bites in order to guarantee their place on the evening news.

When television fills the void left by political parties, everyone save for television loses out. The public is treated to a marathon campaign universally decried as being too long. Choices become more difficult and disillusionment more understandable. Running for office becomes an eternal, sometimes self-destructive battle with the media that few survive. And the victors risk taking office without having to make the political connections that were once a part of partisan accountability. All this makes governance more problematic than in the past.

For television, the presidential election amounts to a great story; to a political correspondent, it is one of the greatest stories—and would be regardless of how the rules of the game were written. In this regard, newsworkers are simply doing what they're oriented to do: find and interpret "the story." If their efforts result in the sort of less than desirable campaign coverage that appeared on cable and broadcast television in 1992, it is not because television has malfunctioned. On the contrary, television is doing exactly what it could be expected to do—responding to running for office, nineties-style. Coverage will always keep pace with the ground rules; the problem comes when the medium is permitted to set the terms of the election. If the selection process were again accountable to the parties, the media-campaign bubble would dramatically reduce in size, longevity, and overall importance. That such a renewal does not happen is the fault of the parties. Similarly, all Americans share responsibility for allowing television to step in and perform functions it is not equipped to handle.

Genuine changes in how network television covers political campaigns are likeliest if parties reinstate centralized control over the nomination process. Fewer primaries would shorten the campaign and change the rules of the horserace. Even "beauty contest" primaries that divorced delegate selection from the popular vote would draw less media analysis than the present system because delegate totals would not be affected by primary results. But the most effective improvements would simply remove as many benchmark measures as possible from the arduous winter and spring campaign stages. Real work could be done in caucuses leading up to the convention. Early caucuses, such as the one in Iowa, might still receive a lot of attention because of their placement, but if current coverage patterns held, later ones would draw far less notice. If a candidate were clearly on the way to nomination, television could and would report that fact just as it did before 1970. But the field would winnow down in a different venue where the media would not find a ready horserace and where reaching the public through the media would be less vital politically for the candidate than it is today.

If this proposal has an undemocratic air to it, that is part of the problem. The reforms that gave us today's media-centered campaign were supposed to replace a system that many argued responded more to elites than to rank-and-file participants. It is still unpopular to argue against the apparent openness of the popular primary. But the old system, while elite-based, was not necessarily closed. "The behind-the-scenes stuff is a bunch of mythology," Hal Bruno recalled, speaking of the image of how party leaders controlled the agenda. "Everybody knew what was happening behind the scenes and reported it. The smoke-filled room had open windows, all over the place."

Reinstating the connection between party and voter would be entirely consistent with democratic norms. From an institutional perspective, it would simply ask existing political structures to perform the tasks they were designed to carry out. It would let television look for political news on its own terms and let the parties set the rules of the game.

The alternative is more of the same and possibly even worse. At minimum, correspondents will continue to hound candidates and their aides, who in the effort to control the agenda will persist in heaping verbal and physical abuse on reporters, who will turn around and report about it. One newsworker, sympathetic to what candidates go through given the way the game is currently played, suggested that the current situation diminishes all involved. She said,

> The press is just impossible. The candidates are just doing what they have to do, and we're impossible. And any tactics that work for them, I really give them that. Because as a group we're so antagonistic and so negative, I could see why they'd want to exert their own control over things. Just out of survival. I mean, nothing is good enough for us. If the candidate does one thing, we complain about it. If he were to do the exact opposite, we would complain about that.

But if the candidate no longer needed the press in the same way, this antagonistic behavior could continue without threatening to drown the entire process. Voters could probably suffer through limited bouts of campaigning on television, such as would be likely to transpire once the nominees were chosen, if the parties regained a share of their lost political power.

Otherwise, 1992 holds strong hints as to the next phase of television's ever-increasing central electoral presence: the talk show as campaign forum. This scenario offers a logical extension of the candidate's quest to control the agenda of the institution running the electoral contest: Use the medium, circumvent the press. Candidates will appear on talk programs, where, say, Oprah Winfrey or Phil Donahue mediates questions called in by home viewers or asked by a live studio audience. Simple in design, the talk show will give the appearance of direct democracy and easy access to the candidate.

The phenomenon, in fact, has already begun. It started on CNN, when Ross Perot appeared on "Larry King Live" and offered himself as an alternative candidate should America respond. According to Larry King, "Perot showed you could start a national campaign on a prime time TV talk show." He is right. Bill Clinton appeared shortly thereafter, with Larry King and a host of others, perpetuating a new forum for getting out the message.

Central to the talk show method is taking calls from the public in a fashion that replaces partisan accountability with public accessibility. Lacking even the press corps as a barrier to the general public, the candidates reach out and touch whoever can get past the busy signal at the network. When I asked Larry King about the way political figures have come to use television talk shows, he drew the comparison to movie stars plugging their latest film, saying, "Michael Douglas is on my TV show next week to talk about his new movie. Michael Douglas is a major star, he's got a movie opening, he wants to sell his movie. That's no different than Bill Clinton. But in my childhood you wouldn't have been able to talk to Michael Douglas or Bill Clinton. Now you can talk to both of them. And the public is beginning to expect it."

King feels the talk show phenomenon adds to our knowledge of the candidates and to our connection to them. He said, "I think we knew the candidates this year better than we ever knew the candidates. It was like a soap opera with these three guys. We knew 'em. They were Ross and George and Bill. We knew 'em from Larry King and Donahue and Arsenio, and all the places they went." Americans, did, in fact, feel they knew these candidates. From Bill Clinton's televised "town meetings" to the evening visits with Ross and Larry, there was the sensation of great responsiveness and the appeal of direct democracy. That only a few people actually got to ask questions is less important than the idea of a candidate fielding queries off the phone. The symbolism of accessibility can be as soothing as the real thing.

But viewers got to know Ross and George and Bill largely on the candidates' own terms. Never mind that talk show host and public caller sometimes asked sharp, pointed questions. It was still one hour with the candidate, out there selling his wares in a setting far more conducive to his direction than anything realized on the campaign trail. So effective was it, in fact, that Bill Clinton has incorporated the technique into governance. Larry King already has a commitment from the forty-second president for at least two appearances a year, live on CNN. The public is left with the pretext that their link to the political system has been strengthened. Television, of course, is about appearances. But the truth of the matter is entirely different from the appearance.

Unless the political parties make an effort to rekindle their importance in the electorate, television will continue to assume greater responsibility for a set of political functions it is not designed to perform. This transfer of power will not simply mean that Larry King will replace Peter Jennings as ringleader. Politicians and consultants have been finding new and creative political uses for the medium since Eisenhower smiled into the camera and read from cue cards, and they will continue to do so, because television is the most effective medium of communication the world has ever known. It simply falls short when it finds itself as the prime institutional bond between voter and candidate, between public and government.

By arguing that change should come from the political parties, I do not mean to acquit television for often self-indulgent election coverage that shuttles between substance and sideshow. Nor do I mean to suggest that newsworkers should cease evaluating their work, although recognition of the orientations that shape it may help alleviate some of the concern that results when the product falls short of the ideal. These are important issues. But if parties were to reinstate an accountable method for choosing a president, television's impact on the political system would not be nearly as large as it will be if present trends continue. There would still be important questions to ask about how television covers elections, but they need not speak to concerns about the health of the political process itself.

Ultimately, whatever the rules, television will be television. It is first and last an entertainment medium, unprepared to act as the political institution it has unwittingly become. Lacking the inclination to change its ways, television will continue to portray politics as it always has. The merchandise will continue to bear the stamp of television's frenetic, self-interested domain. And, looking through the fog and bewilderment of the media-campaign bubble, news-workers will readily confuse their stories with something called objective reality. Just as someone might watch a talk show and think he is interacting with a candidate, so do television personnel believe their product is undistilled. And so will they always. "I get so busy day in and day out, I really don't get a chance to reflect deeply," offered a producer who works in the room without windows. "But when I do get a chance to talk I realize what we're actually do-ing. We're literally showing the world itself."

Appendix

This project employs two original sources of data: a content analysis of CNN and ABC election news coverage and interviews with members of the election news units at both networks.

Content Analysis

For the content analysis, all regularly scheduled broadcasts of ABC's "World News Tonight" and narrowcasts of CNN's "PrimeNews" were monitored from January 1, 1992, through election day, November 3. Both programs air weeknights. "World News" is broadcast at 6:30 P.M. eastern time; "PrimeNews" airs at 8:00 P.M. eastern time. In all cases, I used the East Coast version of the reports. "Special" reports, such as CNN's evening-long coverage of the New Hampshire primary returns, were not included.

Reasons for Selection

These programs were selected for their comparability as evening news reports. Both are early evening signature broadcasts featuring the networks' high visibility anchors. Although only one of many CNN programs, "PrimeNews" is the network's premier prime-time newscast, featuring its star anchors and claiming early selection of the material CNN produces each day. Interviews with the program's producers confirmed that they perceive the two newscasts to be comparable.

The analysis presented in this book is restricted to material appearing on these two programs. Obviously, both networks aired information about the election in settings other than their primary evening news shows. Election coverage could be found regularly on ABC's "Nightline" and "Good Morning America" and on periodic special reports. CNN produced "Inside Politics '92" for the more interested viewer and dedicated blocks of time to campaign coverage on other regularly scheduled and special reports. However, campaign stories appearing on CNN's "PrimeNews" often cycled through other programs, and the thematic content of election news did not deviate greatly from program to program on a daily basis.

The decision to select one broadcast network from the three was informed by research suggesting there are greater content similarities than differences among ABC, CBS, and NBC. For a discussion of cross-network similarities in coverage of the 1992 campaign, see Crigler et al. (1992). ABC was selected to represent network television because of the size of its news audience and the relative health of its news organization.

At one time, CBS was considered the "network of record" because of its large viewership and historical commitment to reporting. Although it lacks the history, ABC today finds itself best positioned to lay claim to this title. Not only do "more Americans get their news from ABC News than from any other source" (as the network is fond of reminding us), but the long-term viability of the ABC news operation is presently greater than that of its network rivals. Recently, the network announced plans to join forces with the BBC, thereby expanding its access to overseas bureaus and facilities.

Coding Scheme Format and Reliability

The content data document thirty-eight distinct attributes of coverage for each statement made about the election on each thirty-minute broadcast of "World News Tonight" and on the first thirty minutes of "PrimeNews" during the ten-month research period. A statement is comparable to the unit of analysis employed by Lichter, Amundson, and Noyes (1988) in their content analysis of the 1988 campaign or the information units (IU) used by Altheide (1976). It is a completely articulated thought about something, generally one sentence in length. Statements introducing or acknowledging correspondents were excluded from consideration.

Examining statements instead of stories afforded great flexibility. Election items mentioned in stories about nonelection topics could be included in the analysis. Connections between actors and their actions could be made with a greater degree of specificity, as could the relationships among actors (discussed in chapter 6). Only items deemed to be about the election were recorded; for instance, matters relating to George Bush in a noncampaign role were excluded from analysis.

A total of 10,329 statements were recorded. For each statement, the subject of the statement (such as a candidate or campaign, the press, the public, and the like) was noted and, where applicable, the specific individual or institution mentioned. If the statement subject was addressed in terms of another individual or group, the latter was recorded as the object of the statement, much as one might parse a sentence for subject and direct object. Indirect objects were not recorded.

Each statement was examined for indications of the five topics addressed in this book (horserace, issue, image, process, and nonissue coverage). Single statements were permitted to have multiple topics. Topic coverage was evaluated using a series of four-point scales indicating whether the statement contained a favorable, unfavorable, mixed, or neutral evaluation of its subject. For instance, a statement that said George Bush was falling behind in the latest opinion polls would note the subject (candidate; Bush) and topic (horserace/opinion polls), as well as the negative evaluation accompanying the topic.

Each statement was coded as to its attribution (whether it was made by an anchor, reporter, or individual in a sound bite) and context (if a sound bite, whether the speaker was partisan, nonpartisan, or news figure). A statement was coded as analytical if it offered an explanation or presumption about its topic rather than a declarative message. Visual imagery was coded using a fairly simple variable that distinguished broadly among commonly used campaign pictures. All statements were coded for their placement in the story, placement in the newscast, and placement in one of the six campaign stages outlined in chapter 1.

Obviously, some of these items were more straightforward to code than others. To ensure the reliability of the data, the coding of select statements was replicated by the researcher and two assistants working separately. Most items yielded high or very high levels of congruity among the coders. As a matter of practice, variables where the coders could not agree at least 80 percent of the time were not employed in this book. This procedure affected some of the topic evaluation measures, which required the most subjective judgments.

Interviews

Data on factors influencing news production come from a set of forty-four semi-structured telephone interviews with personnel in the election news units at ABC and CNN. Correspondents, off-air reporters, and producers who worked on campaign coverage were asked brief, open-ended questions that allowed them to contribute their ideas about why they approached the campaign as they did.

Interviews were conducted in two waves: between July 28 and August 27, 1992, and again between January 11 and February 18, 1993. The two-wave format was designed to control for the effects of memory loss and hindsight, which could influence recollections in the months following the campaign. Additionally, some respondents from the first wave were interviewed again after the election.

Election news units are fairly compact groups. The forty-four individuals interviewed for this book come from the nucleus of the operations at both networks and were intentionally chosen to represent nontechnical workers at several levels, ranging from executive to reportorial (off-air) producer. The intention was to solicit feedback from the core participants at different locations in the network hierarchy.

Overall, forty-eight interviews were requested; four were denied, including three at the executive rank at ABC. Interviews were conducted by position and network as follows:

	CNN	ABC
Executive producers	5	1
Producers	7	4
Field producers	4	–
Reportorial producers	–	8
Correspondents	8	7
TOTALS	24	20

Respondents who granted interviews generally did so during business hours. Consequently, the interviews had to compete with the constant demands of newswork and were occasionally interrupted or cut short by other matters. Almost all of these were completed at a later date. The longest interview was 83 minutes; the shortest, 9 minutes; the average was 24 minutes.

Interviews were open-ended and followed the same basic format. Respondents were asked how coverage decisions were made, how they approached their jobs, and what obstacles they faced in reporting about elections. They were then asked to assess the content of their coverage. Respondents interviewed during the first wave were also asked to speculate about what they thought coverage would look like during the fall campaign. As appropriate, newsworkers were questioned about their experiences covering particular candidates.

Questions were designed to be specific enough to structure the interview but open-ended enough to permit the respondent to guide the discussion. The intent was for the interviewer to set the agenda but not to lead. All respondents were offered anonymity, although many permitted their words and names to be used in this book.

Notes

Chapter One

1. Roger Mudd, "Television Network News in Campaigns," in Devlin (1987), p. 91.

2. Appropriately, *Entertainment Weekly* presents a thorough roundup and evaluation of candidate talk-show appearances through the primaries. See *Entertainment Weekly*, July 10, 1992, pp. 16–18.

3. For a good discussion, see Davis (1992) and Kellner (1990).

4. Daniel C. Hallin, "Network News: We Keep America on Top of the World," in Gitlin (1986), p. 20.

5. Cornfield (1992) refers to "Topic A," the priority item du jour for those in the political subculture, which takes the form of a (usually) short-lived story dominating election coverage. The sequence of Topic A stories comes to define the media agenda as coverage becomes understandable in terms of the conventions of those who create it.

6. See, for instance, Lichter, Amundson, and Noyes (1988) and Patterson and McClure (1976).

7. When critiquing their own performance, newsworkers usually assume that attention to the issues is the hallmark of responsible coverage.

8. Chaffee and Choe (1980) note the high correlation between "image" and "issue" evaluations among a panel of attentive voters during the 1976 election. This observation leads them to question whether the distinction is appropriate when addressing public perceptions. Whereas voter impressions of candidates may in fact amalgamate numerous influences, the topic distinctions utilized here are designed to facilitate an understanding of the nature of the information available to the public upon which impressions may be formed.

9. As more homes are wired for cable television, the potential and real audiences for networks like CNN continue to mushroom. For more on cable technology, see Minow and Mitchell (1986).

10. Goffman (1974) provides a strong conceptual foundation for understanding how news reports, along with other aspects of human experience, are constructed and understood. For a discussion of the portrayal of social reality in the mass media, see Altheide (1991).

11. Literature on the social construction of reality treats portrayals of events on television and in print journalism as socially derived rather than objective. Key studies include Fishman (1980); Gitlin (1980); Gans (1979); Tuchman (1978); Altheide (1976); and

Epstein (1974). A good critique of this literature may be found in Kellner (1990), and a detailed discussion of the various influences on coverage may be found in Davis (1992).

12. In addition to Gans (1979) and Epstein (1974), see Sigal (1973) for an account of economic pressures on print reporters. For an exploration of market influences, see Erfle and McMillan (1989); Boyer (1988); Gitlin (1985); Atwater (1984); Garnham (1979); and McCombs (1972).

13. See Ostroff and Sandell (1989); Robert Smith, "New Technologies in Campaigns," in Devlin (1986); Theodore Peterson, "Mass Media and Their Environments: A Journey into the Past," in Abel (1981).

14. Routines are established in response to a variety of factors, such as corporate economic demands, the roles played by reporters and producers, and the relationships between reporters and sources. They are discussed at length by Tuchman (1978), Altheide (1976), and Molotch and Lester (1974). Fishman (1980) and Tuchman (1978) detail the relationships between reporters and news executives, while reporter-source relationships and coverage of social institutions are discussed by numerous authors, including Brown (1987); Seib (1987); Fico (1984); Nimmo and Combs (1983); Gandy (1982); Hess (1981); Paletz and Entman (1981); Fishman (1980); Epstein (1974); and Daniel J. Boorstin, "From News-Gathering to News-Making: A Flood of Pseudo-Events," in Schramm and Roberts (1971). For a discussion of the limits of pack journalism on the news product, see Sigal (1973) and Crouse (1972).

15. These values, beliefs, and norms are discussed at some length by Davis (1992); Paletz and Entman (1981); and Gans (1979).

16. See Hallin (1989); Gitlin (1980); and Molotch and Lester (1974).

17. See Robinson (1983) and Flegel and Chaffee (1971).

18. See Benenson (1984); Gans (1979); and Epstein (1973).

19. Objectivity is addressed by a host of scholars, including Davis (1992); Kellner (1990); Merrill (1985); Fishman (1980); Hofstetter (1978, 1976); Schudson (1978); Tuchman (1978); Lemert (1977); and Breed (1955).

20. For a discussion of the influences on news production and a good review of the literature, see Shoemaker and Reese (1991).

21. See Asher (1980), chapter 9.

22. Seib (1987), p. 29.

23. ABC's "World News Tonight" appears in most markets at 6:30 or 7:00 P.M. eastern time and runs for thirty minutes. CNN's "PrimeNews" appears at 8:00 P.M. eastern time and runs for sixty minutes.

24. There had been plans for an Iowa caucus stage, in keeping with the media attention given this event in recent past elections. In 1992, however, there *was* no coverage of the Iowa caucus. The presence of Iowa's Tom Harkin in the Democratic field nullified Iowa's horserace significance and as such eliminated virtually all coverage of what was expected to be (and was) a suspense-free event.

Chapter Two

1. The quotation is attributed to Edward M. Fouhy, and appears in Carol Matlack, "Bare Bones," *The National Journal* (November 2, 1991), p. 2671.

2. The key exception here is the greater analytical emphasis found in ABC coverage than in CNN coverage, which impacts directly on how the election is understood. This issue will be discussed in chapter 7.

3. Overall, 61 percent of the election statements (6,304 of 10,329) were broadcast on ABC, constituting 57 percent of the election stories (434 of 766). These figures hardly varied over the course of the campaign. During the primaries, 61 percent of election statements appeared on ABC; during the general campaign, the figure was slightly under 62 percent.

4. On ABC, 15 percent of all statements served to introduce a videotaped report by an anchor. The corresponding figure on CNN was 7 percent. Introductions were typically two or three statements in length at both networks.

5. On CNN, 6 percent of election statements were made by anchors or reporters/analysts in conversation with one another. On ABC, the figure was 2 percent. There was little variation in these figures between the primary stages and the general election campaign.

6. During the New York primary stage, 40 percent of CNN campaign news occupied the second segment of the newscast; during the California primary stage, 40 percent occupied the third segment.

7. Only ABC continued its first-tier presentation through the New York primary.

8. The figures are 29 percent on CNN, 22 percent on ABC.

9. The percentages of statements attributed to news personnel are 77 percent for CNN, 78 percent for ABC.

10. This news consensus may be understood as a common assumption about how to construct a news story—a matter of form with implications for content. From this perspective, similarities of construction stand in contrast to all other matters of form, which differ because of the production requirements of the two networks. Along these lines, it is interesting to note the comparable use of sound bites on the two networks. On CNN, 25 percent of coverage was in sound bite form; on ABC, 24 percent. All statements attributed to people who were not news personnel (along with some videotaped segments of news analysts) appeared in sound bite form.

11. Multiple topics were commonly addressed within a single statement. Consequently, the percentages in Figure 2.3 total more than 100 percent.

12. Lichter et al. (1988) examined primary coverage on the three broadcast networks from February 1987 through June 1988. They uncovered 306 horserace stories, 79 campaign issue stories (comparable to what I call nonissues), and 60 policy issue stories, with little extended issue coverage in campaign news. Their conclusion: "Election coverage is concerned less with measuring the candidates' qualifications for the job than with predicting their chances of winning it" (p. 33). This concern was evident in 1992 as well, although it was tempered by increased attention to other matters, particularly the economy and the role of reporters in the campaign.

13. Lichter et al. (1988) make this case about the 1988 primary race; similar observations about 1984 are made in Blume (1985).

14. Blume (1985) argues that the networks produce election coverage that appeals to the lowest common denominator because television needs to draw revenue from large audiences.

15. A candidate is most surely in a campaign crisis when the content of a press report is that the candidate is trying to get past the content of the press report.

16. "Other" topics are not included.

17. The first deviation represents a difference between CNN and ABC about the news value of a southern contest between Bill Clinton and Paul Tsongas. The second is largely attributable to a series of stories about Jerry Brown's personal life that did not get much exposure on CNN.

18. See Leubsdorf (1976) and Arterton (1978).

19. A combined 1,049 statements were about the public, compared with 6,434 about candidates.

Chapter Three

1. Reported on ABC "World News Tonight," March 18, 1992.

2. Reported on ABC, "World News Tonight," March 6, 1992.

3. Reported on CNN, "PrimeNews," March 6, 1992.

4. The volume of self-referential coverage in the 1992 campaign represents the continuation of a trend begun in recent elections. In 1987, Seib noted that the press was increasingly giving itself a role in the political process by, essentially, covering itself. He pointed to stories discussing how the political parties needed to construct massive facilities at their conventions to accommodate the press (Seib 1987). There were other examples as well. During the 1984 presidential campaign, television was already acknowledging the process by which political operatives interacted with reporters to control the story. By 1988, the operatives were being addressed in the jargon of the newsroom as "spin doctors," and reporters flatly told the audience when they were "being spun." In 1992, terms like "spin" needed little explanation for many people, and process coverage had advanced to the point where the casual viewer could pass a quiz on the intricacies of life on the press plane.

5. Of all statements about the media and the political process made on the two networks, 69 percent were broadcast on ABC. By comparison, 61 percent of all election statements were broadcast on ABC.

6. Reported on CNN, "PrimeNews," March 6, 1992.

7. Reported by Chris Bury on ABC, "World News Tonight," February 14, 1992, emphasis added.

8. Reported by Peter Jennings on ABC, "World News Tonight," February 18, 1992, emphasis added.

9. Reported on ABC, "World News Tonight," April 28, 1992.

10. Reported on ABC, "World News Tonight," January 28, 1992.

11. Reported on CNN, "PrimeNews," January 9, 1992.

12. Reported by Peter Jennings on ABC, "World News Tonight," October 21, 1992.

13. Ibid., Jim Wooten reporting.

14. Reported on ABC, "World News Tonight," January 14, 1992.

15. Reported by Susan Rook on CNN, "PrimeNews," March 9, 1992.

16. Reported by Brit Hume on ABC, "World News Tonight," March 11, 1992.

17. Reported on ABC, "World News Tonight," July 20, 1992.

18. Reported by Chris Bury on ABC, "World News Tonight," August 7, 1992, emphasis added.

19. Reported by Jeff Greenfield on ABC, "World News Tonight," January 20, 1992.

20. Reported on ABC, "World News Tonight," March 24, 1992.

21. Ibid.

22. All reported on ABC, "World News Tonight," March 25, 1992.

23. Peter Jennings to Cokie Roberts on ABC, "World News Tonight," on New Hampshire primary night, February 18, 1992.

24. Reported by Jim Wooten on ABC, "World News Tonight," October 21, 1992.

25. Specifically, process coverage is attributed as follows: to reporters, 69 percent on CNN, 65 percent on ABC; to sound bites, 15 percent on CNN, 14 percent on ABC.

26. An assessment was made of the evaluative nature of each process statement. A "positive" assessment meant an unqualified favorable statement about a political actor. A "negative" assessment meant something unfavorable was said. "Mixed" statements balanced a positive assessment with a negative assessment of the same political actor. "Neutral" statements were nonevaluative; that is, they did not contain an assessment of any sort. Statements were attributed to the individuals who said them (usually reporters or campaign actors speaking in sound bites).

Chapter Four

1. Reported on ABC, "World News Tonight," February 3, 1992.

2. Reported on CNN, "PrimeNews," January 27, 1992.

3. In his study of the 1980 election, Thomas Patterson concludes that viewers are more likely to learn about the issues from television ads than from the evening news. See Patterson (1980). See also Lichter et al. (1988); Robinson and Sheehan (1983); Patterson and McClure (1976).

4. Overall, 29 percent of all statements contained a reference to a domestic or foreign policy issue. Of these, 46 percent were about economic matters. The remainder were about other domestic or foreign policy issues.

5. Overall, there were 557 references to taxes or unemployment, which represented 40 percent of the 1,388 mentions of the economy. In contrast, social security and trade policy were mentioned a combined 113 times, constituting 8 percent of the total.

6. AIDS, for instance, was an "Agenda" topic but received little additional attention.

7. Overall, 32 percent of the 2,813 unambiguous references to foreign or domestic policy were presented as sound bites.

8. The 23 references made during the course of on-air reporter discussion represented only 7 percent of 348 statements made in this context. Analysts surfaced 55 times to discuss issues, constituting 19 percent of 287 appearances during the campaign.

9. The press appeared as the object of issue references only 77 times.

10. President Bush was either subject or object of 65 percent of the foreign policy statements making reference to a candidate on CNN and of 67 percent of these statements on ABC. On economic matters, the incumbent was included 54 percent of the time on CNN and 52 percent on ABC; in turn, Bill Clinton appeared in 31 percent of the statements regarding economics on CNN and in 26 percent of such statements on ABC.

11. See Graber (1987), especially p. 558.

12. Because of how statement evaluations were determined, Figures 4.5 and 4.6 utilize a variation of the candidate subject variable. Sometimes, the subject of the statement was evaluated; at other times, the statement object was evaluated, as when, for example, one candidate (the subject) said something negative about another candidate (the object). These figures, and others like them elsewhere in this book, employ a modified subject-object variable that assesses whether the target of the evaluation was the subject or object and includes the appropriate reference. As a result, the number of references to particular candidates in these figures and tables may differ slightly from the number of subject references to those candidates found elsewhere.

13. Even when the neutral observations are included, one in three statements about Bush and the economy were negative and only 6 percent were positive.

14. As the Bush campaign learned, the president's positive words served to distance him from voters who felt he was out of step with their situation. But that was a strategic problem for the Bush campaign, not the result of negative press.

15. See Graber (1987).

16. Reported by Brit Hume on ABC, "World News Tonight," January 30, 1992.

17. Because issue posturing is assumed to be image-oriented rather than substantive, it is classified thematically as part of the "image" story and will be discussed further in chapter 5.

18. To be considered a nonissue, a statement had to be about a thematic candidate-oriented topic of political concern that could not be classified as a domestic or foreign policy issue and which was more specific in nature than a simple reference to candidate character.

19. Overall, 12 percent of campaign statements made reference to one of the nonissues. The CNN and ABC figures were comparable to each other, indicating a consensus on the appropriate level of nonissue coverage.

20. *Time* aptly noted: "This is national theatre: surreal, spontaneous, mixing off-hours pop culture with high political meanings, public behavior with private conscience, making history up with tabloids and television personalities like Oprah Winfrey. The trivial gets aggrandized, the biggest themes cheapened. America degenerates into a TV comedy." See Lance Morrow, "But Seriously Folks …," *Time* (June 1, 1992), pp. 29–31.

21. Reported by Jeff Greenfield on ABC, "World News Tonight," August 11, 1992.

22. Reported on ABC, "World News Tonight," January 24, 1992.

23. Reported by Jim Wooten on ABC, "World News Tonight," January 27, 1992.

24. Reported by Morton Dean on ABC, "World News Tonight," January 27, 1992.

Chapter Five

1. Reported on ABC, "World News Tonight," May 5, 1992.

2. Reported on ABC, "World News Tonight," April 27, 1992.

3. James Stovall writes, "Political reporters, not journalists who specialize in foreign affairs, economic issues or defense policy, cover the candidates, and what the candidates say and do is analyzed in terms of its effects on the outcome of the campaign rather than for its policy implications." See Stovall (1984), p. 629.

4. See Lichter et al. (1988).

5. The effect would be the reverse of what Stovall (1984) argues to be a liability to incumbents who wish to run on their records but find their achievements overshadowed by horserace coverage.

6. Most of this speculation transpired before the data collection for this project began on January 1, 1992. Cuomo's participation would have provided the makings of a made-for-television slugfest between the New Yorker and his fellow governor from Arkansas in which horserace ups and downs most certainly would have been featured. That his absence left a void in horserace coverage can be verified by Cuomo's appearance on ABC's "Nightline" and CNN's "Larry King Live" after he had made the announcement that he would not run.

7. Reported on ABC, "World News Tonight," April 27, 1992.

8. An additional 13 mentions were made of "frontrunners" and "longshots" that did not name a specific candidate.

9. The consensus was that Bush had done poorly even though he finished first because his opponent, Patrick Buchanan, had no campaign history. However, this same set of circumstances dictated that Bush could not be mortally wounded in these races because a viable alternative did not exist. Consequently, no additional expectations were raised.

10. There were an additional 21 references to momentum that did not address specific candidates.

11. There were 91 references to delegate votes, including delegate vote totals and additional delegates won.

12. A total of 244 of 1,187 general benchmark references were about Perot; despite CNN's tendency to cover the independent more intensely than ABC, 132 of these general remarks appeared on cable, 112 on broadcast.

13. Overall, 88 percent of organizational references were made during the primary campaign stages.

14. For a discussion of the influence of televised debates on the mass public, see Miller and MacKuen (1979). The role of media coverage in public discourse following the 1976 Ford-Carter debates is addressed by Steeper (1978), who finds that repeated postdebate media coverage emphasizing a Ford gaffe penetrated public awareness in a way that the president's original statement had not.

15. One estimate placed the audience for the second 1992 presidential debate, in which the candidates fielded questions from a studio audience, at more than 90 million viewers. See the *New York Times*, October 17, 1992, p. 7.

16. Reported on ABC, "World News Tonight," September 30, 1992.

17. Ibid.

18. Reported on ABC, "World News Tonight," October 15, 1992.

19. The race appeared to close dramatically because CNN began reporting surveys of "likely voters" rather than "registered voters." The apparent tightening in the contest was partly a statistical artifact resulting from the way CNN assessed "likely voters."

20. Bush was the subject of 198 of 436 references to opponent strategies (45 percent); Clinton was the subject of 112 (26 percent); Perot was the subject of only 19 (4 percent).

21. On CNN, this percentage represented 38 of 42 mentions. On ABC, 16 references to campaign ads (31 percent) were about Perot.

22. Reported by Jeff Greenfield on ABC, "World News Tonight," October 27, 1992.

23. Reported by David French on CNN, "PrimeNews," October 20, 1992.

24. Reported by Tony Clark on CNN, "PrimeNews," October 12, 1992.

25. Reported by Bernard Shaw on CNN, "PrimeNews," October 21, 1992.

26. Reported by Peter Jennings on ABC, "World News Tonight," October 27, 1992.

27. Reported on ABC, "World News Tonight," October 20, 1992.

28. Reported on ABC, "World News Tonight," September 30, 1992.

29. Ibid.

30. Reported by Peter Jennings on ABC, "World News Tonight," October 20, 1992.

31. Reported by Susan Rook on CNN, "PrimeNews," October 5, 1992.

32. In contrast, during the general election stage, the comparable figures were 17 percent on CNN and 18 percent on ABC.

33. Even then, it was a second-tier matter warranting only 30 references (20 percent of image coverage) on CNN and 23 references (9 percent of image coverage) on ABC.

34. Clinton actually ended up on the positive end of a small number of references made to his capability during the primaries. There were 17 positive and 7 negative statements made on the two networks combined.

35. Overall, 38 percent of image statements were made in sound bites. The networks posted similar figures: 39 percent for CNN, 38 percent for ABC.

36. This figure is for both networks combined and is based on a total of 623 sound bite statements.

37. By the convention stage, when Perot I was in full swing, the frequency of group supporters appearing as subjects of campaign stories shot up from a handful to better than 6 percent of the horserace subject references on both networks.

Chapter Six

1. Goffman (1974), p. 10.

2. Wattenberg (1982); see especially pp. 225–226.

3. Each statement could have both subject and object. Consequently, the total number of subjects and objects (N) exceeds the 10,329 statements examined for this study.

4. Losers are no longer considered newsworthy; hardly ever did an also-ran gain attention for something he did or said. The one notable exception had horserace overtones: Paul Tsongas received some coverage about the possibility that he would rejoin the race immediately following his departure.

5. Perot "supporters" or "volunteers" were distinguished from Perot "spokespersons," who were identified as campaign workers on the Perot staff. Both networks tended to address Perot in terms of his supporters or volunteers, and he was the only candidate so portrayed. This practice continued throughout the election, even during Perot II, when some volunteers could arguably be considered employees. The classification used here reflects the characterization made on television.

6. The groups portrayed in Figure 6.2 add detail to the institutions and individuals addressed in Figure 6.1. These groups appeared either in terms of support for or opposition to a candidate or as classifications for members of the public.

7. Gans (1979), chapter 1, especially pp. 19–21 and 29–31.

8. Ibid., pp. 29–30.

9. Perot's followers were portrayed as individual supporters of a candidate rather than as partisan figures.

10. Of 81 group references to African-Americans, 64 occurred prior to the general election stage.

11. When multiple objects occurred in a statement, only the direct object was coded.

12. This table includes references to the candidate, his campaign, and his campaign workers.

Chapter Seven

1. Reported on ABC, "World News Tonight," February 6, 1992, about the Bush health care plan.

2. Reported by Jim Wooten on ABC, "World News Tonight," February 3, 1992.

3. Reported on ABC, "World News Tonight," July 20, 1992.

4. Reported on ABC, "World News Tonight," September 29, 1992.

5. Reported by Chris Bury on ABC, "World News Tonight," June 4, 1992.

6. Reported by Peter Jennings on ABC, "World News Tonight," September 21, 1992.

7. Patterson (1980), pp. 25–26.

8. Robinson and Sheehan (1983), pp. 49–52 and 211.

9. The purpose of this analysis is to understand how reporters portray campaign news. Actors speaking in sound bites and all statements by analysts (whom we would expect to be analytical) are omitted from consideration.

10. Unless specified, all quotations are from personal interviews conducted by the author.

11. Gans writes, "Journalists justify their right to individual autonomy by the pursuit of objectivity and detachment; in a way, they strike an implied bargain, which allows them autonomy in choosing the news in exchange for leaving out their personal values. The outcome restricts the news to facts (or attributed opinions), which, journalists argue, are gathered objectively." See Gans (1979), p. 183. See also Tuchman (1978), pp. 158–161.

12. Patterson (1980), p. 26.

Chapter Eight

1. Davis (1992), pp. 15–30.

2. Epstein (1974) makes a strong case for organizational influences shaping television news.

3. Fishman (1980) emphasizes the importance of beat reporting to newspaper coverage.

4. For instance, Gans (1979) sees a prominent role for newsworker values.

Chapter Nine

1. See Epstein (1973). Epstein writes exclusively about network television. For a similar treatment of print journalism, see Sigal (1973).

2. The merger of satellite and computer technology for covering and reporting election news mirrors the use of telecommunications and data processing technology by candidates for targeting and reaching voters. See Robert Smith, "New Technologies in Campaigns," in Devlin (1987), pp. 17–27.

3. For an account of 1970s-era television technology, see Epstein (1973), pp. 102–112.

4. The producer did not indicate *why* he would want to do this.

Chapter Ten

1. I note this tendency toward qualified access to suggest that the decision to cover the presidential race on a campaign-by-campaign basis is neither obvious nor automatic from the standpoint of accessibility. Ansolabehere (1993) writes, "For the political correspondent covering a presidential campaign, the most accessible source is the campaign organization itself" (p. 51). Although Ansolabehere is essentially correct, I would qualify his observation by noting that using the campaign organization as a major source reflects a choice about coverage that follows from how television conceptualizes the presidential election.

2. Jerry Brown himself was inclined to stay in people's houses and tended not to commit to where he was staying until quite late in the day.

3. See Sabato (1991).

Chapter Eleven

1. Hofstetter (1976). For a comparison between structural bias and political bias, see chapter 8.

2. Bennett et al. (1985), p. 67. The authors specifically address how ambiguity can confound the methodology of newsgathering. The particular case involves television coverage of a self-immolation that was intentionally performed for the cameras. For a related discussion, see Eason (1986).

3. Gans (1979), pp. 39–69.

4. The feeling that news coverage ought to be more substantive is not unique to the individuals interviewed for this book, nor is it a new phenomenon. Issues of improving substantive coverage have been the focus of countless forums, starting well before a 1975 Brookings conference on improving political broadcasting and continuing beyond a 1992 Harvard symposium with television anchors. For an account of the proposals stemming from the 1975 meetings, see Cater (1976).

5. David Maraniss, "Down to the Wire and Out of Steam," the *Washington Post* (November 2, 1992), p. D1.

6. Nor, for that matter, is there much difference between either of these and, say, Madonna, from this viewpoint.

7. Comments made by news personnel at both networks reflected the active role they assume in developing stories. These findings were consistent with Robinson and Sheehan's observation that television journalists assume the challenging, interventionist role of "participant," a term used by Johnstone et al. See Robinson and Sheehan (1983), pp. 224–225, and Johnstone (1976), pp. 114–116.

8. Emphasis added.

9. This perspective may well be reinforced by the ritualistic nature of the campaign itself, to which reporters are inextricably bound. Newsworkers no less than the home audience may experience the campaign as a symbolic enterprise in the fashion addressed by Dan Nimmo or Doris Graber. Inclined as they are to fashion news out of elements, newsworkers may find it "obvious" that campaigns, as Nimmo says, are enacted as political dramas where "characters, acts, scenes, purposes, agents, styles, and plot lines have displayed a recurring pattern." See Dan Nimmo, "Elections as Ritual Drama," and Doris A. Graber, "Magical Words and Plain Campaigns," in Devlin (1987), pp. 159–173 and 185–196.

10. Robinson and Sheehan (1983), p. 148.

11. Lichter, Amundson, and Noyes (1988), p. 126.

12. Except, perhaps, on the Brown campaign, where producers and correspondents complained bitterly about the lack of structure.

13. Benenson (1984), p. 764.

14. Larry Sabato (1991) chronicles the process by which pack journalism develops in a campaign.

15. Others have noted how newsworkers employ routines to produce news stories that are defensible as objective. See, for instance, Arterton (1984), p. 132, and Ansolabehere (1993), pp. 56–57.

Chapter Twelve

1. Self-interest continued to permeate ABC's presentation through Labor Day. There were even other instances of the sort of soul-searching Peter Jennings displayed as a rationale for changing the coverage formula. On September 15, for instance, one week after the new policy went into effect, Jennings introduced a story by saying directly to the viewer, "We know from our own audience that a lot of people in a lot of places are unhappy with the media's political coverage this year, and it's very true the question we ask a politician is not always the one on your mind. Thus, we were impressed by an experiment here in Charlotte [N.C.], in which readers of the local newspaper have a greater say in the coverage than they used to have." As sincere as this interest in improved coverage may have been, old habits die hard. That same newscast opened with a self-interested observation of the sort "a lot of people" might be unhappy with: "We're going to begin [tonight] by seeing how the two presidential campaigns have tried again today to make us focus on what they think will work best for them."

2. Emphasis added.

3. At the very least, it provided a reason for him to be invited on "Larry King Live."

4. Also a chicken-and-egg question: Would the other candidates have included Perot in the debates had he not been the recipient of vast amounts of media attention?

5. Reported by Morton Dean on ABC, "World News Tonight," October 1, 1992.

Chapter Thirteen

1. The pioneering study was presented in Campbell et al. (rev. ed., 1980).

2. Graber (1988), pp. 107–115.

3. For a critique, see Combs and Nimmo (1993), pp. 234–235.

4. Again, see Graber (1988), pp. 249–258. Graber claims that television viewers maintain a haphazard but effective approach to sorting out news messages. Among other things, viewers tend to subscribe to an agenda that reflects the dominant themes of election coverage presented here. This agenda includes general acceptance of the American system of government, a negative approach toward politicians but widespread acceptance of their failings, and a lack of understanding of public institutions, which are also largely absent from coverage.

5. See especially Parenti (1986); see also Gitlin (1980).

6. See Lichter et al. (1986).

7. William A. Henry III, "Are the Media Too Liberal?" *Time,* October 19, 1992.

8. An additional 62 nonissue statements were about Dan Quayle.

9. Robinson (1983), p. 60.

10. Hofstetter (1976), p. 188.

11. For a review of the literature, see Davis (1992), pp. 237–253. See also Wagner (1983).

12. Iyengar and Kinder (1987). See also Iyengar (1987) and Iyengar, Peters, and Kinder (1982).

13. Iyengar and Kinder (1987), pp. 112–133.

14. Ranney (1983).

15. Robinson (1977, 1976).

16. Iyengar and Kinder (1987), p. 129.

Chapter Fourteen

1. Cook (1991).

2. In this regard, Cook argues that the media are governmental rather than simply political institutions and that they are essential to the functioning of the executive and legislative branches, and possibly the judiciary as well. He argues, "The American news media need government officials to help them accomplish their job, and American politicians are now apparently finding the media more central to getting done what they want to get done." See Cook (1991), p. 18.

3. Wattenberg (1982).

4. Joslyn (1977).

5. Sabato (1988), p. 9.

References

Abel, Elie (ed.). 1981. *What's News.* San Francisco: Institute for Contemporary Studies.

Altheide, David L. 1991. "The Impact of Television News Formats on Social Policy." *Journal of Broadcasting and Electronic Media* 35 (Winter), pp. 3–21.

_____. 1976. *Creating Reality.* London: Sage Publications.

Ansolabehere, Stephen, et al. 1993. *The Media Game: American Politics in the Television Age.* New York: MacMillan.

Arterton, F. Christopher. 1984. *Media Politics.* Lexington, MA: D.C. Heath and Company.

_____. 1978. "The Media Politics of the Presidential Campaigns: A Study of the Carter Nomination Drive." In James D. Barber (ed.), *Race for the Presidency: The Media and the Nomination Process.* Englewood Cliffs, NJ: Prentice Hall.

Asher, Herbert. 1980. *Presidential Elections and American Politics.* Homewood, IL: The Dorsey Press.

Atwater, Tony. 1984. "Product Differentiation in Local TV News." *Journalism Quarterly* 61, pp. 757–762.

Benenson, Robert. 1984. *News Media and Presidential Campaigns.* Washington, DC: Congressional Quarterly.

Bennett, W. Lance, Lynne A. Gressett, and William Haltom. 1985. "Repairing the News: A Case Study of the News Paradigm." *Journal of Communication* 35 (Spring), pp. 50–69.

Blume, Keith. 1985. *The Presidential Election Show.* South Hadley, MA: Bergub and Garvey Publishers.

Boyer, Peter J. 1988. *Who Killed CBS?: The Undoing of America's Number One News Network.* New York: Random House.

Breed, Warren. 1955. "Social Control in the Newsroom: A Functional Analysis." *Social Forces* 33, pp. 326–335.

Brown, Jane Delano, et al. 1987. "Invisible Power: Newspaper News Sources and the Limits of Diversity." *Journalism Quarterly* 64, pp. 45–54.

Campbell, Angus, et al. 1980. *The American Voter,* rev. ed. Chicago: University of Chicago Press.

Cater, Douglas. 1976. "A Strategy for Political Broadcasting." *Journal of Communication* 26 (Spring), pp. 58–64.

Chaffee, Steven H., and Sun Yuel Choe. 1980. "Time of Decision and Media Use During the Ford-Carter Campaign." *Public Opinion Quarterly* 44:1 (Spring), pp. 53–69.

Combs, James E., and Dan Nimmo. 1993. *The New Propaganda*. New York: Longman.

Cook, Timothy E. 1991. "Are the American News Media Governmental?: Re-examining the 'Fourth Branch' Thesis." Presented at the annual meeting of the International Communication Association, Chicago, IL, May 23–27.

Cornfield, Michael. 1992. "How to Read the Campaign." *Wilson Quarterly* (Spring), pp. 38–46.

Crigler, Ann, et al. 1992. "Local News, Network News and the 1992 Presidential Campaign." Presented at the annual meeting of the American Political Science Association, Chicago, IL, September.

Crouse, Timothy. 1972. *The Boys on the Bus: Riding with the Campaign Press Corps*. New York: Random House.

Davis, Richard. 1992. *The Press and American Politics: The New Mediator*. New York: Longman.

Devlin, L. Patrick (ed.). 1986. *Political Persuasion in Presidential Campaigns*. New Brunswick, NJ: Transaction Books.

Eason, David L. 1986. "On Journalistic Authority: The Janet Cooke Scandal." *Critical Studies in Mass Communication* 3, pp. 429–447.

Epstein, Edward Jay. 1973. *News from Nowhere*. New York: Vintage Books.

Erfle, Stephen, and Henry McMillan. 1989. "Determinants of Network News Coverage of the Oil Industry During the Late 1970s." *Journalism Quarterly* 66, pp. 121–128.

Fico, Frederick. 1984. "A Comparison of Legislative Sources in Newspaper and Wire Service Stories." *Newspaper Research Journal* 5, pp. 35–43.

Fishman, Mark. 1980. *Manufacturing the News*. Austin, TX: University of Texas Press.

Flegel, R., and Steven H. Chaffee. 1971. "Influences of Editors, Readers, and Personal Opinions of Reporters." *Journalism Quarterly* 48, pp. 645–651.

Gandy, Oscar H. 1982. *Beyond Agenda-Setting: Information Subsidies and Public Policy*. Norwood, NJ: Ablex.

Gans, Herbert. 1979. *Deciding What's News*. New York: Random House.

Garnham, Nichol. 1979. "Contributions to a Political Economy of Mass Communication." *Media, Culture, and Society* 1, pp. 123–146.

Gitlin, Todd (ed.). 1986. *Watching Television*. New York: Pantheon Books.

Gitlin, Todd. 1985. *Inside Prime Time*. New York: Pantheon Books.

_____. 1980. *The Whole World Is Watching*. Berkeley, CA: University of California Press.

Goffman, Erving. 1974. *Frame Analysis: An Essay on the Organization of Experience*. Cambridge, MA: Harvard University Press.

Graber, Doris. 1988. *Processing the News: How People Tame the Information Tide*. New York: Longman.

_____. 1987. "Framing Election News Broadcasts: News Content and Its Impact on the 1984 Presidential Election." *Social Science Quarterly* 68 (September), pp. 555–568.

Hallin, Daniel C. 1989. *The Uncensored War: The Media and Vietnam*. Berkeley, CA: University of California Press.

Hess, Steven. *The Washington Reporters*. 1981. Washington, DC: The Brookings Institution.

Hofstetter, C. Richard. 1978. "News Bias in the 1972 Campaign: A Cross-Media Comparison," *Journalism Monographs* 58.

_____. 1976. *Bias in the News: Network Television Coverage of the 1972 Election*. Columbus, OH: Ohio State University Press.

Iyengar, Shanto. 1987. "Television News and Citizens' Explanations of National Affairs." *American Political Science Review* 81, pp. 815–831.

Iyengar, Shanto, and Donald R. Kinder. 1987. *News That Matters: Television and American Public Opinion*. Chicago: University of Chicago Press.

Iyengar, Shanto, Mark D. Peters, and Donald R. Kinder. 1982. "Experimental Demonstrations of the 'Not-So-Minimal' Consequences of Television News Programs." *American Political Science Review* 76, pp. 848–858.

Johnstone, John, et al. 1976. *The News People*. Urbana, IL: University of Illinois Press.

Joslyn, Richard. 1977. *The Impact of Television on Partisan Politics*. Ann Arbor, MI: University Microfilms International.

Kellner, Douglas. 1990. *Television and the Crisis of Democracy*. Boulder, CO: Westview Press.

Lemert, James B., et al. 1977. "Journalists and Mobilizing Information." *Journalism Quarterly* 54, pp. 112–117.

Leubsdorf, Carl P. 1976. "The Reporter and the Presidential Candidate." *The Annals of the American Academy of Political and Social Science* 427 (September), pp. 1–11.

Lichter, S. Robert, Daniel Amundson, and Richard Noyes. 1988. *The Video Campaign: Network Coverage of the 1988 Primaries*. Washington, DC: American Enterprise Institute.

Lichter, S. Robert, Stanley Rothman, and Linda S. Lichter. 1986. *The Media Elite*. Bethesda, MD: Adler and Adler.

McCombs, Maxwell E. 1972. "Mass Media in the Marketplace." *Journalism Monographs* 24.

Merrill, John C. 1985. "Is Ethical Journalism Simply Objective Reporting?" *Journalism Quarterly* 62, pp. 391–393.

Miller, Arthur H., and Michael MacKuen. 1979. "Learning About the Candidates: The 1976 Presidential Debates." *Public Opinion Quarterly* 43 (Fall), pp. 326–346.

Minow, Newton N., and Lee M. Mitchell. 1986. "Putting on the Candidates: The Use of Television in Presidential Campaigns." *Annals of the American Academy of Political and Social Science* 486 (July), pp. 146–157.

Molotch, Harvey, and Marilyn Lester. 1974. "News as Purposive Behavior: On the Strategic Use of Routine Events, Accidents, and Scandals." *American Sociological Review* 39, pp. 101–112.

Nimmo, Dan, and James E. Combs. 1983. *Mediated Political Realities*. New York: Longman.

Ostroff, David H., and Karin L. Sandell. 1989. "Campaign Coverage by Local TV News in Columbus, Ohio, 1978–1986." *Journalism Quarterly* 66, pp. 114–120.

Paletz, David L., and Robert M. Entman. 1981. *Media, Power, Politics*. New York: The Free Press.

Parenti, Michael. 1986. *Inventing Reality: The Politics of the Mass Media*. New York: St. Martin's Press.

Patterson, Thomas E. 1980. *The Mass Media Election: How Americans Choose Their President*. New York: Praeger.

Patterson, Thomas E., and Robert D. McClure. 1976. *The Unseeing Eye: The Myth of Television Power in National Politics*. New York: Putnam.

Ranney, Austin. 1983. *Channels of Power*. New York: Basic Books.

Robinson, Michael J. 1983. "Just How Liberal Is the News? 1980 Revisited." *Public Opinion*, pp. 55–60.

_____. 1977. "Television and American Politics." *The Public Interest* 48, pp. 3–39.

_____. 1976. "Public Affairs Television and the Growth of Political Malaise: The Case of the Selling of the Pentagon." *American Political Science Review* 70, pp. 409–432.

Robinson, Michael J., and Margaret A. Sheehan. 1983. *Over the Wire and on TV: CBS and UPI in Campaign '80*. New York: Russell Sage Foundation.

Sabato, Larry J. 1991. *Feeding Frenzy: How Attack Journalism Has Transformed American Politics*. New York: Maxwell Macmillan International.

_____. 1988. *The Party's Just Begun: Shaping Political Parties for America's Future*. Glenview, IL: Scott, Foresman.

Schramm, Wilbur Lang, and Donald F. Roberts (eds.). 1971. *The Process and Effects of Mass Communication*. Urbana, IL: University of Illinois Press.

Schudson, Michael. 1978. *Discovering the News*. New York: Basic Books.

Seib, Philip M. 1987. *Who's in Charge?: How the Media Shape News and Politicians Win Votes*. Dallas: Taylor Publishing Company.

Shoemaker, Pamela, and Stephen D. Reese. 1991. *Mediating the Message: Theories of Influences on Mass Media Content*. New York: Longman.

Sigal, Leon V. 1973. *Reporters and Officials*. Lexington, MA: D.C. Heath.

Steeper, Frederick T. 1978. "Public Response to Gerald Ford's Statements on Eastern Europe in the Second Debate." In George F. Bishop et al. (eds.), *The Presidential Debates: Media, Electoral, and Policy Perspectives*. New York: Praeger, pp. 81–101.

Stovall, James Glen. 1984. "Incumbency and News Coverage of the 1980 Presidential Election Campaign." *Western Political Quarterly* 37 (December), pp. 621–632.

Tuchman, Gaye. 1978. *Making News*. New York: The Free Press.

Wagner, Joseph. 1983. "Do Media Make a Difference: The Differential Impact of Mass Media in the 1976 Presidential Race." *American Journal of Political Science* 27 (August), pp. 407–430.

Wattenberg, Martin P. 1982. "From Parties to Candidates: Examining the Role of the Media." *Public Opinion Quarterly* 46 (Summer), pp. 216–227.

About the Book
and Author

Sleep-deprived reporters. Spin doctors. Deadlines. All constants in the world of television election reporting. But do they alone explain why television coverage of the 1992 presidential campaign looked the same night after night across the broadcast/cable media divide? Matthew Robert Kerbel says no, pointing instead to the shared interests and perspectives of newsworkers that bridge network differences. *Edited for Television* explores those common orientations as it tells the story of the 1992 election in the voice of a one-time television newswriter and the media personnel he skillfully interviews.

One of the first studies to compare cable news with its broadcast counterparts, *Edited for Television* is loaded with new insights into what gets covered and what gets left out as well as why and to what effect. At once a large-scale media election study and an examination of forces shaping television news, this book answers a host of provocative questions: Under what conditions will television pay more attention to the issues than to the "horserace"? What happened to coverage when Ross Perot redefined how a campaign is conducted? Why is it that cable and broadcast television devote so much air time to the interests and concerns of cable and broadcast television?

For everyone concerned with the effect of the visual media on citizens and the political process, *Edited for Television* is a lively, informative account of how America's most recent bout with democracy appeared on the screen and behind the camera. Original data and election research are combined with engaging interviews of ABC and CNN personnel to produce a work of both scholarly and general interest.

Matthew Robert Kerbel is assistant professor of political science at Villanova University and author of *Beyond Persuasion: Organizational Efficiency and Presidential Power.*

Index